# SENTIMENT, POLITICS, CENSORSHIP

## CENSORSHIP

### THE STATE OF HURT

Thank you for choosing a SAGE product!
If you have any comment, observation or feedback,
I would like to personally hear from you.
*Please write to me at* **contactceo@sagepub.in**

**Vivek Mehra,** Managing Director and CEO,
SAGE Publications India Pvt Ltd, New Delhi

## Bulk Sales

SAGE India offers special discounts
for purchase of books in bulk.
We also make available special imprints
and excerpts from our books on demand.

*For orders and enquiries, write to us at*

Marketing Department
SAGE Publications India Pvt Ltd
B1/I-1, Mohan Cooperative Industrial Area
Mathura Road, Post Bag 7
New Delhi 110044, India

*E-mail us at* **marketing@sagepub.in**

## Get to know more about SAGE

Be invited to SAGE events, get on our mailing list.
*Write today to* **marketing@sagepub.in**

This book is also available as an e-book.

# SENTIMENT, POLITICS, CENSORSHIP

## THE STATE OF HURT

**EDITED BY**
Rina Ramdev
Sandhya Devesan Nambiar
Debaditya Bhattacharya

**⑤SAGE**  www.sagepublications.com
Los Angeles • London • New Delhi • Singapore • Washington DC

*First published in 2016 by*

**SAGE Publications India Pvt Ltd**
B1/I-1 Mohan Cooperative Industrial Area
Mathura Road, New Delhi 110 044, India
*www.sagepub.in*

**SAGE Publications Inc**
2455 Teller Road
Thousand Oaks, California 91320, USA

**SAGE Publications Ltd**
1 Oliver's Yard, 55 City Road
London EC1Y 1SP, United Kingdom

**SAGE Publications Asia-Pacific Pte Ltd**
3 Church Street
#10-04 Samsung Hub
Singapore 049483

Published by Vivek Mehra for SAGE Publications India Pvt Ltd, typeset at 10.5/12.5pt Minion Pro by Diligent Typesetter, Delhi and printed at Chaman Enterprises, New Delhi.

**Library of Congress Cataloging-in-Publication Data Available**

**ISBN:** 978-93-515-0304-0 (HB)

**The SAGE Team:** Shambhu Sahu, Neha Sharma, and Ritu Chopra

# Contents

# List of Photographs

# Preface

Our present untimely times seem to be oriented toward a taxonomy of social threats, staged as a readiness to claim 'hurt' as both lived experience and a cause for political sanctuary. In an attempt to understand the political register of hurt vis-à-vis its conditions of production and retaliation, certain precipitating incidents and the mass-mediated outrage orchestrated around them provided an impetus to frame some of our concerns. Events such as the shootings of the editors of the *Charlie Hebdo* magazine in Paris for depicting hurtful cartoons of Prophet Muhammad, the witch hunt of Perumal Murugan, author of the apparently unsettling *One Part Woman* which led to the author declaring his death-as-author, the furore in Mumbai over a comedy "roast" which was self-admittedly adult in nature, the vengeful responses to Wendy Doniger's *The Hindus: An Alternative History* as also to a public reading from Salman Rushdie's banned novel *The Satanic Verses* at a Literary Festival, the fractious debates in the Indian Parliament over an Ambedkar cartoon in the National Council of Educational Research and Training (NCERT) school curriculum, and the arbitrary removal of a Ramanujan essay on the *Ramayana* from university textbooks were symptomatic of larger tendencies in political expression. These represented diverse yet continuing patterns of offence and counter-mobilization. What also served as a productive entry point into the debate for us was the renewed relevance and the immediate contemporaneity of it. While interrogating the state of hurt as an event and its varied conflictual articulations by groups through volatile emotions and concomitant calls for reparation or revenge, what is, therefore, crucial is an attempt to chart the history of hurt in time, and also a consequent measure of the newness of its articulation at this conjuncture.

Therefore, the first question that we address and attempt an awareness of, is this collectively felt need for the question itself. Why is 'today' the fit time to talk through this debate? Is hurt increasingly becoming a political epidemic, and is history witness to this aggravation of sentiment in contemporary modes of political subjectivization? Or, is it that the urgency of the contemporary moment is not in a disproportionate aggravation of political health over time, but in our own heightened consciousness of it? Simply put, are we really more hurt today than ever before, or are we more conscious today of our being hurt? Is the palpability of our condition of hurt a consequence of 'violence and violation' becoming an everyday, routine experience of the political? Is hurt more real today because it is more immediate, more private, more intimate, more lived than before? Or is it so because it is strategized, circulated, and mediatized now more excessively?

If a discussion on the politics of hurt seemed more timely than ever before, how would one understand the place of 'sentiment' in our political past? If our current understandings of hurt as constitutive of the limits of political well-being have their roots in a postcolonial moment of identity-articulation, how would one understand the use of sentiment in colonial and pre-colonial formations? The proliferative currency of the debate almost assumes an increasing incidence of hurt (or, possibly a strengthening of the clinical consciousness of political being) over successive periods in history.

This leads then to the question of the materiality of hurt as a *felt* sentiment, with its own taxonomies of affect. When and how does a materialist understanding of political rationality make way for *apprehensions* of fear and pain? What is the place of such emotions of endangerment within a progressive tradition of politics? While this feeling of 'being wronged' can be historically evidenced in sustained events of attack on minority communities and alter-publics, how has the positivist regime of law been activated by an otherwise pure realm of sentiment-as-*potentiality*? An order of legality that thrives on empirical notions of 'truth'-as-evidence seems to appropriate this domain of sentiment, and consequently institutes a machinery of censorship. In bringing sentiment within the purview of a statist law, is there an attempt to contain its dangerous excesses—or, is it only a benign constitutional mechanism to protect the alter-subject's democratic right to citizenship? Does censorship safeguard alterity or prevent the proliferation of it through checks and curbs on the right to difference and dissent? The effects of repressive models of power as enforced through the sovereign space of penality are significant to note. Is the censored object necessarily withdrawn from circuits of reception, or does it in turn produce a renewed engagement with the same? Does censorship perpetually not run the risk of being counter-productive, of reinserting the sites of potential transgression within the public order of discourse?

Given that censorship has paraded within different domains of social–cultural production under different names of the "obscene," the "offensive," the "hurtful," the "harmful," this collection of essays is an attempt to exhume the historical debates around each. If hurt is only another analogue for negative determinations of political affect, what gives it the relevance worthy of a current debate? The answer lies possibly in more than a recounting of recent controversies and populist mobilizations of hurt; here we attempt to move along that direction and explore what lies beneath, apart, and beyond.

In conceptualizing this collection, there was a deliberate attempt to identify contributors from diverse spheres of activity to locate the social and political range of hurts and affects distributed across cultural-creative spaces. The privileged totality of the body politic wounds everyone who is a misaligned entity, and is, therefore, both invasive and indiscriminate, treating such misalignment with the curative of hurt or with the threat of expulsion. The contributors reflected in their own personal and public practices, this threat of being both the agents of hurt as well as the affected addressees of hurt.

The affective economies of hurt circulate within all spheres of social relations, and it was this idea of a coincidence-despite-difference of positions that is brought to bear upon this volume. As editors, it was not only imperative to mobilize a cross section of contributors, who belong to a diverse range of professional practice—such as academia, law, film, art, literature, and activism—but we also believe it to be the crying need of the hour to pursue this precise end in order to resist the atomization of our public and private selves that marks the apotheosis of late capitalism. We felt a pressing need to articulate and translate across the increasingly disconnected socially hermetic sections, and create dialogues not only within academia, but with civil society at large. It is this felt expediency that led to the idea of such a collection of understandings and interrogations from voices within and outside of academia; from fields as diverse as law, filmmaking, journalism, and fiction writing. Within this, the heterogeneity of their idiom and the constitutive breadth of their disciplines are retained even as they are aligned by the thematic rubric that hurt assigns this collection.

Thus, the diversity and multiplicity of articulations is the very *raison d'etre* of such an anthology, as we attempt to mine here the space for socially translative practices.

So we begin and continue with questions about pluralities as about binaries, settled identity as about unsettled claims, and hurt not only as an invisibilized but also as a potentially reductive category. In this "marketplace of outrage," has hurt now become recognizable as a mode of affective address, or has it become a vacuous category, shorn of 'real' meaning? Zizek's polemical arguing can perhaps be the point that we leave for conversations to linger and extend the debate on the state of hurt.

> In today's market, we find a whole series of products deprived of their malignant property: coffee without caffeine, cream without fat, beer without alcohol... up to today's tolerant liberal multiculturalism as an experience of Other deprived of its Otherness (the idealized Other who dances fascinating dances and has an ecologically sound holistic approach to reality, while features like wife beating remain out of sight)?... Everything is permitted, you can enjoy everything, BUT deprived of its substance which makes it dangerous. Today's hedonism combines pleasure with constraint—it is no longer the old notion of the "right measure" between pleasure and constraint, but a kind of pseudo-Hegelian immediate coincidence of the opposites: action and reaction should coincide, the very thing which causes damage should already be the medicine[1]

---

[1] "A Cup of Decaf Reality," in *Lacan.com*. 2004, available at http://www.lacan.com/zizekdecaf.htm

# Introduction: Sentimental Sovereignties: Hurt and the Political Unconscious

*Rina Ramdev, Sandhya Devesan Nambiar, and Debaditya Bhattacharya*

# I

## Of Batras and Blasphemies: India as Hurt Capital

Among a spate of recent incidents regarding censorship, on December 5, 2011 the Indian government shut down several social media sites and Internet companies, including Google, Facebook, and Yahoo!, to "prescreen user content from India and to remove disparaging, inflammatory, or defamatory content before it goes online." A day later, in a bid to qualify the move, the then Minister of Communications, Kapil Sibal held a press conference where he stated, "We have to take care of the sensibilities of our people.... Cultural ethos is very important to us." This contradiction of the state's paternalistic protectionism going hand-in-hand with an ensnaring of political rights or freedoms has led, in the recent past, to a vast range of difficult and terrorizing affects in the public arena.

We are now well within what is frequently felt to be the 'Age of Unreason', where the reasonably 'constituted' political being stands witness to the deep forces of the irrational that drive the daily life of democracy. Many recent events bear this out, where a definite tightening of spaces for possible articulation of dissent has been steadily gaining a certain manufactured traction in public discourse. This is evident in the de-recognition (later retracted due to public pressure) of the Ambedkar-Periyar Study Circle at IIT Madras for "creating hatred atmosphere [sic] among the students,"[1] or the beef ban in Maharashtra, or the complete ban ordered by the Central Board of Film Certification (which revels in the habit of mistaking its mandate as a censoring body not a certifying one) on films like *Fire* (1996), *The Pink Mirror* (2003) and *Unfreedom* (2015), or the stay order and subsequent ban on broadcast of the documentary *India's Daughter* which explored the gang rape incident of December 16, 2012, for showing India in a 'poor light' (where discussions shifted from the idea of the ban itself to discussions of an 'outsider' filmmaker Leslee Udwin, commenting on the situation of women in India). We have witnessed college teachers being charged with sedition for setting exam questions on the Kashmir struggle, public intellectuals being threatened with deportation to Pakistan for expressing as much as an opinion about a prime ministerial candidate, writers being forced into an announcement of their 'death' as creative artists or into exile for fears of physical harm, bloggers and social media users being indicted for purported acts of irreverence, fake encounters being staged and 'framed suspects' being hanged in secret to salvage collective conscience, movie posters and theatres being vandalised for screening films deemed 'obscene' or 'blasphemous', drama societies in colleges being warned of bans for nurturing disaffection against ruling parties, elected parliamentarians mandating a loyalty-test for citizen-populations by ordering the drowning of those opposed to certain practices of yoga. Such micro-fascist politics are becoming increasingly routinized through manufactured spectres of demonized others, always looming large on the politico-emotional landscape. The impositions of particular caste/class/religious/gender interests are totalized as the interests of an entire nation, which then can only be achieved through the instrumentalization of a certain prohibitory logic—where all specific orientations and interests incomprehensible to the regime can be put under erasure by recourse to 'public conscience'.

---

[1] Refer to the captioned subject of MHRD letter No. 5-3/2014-TS-I dated 15 May 2015, addressed to the Director of IIT-M and signed by the Under Secretary to the Government of India, seeking explanation on the activities of APSC.

The continued repression of artistic-intellectual freedoms in India, and the consequent shrinking of the democratic space for debate fail to shock us anymore. The 'state of hurt' has scoured into our technologies of self-constitution and self-representation as citizen–subjects, while filtering our everyday encounters with 'ideas'. The claim to hurt has become most easily recognizable as the face of, and force behind all forms of fundamentalism, regulating the public sphere and its now-excessive mediatization. To put it rather simply, the prolonged history of censorship and legal–legislative curbs on free speech has made it the most predictable experience of print-modernity now. In fact, there is a certain proverbial legitimacy in the 'popular' belief that the success of a writer today is directly proportional to the number of readers that can be potentially hurt by his work and the amount of resentment that, thus, gets inspired. Conversely, the number of court cases or bans that an author is laboring under is, in most instances, very nearly an accurate measure of his claim to posterity.

Positioned within such an epidemic of sentimental outrage, it comes as no surprise to have a former general secretary of the education wing of Rashtriya Swayamsevak Sangh (RSS) wage wars on A.K. Ramanujan's "Three Hundred Ramayanas", and Wendy Doniger's *The Hindus: An Alternative History*. What is, however, alarming, if not new, about this moment of intellectual volatility is the act of betrayal on the part of what were institutionally and traditionally regarded as the repositories of 'ideas'. In this, it can be seen as a breach of the ethical responsibility that universities or publishing houses bear toward their reading-publics as spaces that enable the reception and circulation of alternative knowledge practices. The heightened susceptibilities of those entrusted with the task of archiving the life of thought only confirm our perpetual coincidence and cohabitation with a 'state of hurt'.

Early in 2014, Penguin Books India settled for an out-of-court agreement with Dinanath Batra—the convener of Shiksha Bachao Andolan and one behind the legal campaign against Delhi University's inclusion of Ramanujan in its curriculum—to withdraw all copies of Doniger's fascinating alter-reading of Hinduism. After a protracted legal battle that spanned over four years, Penguin Books India's sudden decision to pulp a book because it was allegedly written by a "woman hungry for sex"[2] and "with a Christian Missionary Zeal and hidden agenda to denigrate Hindus and show their religion in poor light"[3] was indefensible to say the least. Faced with acerbic criticism from academic and intellectual communities across the world, Penguin Books India issued a public statement as an afterthought to vindicate its position. Avowing still an unflinching commitment toward "every individual's right to freedom of thought and expression," the statement went on to justify the publisher's metamorphosis into an agent of censorship in the cause of a "moral responsibility to protect [our] employees against threats and harassment."[4]

Penguin Books India's point about professional "responsibility" brings into evidence a necessary relationship between instances of epistemological violence and the organized ritual tactics of 'real' corporeal violence that surround the event of a ban. The issuing of *fatwas* by Muslim fundamentalist groups as a response to blasphemous knowledge production, or the periodic vandalism engaged in by Hindutva proponents as a means of resisting anti-Hindu 'corruptions' of Indian history can conveniently substantiate this inalienable network of violences/violations that censorship works its way through. But Penguin Books India, while significantly granting visibility to the related threats to life and property that any censorial maneuver bears within itself, refuses to put up a fight. Rather than acknowledging the criminality in these potential sites of exogenous violences around knowledge and combating them through punitive processes, it proposes a martyr-policy of self-censorship as the easy way out. A presumptive 'claim to hurt', coupled with a preemptive threat to counter-hurt, ends up actualizing an event of self-injury in the murder of free expression. This is not violence *against* the law or even *of* the law (in the Benjaminian sense [Benjamin, 1986]), but in fact violence *in fear of* the law. It not only helps detract from the principle of fearless academic publishing that Penguin Books India had historically staked its right over (through its successive decisions to publish some of the

---

[2] Excerpted from Point 9 of Batra's legal notice Ref. No. 254/LN/0310, March 3, 2010, sent to Wendy Doniger, Penguin Group (USA) Inc. and Penguin Books India Pvt. Ltd., available at http://www.bharatiyashiksha.com/?p=217

[3] See Note 2, Point 5.

[4] Available at http://www.penguinbooksindia.com/en/content/penguin-india%E2%80%99s-statement-%E2%80%98-hindus%E2%80%99-wendy-doniger

most controversial authors/texts), but also sets a dangerous precedent that was soon to be mimed and repeated. Emboldened by his success against an erstwhile champion of creative freedoms, Dinanath went on to bully yet another publisher of Doniger—Aleph Books Company—to cancel the reprint of her 2013 book *On Hinduism* and order its review by a panel of lawyers and independent scholars for suitable publication advice. The crusade of a mindless cultural holocaust continued. Now targeting Orient Blackswan, it sought to avenge its 'hurt sentiments' by threatening legal action against acclaimed historian Sekhar Bandopadhyay's celebrated work *From Plassey to Partition: A History of Modern India*, which had, with sufficient historical legitimacy, associated Gandhi's assassinator Nathuram Godse with the RSS. Cowering under the attack, the publisher took a policy decision to undertake a "pre-release assessment" of such books as may be deemed to appeal to the constituencies of popular sentiment, and suggest "revisions" (read: omissions) of the same on the advice of lawyers. While such a shameful attempt at preemptively excising academic content in heeding tendencies of extremist political lumpenism gives a greater legitimacy to the 'sovereignty of hurt', it soon found a fit target in Megha Kumar's *Communalism and Sexual Violence: Ahmedabad Since 1969* to be published by Orient Blackswan. Already peer-reviewed and sent to the press and made available for online pre-booking sales, Kumar's empirical study of the relationship between communal riots and sexual violence in Gujarat was suspended "for the present,"[5] not without a hint of apprehension at the electoral rise of the Hindu right wing. Taking a cue from Penguin Books India's example, the management of Orient

---

[5] In a letter dated May 16, 2014 to Kumar, the President of the Humanities and Social Sciences Section at Orient Blackswan, Uday Rao, writes: "On 14 April 2014 we received a notice from Mr Dinanath Batra's lawyer accusing us of publishing a book that is defamatory and derogatory to the RSS.... It is a book that is a careful history, written in the best traditions of historical writing. As a company we believe strongly in the freedom of expression and in academic freedom.... However, because of the above issue, the Board of Directors of the company has been advised by legal counsel to undertake a pre-release assessment of books that might attract similar reactions. Such assessment may extend to examining the possibility of legal proceedings, especially under the Penal Code, being filed against authors, the company and its employees. Quite apart from the legal proceedings, our concern is that our authors, our staff, and the families of both, could be exposed to the risk of violence, endangering their life and safety." The entire correspondence between Kumar and her publisher, through successive letters written between May 16 and June 13, 2014, is available here on the author's website http://www.meghakumar.org/news.html

Blackswan re-cited its professional pledge to the safety of its "authors" and "staff" against "threats, legal or otherwise."

The point where institutions of knowledge dissemination begin to perceive law as a "threat" to the safety of its "authors and staff" is a moment of deep crisis. This is particularly ironic, given the exactly antithetical role of the legal apparatus in protecting life and its claim to reason. The consequent chronicle of a retreat of despairing publishers into zones of 'safety', well-guarded from the *terror of hurt* does not bode well for either the state of democracy or its machinery of justice dispensation. We have reached a state where even the hint of law— supposedly a defender of the citizen's right to free existence—'realizes' the possibilities of violence for both producers and preservers of academic thought. At such a moment when the slightest reference to "legal action" comes cloaked not with a promise to heal but with multiple threats to hurt—when *what was to redress only encourages repression*—it is not entirely unexpected of a Penguin Books India to publicly justify its betrayal in the name of "respect[ing] the laws of the land, however intolerant and restrictive those laws may be." To use the legal pledge as a suicidal excuse for self-censure is alarming, though not entirely unfounded. Further, the repeated references by publishers to Section 295A of the Indian Penal Code as running counter to the rights enshrined in the Constitution and often activating a chain of ideational violence summon forth a dire need for introspection. The statement of "commitment" to serious scholarship issued by Penguin Books India, while alternating between the self-righteous and the exonerative, mourns in an almost elegiac tone,

> We believe, however, that the Indian Penal Code, and in particular Section 295A of that code, will make it increasingly difficult for any Indian publisher to uphold international standards of free expression without deliberately placing itself outside the law. This is, we believe, an issue of great significance not just for the protection of creative freedoms in India but also for the defence of fundamental human rights.[6]

Notwithstanding the debate about what Lawrence Liang (in his sardonic legal notice against Penguin's cowardice) calls a "moulting"

---

[6] Penguin Books India's statement on Wendy Doniger's *On Hindus: An Alternative History*. Available at http://www.penguinbooksindia.com/en/content/penguin-india%E2%80%99s-statement-%E2%80%98-hindus%E2%80%99-wendy-doniger

act of the penguin's becoming a chicken,[7] it is important to note the equation made by the publisher with regard to the circulation of daring scholarship as "deliberately placing itself outside the law." The seemingly obvious illegality of the 'unpopular'—that is, whatever challenges the accepted 'popular' canons of thought—is but an ominous sign of our times. It is this same concern that Doniger accurately addresses in the May 8, 2014 issue of the *New York Review of Books*, albeit with a discerning attempt to bail her publisher out of the intellectual climate of wholesale condemnation:

> Some writers argued that Penguin India could have won the case had it seen it through to the end. After all, these accusers said, how can you prove malicious intent in a book? Alas, in some courts it could be very easy. To satisfy the terms of Indian law, statements in the book in question need merely be expected "to outrage religious feelings." If you got the wrong judge—and India is a place where the Supreme Court has recently reinstated a law criminalizing homosexuality—you'd be convicted just for publishing a statement that you had good reason to believe might well offend someone. It's hard to imagine how you could write about any subject as sensitive as religion or history without outraging someone; such a rule would mean the end of creative and original scholarly thought.
>
> Any new idea offends people who are committed to the old idea, which is to say, most people. Even in the hands of someone as intellectually challenged as Batra, Article 295A is a weapon of mass cultural destruction.
>
> I still believe that the Indian law is the main villain in this case…. (Doniger, 2014)

The Victorian colonial inheritance of a particularly outrage-prone economy of 'feeling'—which right-wing nationalist forces have subsequently identified with the cultural character of India as a

---

[7] Quoting from Liang's "Legal Notice for Violation of Rights of Readers," to Penguin Books India Pvt. Ltd., February 14, 2014: "In effect you have withdrawn the book on the basis of a legal threat thereby granting unauthorized groups and individuals the right to censor books. These groups and individuals believe that the threat of force is the best way to counter the written word and when publishers succumb to such pressures they perhaps need to rethink why they are in the book business at all. While they may both be birds, there is a world of difference between a Penguin and a chicken and the last time my clients checked, the penguin had not changed his feathers in the natural world…. [But] if not in the natural world, then at least in the publishing world the Penguin is mutating into a chicken." http://altlawforum.org/campaigns/penguin-india-served-legal-notice-on-agreement-to-withdraw-and-pulp-the-hindus-an-alternative-history/

homogeneous space of non-difference—has become the cornerstone of blasphemy laws here. In this respect, the 'terms of Indian law' promote a culture of offence as the legitimate guarantor of justice while on the other hand, discouraging any effect of 'difference' (in opinion or identity) as evidence of punishable deviance or disharmony. Remembering Hegel, the harmony of ideas is never a proof of civil harmony but instead of a stifling climate of intolerance. It brings in its wake what Doniger appropriately names as "mass cultural destruction" in abidance and complicity with the law. The privileged appeal granted by the Code to states of aggravated sentiment as inhering in and disruptive of a larger numerical coincidence of 'feeling', more often than not runs the risk of suppressing the dissenting voice of reason. In other words, a law that regards a proneness to emotional hypersensitivity as the only integrative condition of community formation is one that threatens the right to alternative thought and practice. It poses serious dangers on the task of the intellectual by pitting her against an imagined consensus of vulnerabilities. History, for such a 'law-abiding' society, is a project of producing fantasies of immanence and religion is but a means of achieving it. A professional historian of religion, as Doniger rightly points out, is by the very description of 295A an outlaw with criminal tendencies of "outraging someone [or another]."

To turn attention to the letter of the law, IPC Section 295A—which has veritably become the unique identification number [all puns intended!] for any community's claim to collective determination—states,

> Whoever, with *deliberate* and *malicious intention* of *outraging* the religious *feelings* of any *class of citizens of India*, by words, either spoken or written, or by signs or by visible representations, *or otherwise* insults or attempts to *insult* the religion or the religious *beliefs* of that class, shall be punished with imprisonment of either description for a term which may extend to three years, or with fine, or with both. [emphasis added]

The litany of terms such as "deliberate," "malicious," "intention," "outraging," "religious feelings," "class of citizens," "insult," and "beliefs of that class" inserts a calculated ambiguity in the possible interpretations of this section. One could reasonably ask: how could a work of professional history writing hope to pass itself off as 'indeliberate' and 'unintentional' to avoid attracting penalty under

IPC? Is all work of history therefore—given the arduous process of 'deliberation' and 'intention' that necessarily precedes it—liable to be convicted of 'malice'? Further, what is an exact measurable quantum of malice—and of what proportions of intention and deliberation—that is deemed sufficient for 'outrage'? Is one word enough to outrage an entire "class of citizens" or one phrase or one sentence? More precisely, what unit of meaning is legally permissible as an adequate ingredient of 'outrage'? Might the historian—who treads a perilously thin line between reason and prison—know the difference between 'outrage' and 'insult', though both have been deemed equally punishable? It is worth noting—though we shall revisit this point later again—that not all of the same "class of citizens" might necessarily share the same "religious feelings" or "religious beliefs." How many then must share a feeling for it to be 'outraged' or 'insulted,' and how again would all of those 'many' prove the equivalence of their feeling or belief? By virtue of being born into a religion, or through material evidence of its everyday practice? To assume a numerical consensus within a community of "feeling" would amount to a breach of legal positivism, though it is at this point that Indian blasphemy laws meet a crucial disjuncture and one that we shall come to in a minute.

Finally the twin words—"or otherwise"—in the Code, hinting at the potential innumerability (and unnameability) of the means/media of offence, are most significant. They point at the moment of the aporetic at the heart of law, the scourge of the indefinable that functions as the internal logic of the law. Though the word of law is the mark of the limit, its jurisdiction is a limitless possibility. The element of deliberate ambiguity within its own self-definition tames every exception into a state of emergency and a call unto itself. The words—"or otherwise"—therefore open up an infinite space of the criminal-as-possible and never exhaustible within the literality of the law. What is not named can also and at any time be construed and contained within the ambit of its jurisdiction.

The terminological puzzle that Section 295A presents has often come up for discussion in court judgments relating to charges of blasphemy, and the verdict delivered by the Calcutta High Court on September 22, 2005 in the case of Sujato Bhadra vs. State of West Bengal famously touched upon the debate. Relating to Taslima Nasreen's *Dwikhondito* which was banned by the Government of West Bengal under Section 95 CrPC, the bench of judges decided to set aside the state's declaration of forfeiture by deeming the book as not violative of the concerns in Section 295A IPC. Addressing the issue of the framing and semantic applicability of the law, the judgment maintained at one point

> The outrage to religious feelings or insult to religion or religious belief, if made unwittingly or carelessly or without any deliberate or malicious intention, then the same would not come within the purview of Section 295A IPC.[8]

A question, however, lingers on. How might a scholarly or creative piece of work convicted of mischief under IPC prove itself as 'unwitting', 'careless', or 'intentionless', when its mettle precisely lies in the nature and duration of its premeditation? The question of 'malice' of course takes us back into the domain of morality, which again largely depends on the readership and its constituency of belief.

It is this issue of membership within a belief-system vis-à-vis the collective sanction of its hurt that got highlighted in a landmark judgment of the Supreme Court on August 25, 1958 in the case of S. Veerabadran Chettiar vs. E.V. Ramaswami Naicker and Others. A judgment that even Batra makes an out-of-context reference to in his notice to Penguin Books India–Doniger, the above case appealed under Section 295 of the IPC (relating to defilement/destruction of objects held sacred) against an incident of public demolition of a Ganesha idol by the members of an anti-idolatrous Dravida Kazakam party in 1953. The petitioner successively went from the court of the Additional First-class Magistrate to the Sessions Court and then, to the Madras High Court, but only to have his appeal dismissed on all three occasions and on the same grounds. It was contended by the learned judges in all three instances that breaking an idol is not tantamount to an object held sacred, since what grants sacrality to an image or an idol in the likeness of a god is its consecration in a place of worship. Therefore, any object removed from its consecrated site of religious practice cannot be deemed sacred and liable to defilement. At this, the petitioner moved the Supreme Court with his thrice-rejected plea—which historically proceeded to overrule the interpretations of the lower courts and pronounced its judgment thus:

---

[8] From the Calcutta High Court Judgment, Sujato Bhadra vs. State of West Bengal on September 22, 2005, p. 4.

In our opinion, placing such a restricted interpretation on the words of such general import, is against all established canons of construction. Any object however trivial or destitute of real value in itself, if regarded as sacred by any class of persons would come within the meaning of the penal section. Nor is it absolutely necessary that the object, in order to be held sacred, should have been actually worshipped. An object may be held sacred by a class of persons without being worshipped by them. It is clear, therefore, that the courts below were rather cynical in so lightly brushing aside the religious susceptibilities of that class of persons to which the complainant claims to belong. The section has been intended to respect the religious susceptibilities of persons of different religious persuasions or creeds. *Courts have got to be very circumspect in such matters, and to pay due regard to the feelings and religious emotions of different classes of persons with different beliefs, irrespective of the consideration whether or not they share those beliefs, or whether they are rational or otherwise, in the opinion of the court.*[9] [emphasis added]

The Supreme Court, thus providing a massive vindication to "religious susceptibilities" and their fetishization of "any object however trivial or destitute of real value in itself," makes way for the frightful tyranny of the sacred that was soon to be compounded with the renewed rise of fundamentalist forces in India. The caution issued by the apex court about the need to be "very circumspect in such matters, and to pay due regard to the feelings and religious emotions" breeds a vision of the 'state of hurt' that successively goes to claim a Rushdie, a Ramanujan, a Doniger, or a Muslim techie in Pune.

Interestingly, there are two clauses in the text of the Supreme Court judgment that strikingly sound a discordant note in the legal discourse on hurt, and in examining which we shall devote much of our labor through the rest of this essay. The first of these clauses—"irrespective of the consideration whether or not they share those beliefs"— appears to strike at the root of the liberal democratic paradox that underlies mechanisms of justice dispensation. While the currency of 'feeling'/'emotion'/'belief' can conclusively derive legitimacy only from its inherence in an imagined *collective* of the "class" (or religious community), the allowance for a non-sharing participation-cum-cohabitation with this class grants every individual a sovereignty of sentimental claims. It apparently goes on to carve out an autonomous

---

[9] From the Supreme Court of India Judgment, S. Veerabadran Chettiar vs. E.V. Ramaswami Naicker and Others on August 25, 1958, p. 5.

space of alternative practice for the individual, but only to be finally swallowed by an overarching vow of allegiance to larger "class" beliefs in claiming offence. The individual is, thus, legally empowered to make personal claims of hurt, albeit always in the name of 'belonging' to the community. This is a potentially disruptive moment of empowerment, as we shall go on to discuss later.

The second and final clause in the text—"whether they are rational or otherwise, in the opinion of the court"—ascertains the place of the non-rational and grants singular credence to 'states of sentiment' as legally admissible claimants for redress. In dealing a decisive blow to the cause of rational inquiry and thought, the judiciary rules in favor of a differentially distributed space of "religious feeling" *separable from* "the opinion of the court." In effect, it orders an event of self-suspension, only to reorganize the legal object in deference to the currency of hurt. When it comes to matters of religion, the law self-admittedly stands to witness its own dissolution and abrogates its sovereignty unto the irrational. This is tantamount to an acknowledgment of law's ownmost fears, when pitted against the superior sovereignty of God. At the heart of the law's failure to safeguard the voice of reason is an event of its own censorship by the community of sentiment.

What then can Penguin Books India do, but rant at the 'state of hurt' that resides *within* the [self]repressive "laws of the land?"

# II

# Em-bodying Hurt, Enacting the Political

Now, what is the state of hurt? Within a commonsensical understanding, it indicates an aggravated pathology of being. Crucially, hurt signifies the abstraction of an intimately private experience of 'pain'—made recognizable through certain marks on or contortions of the body. It evidences itself as 'real' and proves the objective validity of its claim through what one can call a staging of the body—in either the 'trace' of a wound or the 'effect' of a mourning. What becomes paradoxically relevant in this biomedical definition of hurt as a symptom-begging-cure is its concurrent public and private nature. Experientially part of the inner life of an individual, hurt must render itself susceptible to the eye of the diagnostic apparatus. It must become a sign that can effectively approximate the value of its inner meaning—that is, pain. In classical terms, hurt can legitimately lay its claim to healing only when it gains in bodily aspect and visibility.

This antithetical character of hurt as the mark left by traumatic experience binds it analogically with the next two terms in our titular series: "sentiment" and "politics." Much like the way in which 'sentiment' as 'inner experience' is lent a degree of evidential truth and mobilizational validity through the publicness of the political, hurt too must make its presence felt via the technologies of staging. The process of 'staging,' however, as already stated, concerns the body as an anatomical totality that has now been dis-ordered by violence. Incidentally, this 'hurt-in-and-as-the-body' can—in its political uses— refer to either the body of the individual or of the community. Politics thus, through its conscious articulations of sentiment, comes to relate to its welfarist sense of the health of a polity at large. Inasmuch as every political claim to hurt implies an event of assault on the 'body politic,' it carries with it a necessary aspect of the 'grotesque' often bordering on the obscene.

The associations of the 'grotesque' within our political imagination of hurt possibly beg further explanation. In Rabelaisian terms, the "grotesque" is an effect produced by the severing of a biologic order to the body (Rabelais, 2006). In other words, the body is proverbially in good health only as long as it is ordered as a coherent and connected whole. It is precisely the moment when the anatomical aggregation of the 'connected whole' is disturbed or disarranged that Rabelais notices an act of grotesquerie. This is the state of hurt. And in being thus imagined as an event of disaggregation of the 'body politic', the saying of hurt is most typically an intolerable measure of the obscene. Hurt characteristically enters the prohibitive space of law, and it is no wonder, hence, that it must as a rule validate the call for censorship.

Simply put therefore, the 'state of hurt' acquires political expediency only by em-bodying an event of disruption that necessitates further repression. Contrary to a clinical rationality of healing as the immediate 'need' of the hurt object, it seems that the latter—by its very principle of exceeding the sovereign insistence on order and totality—becomes the condition of possibility for renewed instances of hurt-as-expulsion.

In order to understand how hurt gains credence within discourses on governmentality, one needs to trace the strategic insertion of the body in the history of liberal democratic politics. In this historical chronicle of what we might call "body-politics," the rationalistic biases of the Enlightenment seem to belie some fundamental contradictions. Consequently, the move toward a democratic configuration of 'popular sovereignty' will only appear as an excuse for a bourgeois individualism premised on a legislative–punitive right to (and command over) the body.

Analytically, it is but imperative that the politics of hurt (or conversely, what contemporary commentators have preferred naming as the "politics of sentiment," almost hinting at an interchangeability of the latter categories) must historically begin at the conjuncture where the body becomes an institutional field of power. And this again has interestingly coincided with a new order of legal modernity, relying for its absolutism on a procedurally (re)produced experience and exercise of violence.

# III

# Historicizing Hurt as Affect

The project of European modernity, as much of the Frankfurt debates would confirm, began with the rationalistic tendencies of the Renaissance. The Cartesian cogito set the stage for the coming to being of the modern subject of power, consciously driven by an act of will. In an almost Platonic precedence given to the *anamnesic* order of 'thought', Descartes heralded the political philosophy of the modern age. Opposed to the sovereign powers of the 'mind' as instrumentalizing action, was the physical dimension of space as ordered by and contained in the body. Conceiving of the proto-bourgeois subject as instituted and individuated by a default capacity for ideation, his body was, on the other hand, relegated to an extensional materiality requiring conquest or control. In this sense, an ethical economy of human action was formulated through the operational dichotomies between reason and passion. The former, it was thought, enabled a productive reining in of the latter such that the ends of action could correspond to a modern theory of moral consciousness. As a result, anything that had to do with an experience of emotion was to be mastered and contained within the body through the superior command of thought. The body thus, as the singular space for passionate or sentimental investments, had to be absented from the discourse on political subjectivity as a form of agential individualism.

Significantly, in the latter half of the 17th century, this ethico-political dimension of modernity was nuanced through a symptomatic unification of the body and mind. This became the defining moment for an emergence of the Enlightenment principles of bourgeois subjectification. In a Spinozistic performance of the integral subject of ethics, the schizophrenic self-division of body versus mind was swept away. Both attributes of the ideational and the extensional (the Cartesian duality between mental versus material) were now considered to inhere in the same substance of nature. Through an elaborate theory of affect as determinative of the 'power to act', Spinoza reinstated the body-acted-upon within signifying orders of agency. Contrary to what is believed as simply a retort to Descartes' hierarchy of rational action and a resuscitation of the organic powers of emotion, Spinoza actually takes on the task of remedying his predecessor's somewhat-lopsided model of individualism through the integrative category of the body. By painstakingly reviewing the basis of ethical action as contingent on pre-political interactions and modifications of bodies, he makes the 'will to act' seem dependent not on solipsistic rational dispositions/ decisions but collective bodily determinations. In this, Spinoza attempts to solve the ethical crisis of bourgeois rationalism through a theory of liberal democratic action via affective intersubjective alliances. He says:

> The power of any particular thing, and consequently the power of man, by which he exists and works, is determined only by another particular thing whose nature must be understood through the same attribute, through which human nature is conceived. Therefore our power of acting, in whatever way it may be conceived, can be determined, and consequently aided or hindered, by the power of some other particular thing which has something in common with us.[10]

According to Spinoza's logical postulations, the "power of acting" is necessarily a consequence of being 'affected'. Bodies interact

---

[10] Spinoza. *Ethics* IV, prop. XXIX, proof.

with each other as with all proximate objects to produce certain modifications of pleasure or pain that he calls "affect." Incidentally, the modifications manifest themselves in the affected body through differential capacities of action. Spinoza suggests that while on the one hand, the 'will to act' depends on the interactive potential of bodies in space, the extent of action on the other is determined by the emotional import of these interactions. Through a re-ascription of "the power of man, by which he exists and works" to the possible orderings of his body, not only does the 17th-century philosopher bring back the physical into emergent discourses of power but also hints at a new currency of the 'affected body' as 'active agency'. In other words, the field of ethical determinations now shifts from a forceful disciplining of the body to a tactical maneuvering of its 'emotions' as productive of action.

> A man does not know himself except through the modifications of his body, and the ideas thereof ... wherewith it is able to conceive itself and its own power of activity.[11]

The central thesis of Spinoza's ethical doctrine is in the relationship between two spatially ordered bodies as productive of the "power of activity" in each. The apparent championing of affect as the potential cause of action gives a degree of political importance to the "modifications of the body." Also, the event of interaction as capable of violent "modifications" becomes a case in point. The adversely "affected" body, Spinoza maintains, is inversely disposed toward action. But inasmuch as the category of hurt becomes determinative of a body's power to act, victimhood asserts a right to 'limited' political legitimacy. Hurt, as experienced in the negative affect of pain, becomes potentially constitutive of the modern ethical subject of action. The latter's relationship with every individual other is now the condition of possibility of a liberal politics of affect.

But, there is the shadow of a contradiction at the heart of Spinoza's claims about the relationship between negative affect and the agential body as productive of action. Though corporeality is reinstated as a self-generative medium of social–political interactionism, the subjective experience of pain (as evidence of 'hurtful' interaction with the other)

---

[11] Spinoza, *Ethics* III, prop. LIII, proof.

is at the same time delegitimized as minimally disposed to action. The hurt body—overcome by the affective jurisdiction of 'pain'—is, Spinoza maintains, naturally deprived of motility-as-agency and almost tending toward the inactive. What this amounts to saying is that, despite the increased political credence granted to a corporeal subjectivity, the sentiment of hurt is potentially un-/anaesthetic and, therefore, corresponds to a measure of latency as opposed to agency. It has a limited claim to political felicity by virtue of a restricted amplitude of its field of activity.

# IV

# The Hurt as Hideous

There are three implications that follow from Spinoza's theory of negative affect that we began by marking as a crucial intervention in contemporary discourses on the political. The first, being the most obvious, is his withholding of determinative rights from the hurt body to reorganize its immediate (often malignant) social field of movements and alliances. The state of passivity that the violated 'corpus' is supposed to exhibit, of course, forestalls the future of its participation in an otherwise self-renewing order of the political. The passive here does indeed become an index of powerlessness, explained by a quasi-medical rationality of 'injury' as seeking retirement and reclusion from flux. Second, Spinoza's attempt at identifying a desire for withdrawal and a consequent self-absorption in the 'pained' subject conveniently (and rather deviously) merges with the narrative of repression that we had earlier discerned in relation to the grotesque body. Insofar as the anaesthetized object is also an antonym of the aesthetic principle (and its constitutive experience of 'pleasure'), it necessitates a forceful elimination of itself from the field of public visibility. The Spinozistic definition of the hurt body is alarmingly susceptible to the charge of obscenity and thus begs censure and exclusion from the filiative and intersubjective 'polis'—the public domain. The third and final implication of Spinoza's ethical postulations on the category of affect relates to the afterlife of the now-excluded and incarcerated subject of hurt. The habitual passivity—translatable into helplessness—of the hurt body seems to appeal to an ethical responsibility of the state to grant 'care' and 'healing'. Itself incapacitated of the autonomy of action and thus incapable of every assertion of sovereignty, the ailing hurt body must by default surrender to the sovereign power of the other-as-state—which, consequent on this act of recognition, might grant asylum and healing as charity. This returns us to a status quoist imagination of power, that symbolically transforms and transfigures the historically 'injured' as minority. The latter again is deemed deserving of an 'ethical' safeguard of state protection only as long as it pays a routine obeisance to the sovereignty of the majority (of 'acting'/'active' subjects).

The political imaginary of the hurt-as-minority, thus, contains a welfarist plea for social protection from dominant structures of power. But, the 'deep' ethical responsibility of protection must first necessitate rigorous scrutiny of and routine corrections in the minority body, lest the excommunicated object ends up posing a threat to both the sanctity of order and the order of sanctity in the sovereign. In plainer terms, the activity enabled by regimes of 'negative' affect should as a rule pass a positivistic test of legitimacy. An injured body is always-already in excess of the order of forms and institutes what Jacques Ranciere calls a 'dissensus' in the sensory distribution of power; and hence its claim for recognition begins by being a criminal act of normalizing difference. At the very outset, therefore, the transgressive properties of an 'active hurt' call for stringent surveillance and closer examination. The affected-as-(minimally)-active body must nonetheless be summoned into presence within the court of law and scrutinized for the remotest evidence of culpability. Consequently, the most significant moment of modern legal reform was in the introduction and amendment of the Habeas Corpus Act in 1679 (only two years after the publication of Spinoza's revisions of early modern subjectivity). Dubbed as a historic championing of the right to individual liberty, the writ of "habeas corpus" could literally be translated from Latin as "you are entitled to have the body." Granting the promise of respite from unlawful custody or motivated state-sponsoring of violence, such a petition relies on the technologies of staging the hurt body to assess its claims of being-hurt. In this process, the making public of pain involves not only a conscious advertisability of the 'traces' of hurt, but also a simultaneously ironic giving away to law of the right to one's body. Hurt finally becomes the pretext for the state's exercise of sovereignty in a verdict of its permissibility or relative impropriety.

# V

# A Politics of (Hurt) Identity

Even as liberal democracy envisions a unified 'aggregate' of the people as the gestalt of political agency—as whole and undivided, undifferentiated by divisive communitarian claims—the very framing of a Constitution enshrining a discourse of Rights acknowledges the state's predilective will to violence, its invisibilizing of adjunct histories in favor of majoritarian interests. These historically evidenced omissions create counter-publics negotiating for privilege and power, just as they devise interventions to publicize their exclusion through a cohesive solidarizing language of identity. The moment of identity politics begins when the disenfranchized body, subsumed within majoritarian discourses that structure and define the liberal state, is recalled and reinserted in its singularity. Even if it still seeks redressal, the symbolic enumeration of the untouchable-as-insensible within a social–democratic imagination of numbers and the ritual inclusion of the minority as a "unitary" entity force one to now conceive of the hurt body as an integral source/site of political action. In its re-inscription, the minority demands a Constitutional acknowledgment of the historical wrongs of the state that have led to an experience of injury and hurt while at the same time attempting to mobilize a penitential system of political recompense. In this—in its originary moment that puts 'pain' beyond the experiential and into the historical—the idea of 'hurt' posits an affective community that binds and works as an adhesive force to empower and grant political agency to a neglected public. And within this frame, hurt is mobilized as a category of coherence, predating what is seen as its axiomatic disruptive alignment against the state. It is this political legacy of hurt as not always being presumptively detrimental to the larger vision of progressive politics that also needs acknowledging as it works through ideas of inclusive social justice to provide a crucial entry point for the consolidation of communitarian identity and claims.

This moment of inception through which identity politics defines itself is concomitant with the proliferating rise of multiple publics demanding political safeguards from the state. It is at this point that the state opportunely invokes the language of hurt and moves between offering its protectionist power at the behest of minoritarian claims and at other times censures/censors such claims to regulate the rise of these excluded publics and their assertions of counter-sociality. Through its organized structures of legislation and control, the state is also able to arrogate to itself agencies of both hurt and redressal—being the site, the source, and the 'hurting' state all at once. When pitched against a hurt counter-public, the state vacillates between the democratic dualism of entitlement versus responsibility to make the former governable.

It would be useful here to remember Hegel's contention in *The Phenomenology of Spirit* that the only logical outcome of the bourgeois-democratic energies unleashed by the French Revolution could be the "Reign of Terror"—philosophically speaking, the threat of a negation of individual self-consciousness. The revolution, Hegel maintains, of course ushered in a new conceptual economy of the community representable in the abstract general will of the people. It notionally restructured the collective as the new locus of governance, thereby granting legitimacy to every individual consciousness as an empowered effective participant in compounding the general will. The absolute claim of 'liberty' made by the essential Being-for-self was abstracted and enshrined within the inclusive space of the community. But it was here that the profoundest paradox of democracy resided—and one that the instrument of the Constitution takes serious cognizance of. Insofar as the communitarian principle embodies a shared generality of the will, this same will could not be acted except in and through a determinate agential individual. Every manifestation of the self-identical communal will was always already a pretext for the differentiated action of the pure self-consciousness, and therefore a cause for 'terror' and threat. The sole work of the community, Hegel continues, was the work of death—a punishable event of supersession that hurt and threatened both the forged unity of the communal and the fearsome agency of the individual. A mortal potentiality of hurt and the consequent call to censure difference were but incipient in the imagining of post-revolutionary society. In other words, liberal democracy was the very condition of possibility of the event of hurt—whether in its nominal acknowledgment of the individual's sovereign rights or in its actual instances of suppressing the self-differentiating effects of the same.

[B]y virtue of its own abstraction, [the universal will] divides itself into extremes equally abstract, into a simple, inflexible cold universality, and into the discrete, absolute hard rigidity and self-willed atomism of actual self-consciousness…. The relation, then, of these two, since each exists indivisibly and absolutely for itself, and thus cannot dispose of a middle term which would link them together, is one of wholly unmediated pure negation, a negation, moreover, of the individual as a being existing in the universal. (Hegel, 2010)

Ideas and beliefs that communities are crystallized around grant a shared identificatory site—the 'universality' of the will—for individuals to cohere. And yet the volatility of individuals contained within the collective remains at the level of a potential threat to any kind of unitary projection that it strives for. The disaggregated individual is capable of reordering the community ethic, rendering it contingent and, thus, replete with the possibility of being both a producer and consumer of hurt in the most proliferative of ways. The possibilities of multiple publics within the community, articulating diverse and often competing claims of hurt, constitute a fraught consolidatory ideal—one that can both be destabilized and splintered. This matrix of excess within communitarian forms of sociality creates a circuit of public consumption within which the staging of hurt has a perpetual site and audience.

# VI

# Private Perfidies, Contested Communities

In asking for a censuring of writers as they famously did in 1989 of Salman Rushdie for *The Satanic Verses*, and in more recent times, Ramanujan for "Three Hundred Ramayanas", communities enact extrusions of their own members over a perceived moment of hurt. A disavowal of the community's ownness in a member-individual is born of a perception that views them as latently disintegrative and a threat to the homogeneity that defines the (af)filiative space. It is at this moment that the operative expression of hurt seems to deflect from its progressive communitarian legacy. The anticipated splintering by the One takes its cue from the liberal bourgeois ethic that foregrounds the individual as the effective-agential site of political action. From being rallied for the collectives of minority politics, hurt is now reassigned into a liberal vocabulary that argues for the single constituted citizen as the bearer of political agency. The exigential occasion is not staged between communities but is played out as an endogenous confrontation *within* the collective. The crisis is commuted to the One, the individualized subject who becomes the potential source and bearer of violence within the community. In attributing a certain political capacity of destabilization and disruption to an atomized individual against the power of its coherent whole, the community in effect signals its own moment of weakness. In even allowing for a foretold moment of certified splinterability, it acknowledges its own fear of a breakdown of solidarities and commonality that define its identificatory force. Within this, the offending individual is castigated and proscribed not for what the community views as either an appropriation or infringement upon its entitlements or rights, but for every dissenting and nonconformist position taken. The perceived threat is, thus, from the heterodoxy—the 'dissensus'—that he introduces within a largely cognate space. To counter its own fear of the threat the community in turn attempts the marshaling of a thwartive, interventionist machinery to censor and censure the detractive agent.

In the case of minority communities, this moment of perceived detraction brings about a significant reordering of its relation with society (and the state) at large. The general tradition of identity politics within a majoritarian polity had in the past used the currency of hurt in the defense of the collective, arguing for a reinstatement of partial, excluded publics. In the first place, a marginal group's assertion of hurt works within an affirmative discourse mobilizing as it does a constitutional commitment to social justice and the coterminous protection of rights. Its protests devolve from a position of ascribed subalternity within the social ethic, as it seeks to expose the economy of power that creates differential relations of excess and impoverishment between the perpetrator and the hurting body. As a counter-public forged out of a minoritarian axiom, its confrontation now weighs against the very epistemology of emotion it had in the past sought to strategize its visibility through. Numerically, the majority is always advantaged against it, but in seeking a requital now from an individual, every community seems to articulate a negative assertion of hurt. *It demonizes dissent as localizable in an absolute imagination of minoritization (in the individual non-believing dissenter) and uses its own numerical force of being-larger-than-the-exception to amputate hurt.* In this, it replicates the statist semiotics of power and galvanizes an entire apparatus of coercion against the offending individual. Here, hurt, which had otherwise been a mark of its marginality, becomes for the community the point when it reassembles its constituent mode into dominance. The classic position of its minoritarian subalternity is thus complicated by a self-signifying sovereignty that it seizes in order to assert power against an atomized individual, whether through the courts of law or its own coercive machinery. This claim of being the hurt body, thus, encodes a paradox, for in recording a moment of hurt against the singular "hurter"/transgressor it grants it a spectral power while articulating a vulnerability despite its own numerical strength. The logic of numbers underlying the liberal representative political model is internalized even by the co-ethical counter-social community-space, which inevitably reorganizes itself as a default majority.

Herein lies the fracturing of the community and also the endless possibility of the same in the future. Hurt is privatized to a point where it, at the very least, potentially and notionally empowers individuals with the capacity to break and splinter erstwhile solidarities forged through a similar vocabulary of historical wrongs. This infinite privatization of hurt to the extent where every atomized affective organ of the feeling subject registers a right to aggravated vulnerabilities not only crumbles the field of ethical determinations available within the community, but also imputes to the latter a character akin to the repressive apparatuses of intolerant sovereignty.

# VII

# Speaking Otherness: Languages of/That Hurt

In his Preface to the *Order of Things*, Foucault had referenced a ubiquitous Borges story, which in typical Borgesian fashion had spoken of a "certain Chinese encyclopedia" where "animals are divided into a vast array of dizzying classifications, both fantastical as well as 'real'." Foucault subsequently remarks on the strangeness of this universe as attaining fabulous proportions only because of the limitation of our system of thought—the impossibility of thinking the Other. But it becomes possible to attempt this leap of imagination because of the "proximity of extremes," or, "the sudden vicinity of things that have no relation to each other"[12] where the mere act of proximation leads to a state of fantastical enchantment.

This enchantment effected by the epistemic awareness of the Other is constantly brought to us through language, which closes aphasic gaps and allows things in conflict to coexist in mutual awareness of the other, and the infinite ability of the other to hurt, to damage or structurally alter not only the relation but also the very structures that construct the Self. This knowledge is potentially threatening and is always kept at bay, lest it already change what is assumed to be given. But the language and the order of the Other make it possible also to articulate the self, and to order the structures that govern the biopolitical regimes of the self. It also makes it possible to name the hurt as well as the hurting self and reascribe it in social terms. It is the ordering of experience that renders it an element of a particular order of experience altogether. The nomination of felt experience in particularized terms makes it possible to formulate it conceptually and experientially iterable—it becomes possible to recall the hurt and restore it to imaginative experience.

In Nietzschean terminology, hurt is a transactional category, since one hurts another not only to actually cause harm and to conquer the other, but also to become aware of one's own strength. For Nietzsche, hurt is, therefore, contractual and axiomatic, manifesting not only the action in return, but also the epistemic coagulation of the self. The very knowledge of hurt or the recognition of being hurt engenders also the very idea of the *hurt self*, an ontology of hurt.

Language attains the paradoxical quality of retaining the capacity to frame the very terms of the epistemology of hurt, as also possessing the agential capacity to cause the hurt. One becomes vulnerable to language precisely because one is constituted by it and is denoted by its nominating capacity. The *ekphrastic* power of language precedes our ontic existence and possesses the prior power to name and injure. The hurt body is a body that claims political articulation and sovereignty

---

[12] "We are all familiar with the disconcerting effect of the proximity of extremes, or, quite simply, with the sudden vicinity of things that have no relation to each other; the mere act of enumeration that heaps them all together has a power of enchantment all its own" (Foucault, 1971).

for itself on the basis of hurt caused by a precisely sovereign other, which negates such sovereign claims. To claim hurt, is to also claim posteriority, and the primacy of the hurting action undertaken by the Other against the self. It, thus, achieves recognition through an interpellative action that exists within the realm of *potentia*. There always exists the possibility of being hurt as well as of hurting another. But this possibility is not always followed into the plural realms of its actualization, where hurt actually takes place and *is* materially felt and experienced. The sensation, therefore, of being hurt depends not only on the actual material condition of hurt, but also on the pre-figured spaces of possible hurt, which threaten actual articulation.

In Althusserian terms, language interpellates our being and "hails" it into particularized existence. One 'exists' not only by the particular instance of being recognized through language but by the prior instance of being 'recognizable' as a hurt entity.

This recognition rests precisely on the capacity to articulate the hurt itself in terms acceptable to law and the social structures that govern articulation. The subaltern can speak, provided of course that it speaks in the prescribed language of law—and a law which recognizes at the same time the political existence of the other who wields the capacity to hurt.

# VIII

## Agency and Responsibility

This brings us to the question of agency: Is agency for language the same as agency for the subject? The act of making the threat, and the threatened act both issue from the body but are not identical. "I condemn you" becomes effective as a blandishment only if the subject wields sufficient power to substantiate the claim, otherwise it is rendered a 'failed performative'. For Bourdieu, the distinction between performatives that work and those that fail is to do with the social power of the one who speaks, and is to be understood within established contexts of authority and instruments of censorship. The law provides the dimensions of possibilities available to the speaking subject, as well as the reference-frame for norms that are embodied in the habitus of the body.

The subject who speaks hate speech is particularly responsible for what has been spoken, but can the subject be held responsible also as being the decidedly singular origin of that speech? This fixing of articulated responsibility becomes the uncomplicated, 'detached' concern then of the law, which takes upon itself the mantle of sovereignty and sets itself up as 'neutral' against the injured parties. This assumption camouflages the nature of the law which is complicit in the creation of speaking subjects, where speech itself demands censorship. To transgress against the limits of speakability is to risk one's position as subject. Speech then legitimizes a certain kind of subject, producing and silencing it at once. The law is not external to speech and speech is not the privileged venue for freedom. The law and speech are one in the moment that they both name the subject as subject, inaugurating it into social existence and visibilizing it toward surveillance.

To be "called a name" is one of the first forms of linguistic violence, since it imposes an identity which is not of one's choice, but not all names are injurious—they inaugurate the subject, but their denotative agency is not felt to be injurious at the inaugural moment and is rather taken to be an evental moment denoting agency rather than vulnerability.

But while language can sustain the body, it can also threaten its very existence. Words can wound precisely because words also fashion the subject through the articulation of multiple fluid selves and the mobilization of identities. There is presumably then the deliberation upon and selection of arenas of hurting capacities, which are willfully entered into and transformed into arenas of vengeful social identification in time. Words wound because they 'mark' and allocate the hurt subject as separate beings. To be injured or hurt through speech is to be decontextualized and destabilized from a particular location which was possibly an arena of identification and the comfortable negotiation of social position. It is through this denomination that the comfortable subject undergoes a disenfranchisement and, therefore, a profound loss of subjectivity.

In her Nobel Prize-winning speech, Toni Morrison stated that oppressive language is not constrained within the limits of representability. It instead IS violence, where the threat is not in the promise of actualization of the violent potential contained within language but is performed in the very moment the promise is made and enacted.[13] Hate speech is, thus, placed in opposition to ordinary speech, which is not presumed to be manifestly oppressive. But ordinary speech is what makes hate speech possible. The cunning of ordinary speech lies in its power to invisibilize the effects of its power and normalize the negotiations that are carried on in its terms that regularly mobilize the idea of the norm and oppress all those who claim disparity. On the other hand, hate speech uses what Pierre Bourdieu calls the *strategies of euphemization* (Bourdieu, 1991) in order to make itself 'felt', but at the same time, hate speech is always a citation of itself—its force is governed by its prior instance and places it in a continuum of emotional effect. The iterability of hate speech is effectively disseminated by the next subject who speaks the speech of hate—thus rendering it a historical testament.

Although language can denote the violent power potentialized within the promise of harm, language can also suffer cessation at the moment of confession. Writing in the *Body in Pain*, Elaine Scarry suggests that the threat *of* violence is a threat *to* language—its sense-making possibilities. She cites the example of a tortured body where the instance of torture renders the victim incapable of documenting it in speech. One is literally "struck dumb," and therefore one of the effects of torture is to efface its very victim as witness (Scarry, 1985).

Such effacements are precisely what have been producing their traces through the acts of self-censoring and the delegitimation of authorial communities and voices through the threat of unnamed and unnameable violences; we have been witnessing the enforced *pati in silentio*—the suffering in silence of the many texts and articulations, whether as evidenced in the Wendy Doniger cases or the irruptive violence exploding over texts such as James Laine's *Shivaji: Hindu King in Islamic India* or the Ambedkar cartoons. However, this is not to say that the provenance of hurt sentiments is circumscribed only within the self-professed logic of nationality or region. Such an emotional economy is also an investment in a Foucauldian conduct of governmentality, staking claims and apportioning/manufacturing blame across regimes of power, wherever it may find itself. Such an

---

[13] "Oppressive language does more than represent violence; it is violence; does more than represent the limits of knowledge; it limits knowledge." Nobel Lecture, December 7, 1993. Available at http://www.nobelprize.org/nobel_prizes/literature/laureates/1993/morrison-lecture.html

exercise in the cartography of hurt sentiments and the politics thereof is what is explored in the essays contained here—the attempt to chart the fluidic pluralities of identities and the multiple structurations of calculated subjectivities that are buried, exhumed, and 'molted' within these assemblages of identity, emotion, and politics.

We embarked on this course with the idea of scrutinizing these unsettled and unsettling claims of political crises, presenting a bio-political array of sentimental impedimenta to nativized and narrativized belongings. We hope that the very range, quality, and depth of the essays comprising this volume shall make explicit the many traces and inquiries into the organization of the politically abject subject.

# References

Benjamin, Walter. 1986. "Critique of Violence," in *Reflections: Essays, Aphorisms, Autobiographical Writings* (trans.) Edmund Jephcott. New York: Schocken Books.

Bourdieu, Pierre. 1991. *Language and Symbolic Power* (trans.) Gino Raymond and Matthew Adamson, (Ed.) John B. Thompson. New York: Polity Press, p. 20.

Doniger, Wendy. 2014. "India: Censorship by the Batra Brigade," *New York Review of Books*, May 8 Issue.

Foucault, Michel. 1971. *The Order of Things: An Archaeology of the Human Sciences.* New York: Pantheon Books, pp. xvi.

Hegel, Georg Wilhelm Friedrich. 2010. *Phenomenology of Spirit* (trans.) A.V. Miller. Oxford: Oxford University Press, pp. 359–360.

Rabelais, Francois. 2006. *Gargantua and Pantagruel* (trans.) M.A. Screech. New York: Penguin Classics.

Ranciere, Jacques. 2010. *Dissensus: On Politics and Aesthetics* (trans.) Steven Corcoran. London and New York: Continuum Publishers.

Scarry, Elaine. 1985. *Body in Pain: The Making and Unmaking of the World.* Oxford: Oxford University Press, p. 27.

# Overture

# 1

# How Far Can You Go?

*Mukund Padmanabhan*

Freedom of speech is the freedom to offend. It has become something of a cliché to say this and, heaven knows, I may well have used it myself in a couple of newspaper editorials.

But is it really? In a sense, of course. Deprived of the license to offend, freedom of speech and expression simply amounts to very little. Imagine a world stripped of scorn, shorn of satire. One in which it was forbidden to send up a pompous bigwig or deflate a political windbag. Life would be dreary and lackluster in such a world, but that is hardly the main problem. The injunction to never offend people's sentiments has far more serious implications. It is inimical to the very foundation of liberal democracy—the free exchange of ideas and the peaceful pursuit of knowledge and truth. We can all think of circumstances when offending someone—a racist, for example, a bigot, for another—is not a matter of choice, but of obligation. Merely telling the truth can cause offence. Copernican cosmology or Darwinian evolutionary theory, to understate the point, did not exactly endear itself to the church.

On the face of it, the idea of proscribing hurtful criticism may seem grounded in a sense of tolerance or compassion. Far from it. Invoking compassion to censor words that 'wound', is usually a cover for those whose worldviews are fed by intransigence and dogmatism. Causing offence is one of the necessary by-products of free speech. It is more than just an unpleasant derivative and is in fact very much an integral part of it. This is why free societies protect those whose words may cause offence.

But it is important to understand the cliché for what it is, or what it should be. Yes, freedom of speech includes the freedom to offend but this does not mean—as it is sometimes misinterpreted—that there is an unfettered liberty to do so. For example, defamation, which involves hurting someone's reputation, is unlawful and is an accepted limitation on free expression.

So, the question really is: when does one person's right to free speech trump another's sensitivities? When and under what conditions does offending a person, a group or the public at large get complicated? Where do you draw the line? Or, as David Lodge asked in a completely different context in his eponymously titled novel, "How Far Can You Go?"

# I

# Not all the Way

The short answer is not all the way.

The right to speech is never absolute and every country places restrictions on it. Article 19 (1) (2) of the Indian Constitution itemizes these restrictions in a list. It allows the state to impose 'reasonable restrictions' on eight specific grounds. They are the sovereignty and integrity of India, security of the state, friendly relations with foreign states, decency or morality, contempt of court, defamation, public order, or incitement to an offence.

Some of these restrictions are universal and, one may argue, perfectly reasonable. Free expression is rarely, if ever, an authorization to divulge state secrets, distribute child pornography, or indulge in unregulated slander. The legitimacy of some others is questionable— why, for instance, should anyone be constrained to promote friendly relations with foreign states?

Friendly relations with foreign states was one of the three additions to the list of restrictions brought about by the First Amendment, which was passed a year after the Constitution came into force in 1950. There is an odd irony to this, given that the First Amendment in the United States protects Congress from passing any law that abridges freedom of speech. Our First Amendment, the first of many retrograde changes to the Constitution, restricted free speech also on two other grounds, public order and incitement of an offence.

These two grounds are vitally relevant to any discussion on hurt sentiments and the issue of giving or taking offence in India.

Governments at the Central and State levels routinely ban inconvenient books and films on the ground that they endanger public order. And the distance between what merely offends some people and what is an actual incitement to offence is often blurred to discourage, even censor, free speech.

It is widely accepted that an explicit and unequivocal incitement to violence is a suitable ground for curbing free speech and expression. This follows from John Stuart Mill's so-called 'harm principle', which he laid down in his classic defence of free speech in *On Liberty*. According to Mill, the only justification for silencing a person against his will (or restraining him from living the way he wants to) is to prevent him from causing harm to others. For Mill, mere offensiveness does not constitute a ground for proscription.

As in many other countries, the deliberate use of hate speech is a criminal offence in India. Under the Indian Penal Code (Section 153 A), it is an offence to say anything that "promotes disharmony or feelings of enmity, hatred or ill-will between different religious, racial, language or regional groups or castes and communities." Section 295 A of the Code singles out religious sentiment and punishes those who intentionally outrage religious feelings or insult any religion or religious belief held by Indian citizens. Introduced in 1927, this provision gives protection to all religions on an equal basis—a kind of egalitarian and abridged blasphemy law.

The law takes the feelings of offended groups—religious fundamentalists, language chauvinists, and caste formations—very seriously. It has helped to feed what Monica Ali described in another context as a "marketplace for outrage"—a new economy which thrives on emotion, where "if the feelings run (or are seen to run) high and deep enough, a good price will be fetched" (Ali, 2007).

# II

# The Republic of Hurt Sentiments

We are quick to take offence and the most common source of such outrage is religion. Section 295A is intended to apply only in cases of a 'deliberate or malicious act' that is intended to outrage religious feelings, but it has become a handy tool to harass all manners of people, including writers, artists, and filmmakers. Complicit in this harassment is the state, ready to appease some irate religious grouping or another, and the courts, which often fail to make a distinction between frivolous litigation and a really malicious act.

People are routinely offended by what lies in the personal realm. Three years ago, former Test cricketer Ravi Shastri declared his love for Biltong while commentating for a sports channel in South Africa. His partiality for this dish of cured beef apparently offended the religious sentiments of a certain Manoj Malpani, a Bajrang Dal functionary; a case was filed before a court in Indore, which took the trouble to issue a notice and record the statement of the petitioner.

A few years ago, a spy camera caught a Godman and a Tamil actress having sex. The visuals were splashed in a magazine and found their way into television news channels. On the basis of a complaint, filed by a disgruntled devotee of the Godman who secretly filmed the encounters, a case was registered for, among other things, offending religious sentiments. Ironically, no action was taken against this gross violation of privacy committed by the devotee or the media, which went into a feeding frenzy over this 'exclusive'. Eating beef is not illegal, nor is consensual sex between single adults—but does anybody care? They are what Mill would have described as self-regarding behavior, activities to which the harm principle does not apply. Yes, you are free to criticize such activities, to persuade people from indulging in them. But they do not justify any form of coercive interference.

More seriously, hurt sentiment in this country is often a euphemism for aggressive moral vigilantism, an excuse to take the law into one's own hands, to perpetrate violence in the name of emotional victimhood. Our artistic and cultural freedoms are threatened routinely by such violence and vandalism—as during the controversies over M.F. Husain's paintings, Taslima Nasreen's novels and articles, Deepa Mehta's *Fire* and *Water*, Jaswant's Singh's book on Mohammed Ali Jinnah, Pakistan's cricketers playing in India, CNN-IBN broadcasts, and so on. The irony is that these aggressive vigilantes usually belong to organizations that make a living out of promoting enmity between different communities and religious groups—the very thing they accuse artists, filmmakers, writers, and journalists of doing.

In our Republic of Hurt Sentiments, we are confronted by two kinds of failures. The first is that of governments, which go out of their way to appease the offended. In the conflict between hurt sentiment and freedom of expression, between angry mobs and defenseless writers, governments and authorities prefer to take the safe route and ban the 'offending' book or play. Often, the mere threat of violence or some disturbance is sufficient for proscription. This happens despite the Supreme Court having laid down time and again that a mere threat to public order cannot be a ground for suppressing freedom of expression. In the landmark S. Rangarajan vs. Jagjivan Ram case, the Court observed that were this to happen, it would be "tantamount to the negation of the rule of law and a surrender to blackmail and intimidation."

We were the first country in the world to ban Salman Rushdie's *The Satanic Verses*, the import of which was forbidden in 1988 under customs law. But the real power for forfeiture vests with state governments which, under Section 95 of the Code of Criminal Procedure, may ban books (and newspapers, paintings, and photographs) for being seditious, obscene, and—yes, of course—for outraging religious feelings. Unlike books, films are subject to 'prior restraint'.

Moving images are regarded as having much greater potential in swaying emotions and influencing behavior than the printed words. The Supreme Court has held film censorship as "not only desirable but also necessary." But the Censor Board is not always the last word on the subject. In 2006, seven states banned the *Da Vinci Code* following representations and protests from Christian organizations; this was affected by directing local authorities all over the state to invoke Section 13 of the Cinematograph Act, under which films can be prevented from public exhibition if they are "likely to cause a breach of the peace." The governments defended their action on the ground that the film was likely to offend religious sentiments.

Despite the Supreme Court ruling in the S. Rangarajan vs. Jagjivan Ram case, governments routinely invoke public order to ban films, as the Tamil Nadu government did following a campaign by fringe Muslim groups against actor Kamal Haasan's *Vishwaroopam*. The ban could have been swiftly overturned, citing a strong body of judicial precedents, if the Madras High Court's dismissal of the petition challenging the Tamil Nadu government's ban on the release of *DAM 999* is an example.

The history of banning books and films in India on grounds that someone is offended is long and notorious, one of the earliest cases being Aubrey Menen's rationalist retelling of the Ramayana, *Rama Retold*. In 2003, the West Bengal Government banned Taslima Nasreen's *Dwikhondito*. Far worse, the Left Front government was complicit in forcing her to flee Kolkata a day after a group of Muslim fundamentalist demonstrators turned violent. Rather than declare that they would make the city safe for her, a senior Communist official complained to the press that her presence posed problems and said "the city would be safer without her." The same government was responsible for arresting the Editor and the Publisher of *The Statesman* for carrying an article that was reproduced from *The Independent*, which "outraged the religious feelings of Muslims."

If our first failure is the tendency to appease the offended, the second is the failure of the courts, particularly the lower ones. Rather than properly applying their minds to petitions before them, the courts summarily issue summons and non-bailable warrants in cases invoking hurt sentiments. The harassment of M.F. Husain exemplifies how the process itself becomes the punishment. More than one court issued non-bailable warrants against him in cases relating to his 'obscene' paintings of Hindu goddesses. By the time cases against the grand old man were clubbed together, transferred to the Delhi High Court and eventually quashed, Husain—who had received death threats, seen his house ransacked and his paintings defaced by Hindu fundamentalists had been forced into exile. All we seem capable of doing now is a hand wringing that before his death Husain could not return home and reclaim his original nationality.

# III

# Giving and Taking Offence

We are so used to being offended in the name of religion that we rarely stop and ask the philosophical question: why should religious belief or sentiment receive special protection under the law? Is there any reason for not extending this privilege to atheists or agnostics? Is there any rational basis for maintaining that religious beliefs or religious figures should not be exposed to scorn or ridicule in the manner that secular, worldly figures are?

Such questions are likely to lead us to a typically inconclusive philosophical debate. But they draw attention to an important truth. If we must have laws that prohibit offences against religious sentiment, then the very least we must do is to ensure that they apply only in cases of deliberate provocation, where the form of expression—whether words or visuals—is principally designed to humiliate or debase believers. This applies to all hate speech laws, including those that apply to causing offence on the basis of class, race, gender, or sexual orientation.

The mere criticism of a religion, that is its religious tenets, can hardly be the basis for taking offence. If no one else, surely the devout should understand this. Whether we like it or not, many of the world's religions do not portray—to understate the point—those who are non-believers in a kindly light. Implicit in the very nature of some religions are the criticism of certain others; this finds expressions in a variety of terms such as infidels, idolators, pagans, and so on. So is it not somewhat hypocritical to be deeply religious—at least in a conservative sense—and at the same time take offence very easily at criticism against your own religion?

Our laws are not the problem, but a messy combination of things. We take offence too easily—as caste formations, ethnic groups, language groups, and individuals. Political or politically affiliated organizations play the hurt sentiment card and indulge in violence in order to court some constituency or the other. We ban books, plays, and films in the face of protests with no concern about whether the offending material satisfies the two conditions required in any hate speech law—that it is a 'deliberate and malicious act' and that it poses a clear and present danger to (as opposed to something "remote, conjectural and far-fetched" in the Supreme Court's words) to society. And we use the deficiencies in the judicial system to harass those who have ostensibly offended us.

The controversy over the James Laine book on Shivaji is one of the many examples that typifies this messy state of affairs. An academic work on a Maratha King is declared offensive by a group calling itself the Sambhaji Brigade, which attacks a Pune institute, damaging works of historical and literary importance. The book is banned in Maharashtra on the ground that it intended to cause riots and promote enmity between different groups. The author is charged and threatened with arrest if he returns to India.

# IV

# Obscenity and the Law

Obscenity, in one form or another, is a restriction on free expression in all legal systems. Our obscenity laws are dealt with in Sections 292 to 294 of the Indian Penal Code which, among other things, make it an offence to publish and distribute material that is "lascivious or appeals to the prurient interest." In the context of hurt sentiment, the contentious part of the law is Section 294, which makes it an offence to participate in "any obscene act in a public place" to "the annoyance of another."

The use of these sections in controversies such as that involving M.F. Husain's paintings or the art student in Vadodara's M.S. University highlights how artistic expression has come under fire from religious vigilantism. But our form of moral policing often spills over into the personal realm. Marriages between Muslim boys and Hindu girls have evoked ugly campaigns against a so-called love jihad, young people drinking in pubs have been brutally attacked, and couples have been accosted on Valentine's Day for deviating from Hindu culture.

Filmstars have been a special target for complaints under Section 294. The fuss over the Richard Gere–Shilpa Shetty kiss may have caught international attention, but a slew of other actors have been caught in the crosshairs of moral police fire. A few examples: Sushmita Sen had a case slapped against her for her comments on pre-marital sex, similarly, Tamil actress Kushboo was embroiled in a huge controversy for saying that educated men should not expect their brides to be virgins, Akshay Kumar was arrested for an 'obscene' act involving his wife Twinkle at a public function, a non-bailable arrest warrant was issued against Reema Sen for pictures published in a Tamil weekly.

Our attitude to obscenity in cinema is paradoxical. On the one hand, we are comfortable with watching suggestive dance sequences and hearing crass double entendres on screen, at ease with sex when presented as insinuation or wrapped as fantasy. On the other, we expect our filmstars, particularly women, to be prim and straitlaced off it.

The *Savita Bhabi* episode illustrates we can be strangely paradoxical about pornography too. Scores of websites peddling hardcore Indian porn are available to Internet users. So what rationale could there have been for the Centre to single out and ban this adult cartoon site?

Leave aside the absurdity that the site was blocked through a section in the Information Technology Act that deals with sovereignty and security of the state. If pornographic obscenity was the issue, then surely it is hardcore porn sites featuring real men and women that should have been the principal target. One of the central arguments against pornography is that it is a form of oppression and enslavement, one that represents women solely as sex objects, as creatures deserving of such things as humiliation and abuse. A parallel to this argument at the empirical level is based on the nature of the porn industry, which is said to employ poor desperate women to perform acts against their will and at the cost of severe physical and psychological harm. Remember Linda Lovelace of *Deep Throat*, who claimed she was forced to perform sexual acts at gunpoint?

To many Indians, the spirited freewheeling *Savita Bhabhi*, who enjoys a successful marriage and an extremely varied sex life, seems anything but exploited. Pritish Nandy went as far as describing her as "a symbol of freedom, of empowerment," an *iconic* figure "who can take all her sexual decisions on her own without fretting about them." Since the *bhabhi* series was a cartoon strip, the argument about physical and psychological harm clearly does not apply.

So why did the Centre single out *Savita Bhabhi*? Why did it find the website particularly offensive? Was it because one of the strips dealt with her affair with a man, who resembles a Bollywood star? If this was so, then surely the appropriate response was a defamation case and not a blanket ban. Or was it because of our sense of discomfort about a saree-clad desi *nari*, a *mangalsutra* around her neck and vermillion on her forehead, who keeps her cuckold happy while having it off with everyone from a travelling bra salesman to a couple of adolescent boys? Did this overtly sexual *bhabhi* threaten the Indian male psyche even as she titillated it?

# V

# Slippery and Subjective

Quite possibly, it did. But the *Savita Bhabhi* episode illustrates just how utterly unpredictable this entire business of taking offence is. Offence is much too slippery and subjective a term for it to deserve a place in the statute books and become a handle for punishing those who think, act, and speak differently from the rest. There is no way of objectively determining what causes offence and what may not. The person who has caused such offence has no clear way of knowing what line he should not cross, or even where it is drawn.

In this respect, taking offence is rather like contempt of court. We have no way of gauging when and under what circumstances a judge believes that someone has incurred contempt of court. If a particular judge is *scandalized* or *offended*, then this is enough to constitute contempt.

Similarly, it is always going to be hard to tell who will get offended, how many will get offended, or how seriously they will get offended. This is especially problematic in a country where people's sentiments are hurt by just about anything—from expressing a preference for beef to holding hands on Valentine's Day.

In such an environment of uncertainty, how far can you go? The problem is we will never know until somebody somewhere thinks we have gone further than we should have.

# Reference

Ali, Monica. 2007. "The outrage economy," *The Guardian.* October 13. Available at http://www.theguardian.com/books/2007/oct/13/fiction.film (accessed on January 30, 2013).

# The Hermeneutics of Hurt

# 2

# What, If the Hurt Is 'Real'? Psyche, Neighbor, and Intimate Violence

*Anup Dhar*

This chapter looks at 'hurt' at two related levels. One is at the level of the *experience* of hurt. The other is at the level of the *response* to hurt. In the process, the chapter argues that the nature of the response—however problematic, however non-Left, not-so-Left-like (Left in the official and orthodox sense)—cannot drown altogether or render redundant the 'truth' of the experience of hurt or the need to attend, even if painstakingly, to the sometimes longstanding nature of the experience of hurt—for example, the experience of domestic violence in women, the experience of being untouchable, the experience of being poor, and the experience of being minoritized and branded 'terrorist'.[1] Hurt has a psychological substratum; marked by otherness, marked by loss, repeated loss, loss of land, loss of home, the bringing down of the mosque on December 6, 1992, loss of near ones, and the sexual violation of the loved ones in Gujarat 2002 and the trauma therein, all contribute to an experience of hurt. Nearness also contributes to the experience of hurt: how could *they* do it? We have lived together for so

[1] This is of course not to suggest that response cannot as such be examined. This chapter indeed puts response to critical scrutiny primarily in terms of the critical examination of the invocation of *blasphemy* in politics around hurt.

long; our children have played together. This chapter argues that one needs to take 'hurt seriously', and not judge it only by the barometer of the political correctness of response.

One needs to ask further, who is hurt? Who can get hurt? What is the condition of getting hurt? Is hurt a psychological state? Who can hurt? When and how is one hurt? Is nearness/relatedness the condition of being hurt? Does detachment preclude hurt? Does detachment make hurt 'hate'? What hurts? It also asks: what could be the response to hurt: sublimated aesthetics—unpublished woman writing after partition? Introjected violence—self-immolation among Tibetan refugees? Extro-jected violence—26/11? Violence in-between the purportedly introjected and the extro-jected—9/11—the suicide bomber who kills self-and-Other in a deadly and deadening deconstructive embrace? Aggressive counter-cathectic majoritarianism in the mainland—after Hindus have been displaced from Jammu? This leads us to one other question: would the experience of (and response to) hurt be different in the case of the (purportedly) powerful and the (purportedly) powerless? Or, more radically, is hurt an experience that is limited to the powerless; because in the powerful hurt is perhaps a nascent state; it quickly turns to either hate or rage; geared at times to (retributive) action; while the experience of hurt in the powerless does not necessarily translate to action, to an undoing, but remains cocooned, and encrypted[2] as a traumatic spur, a thorn stuck in the flesh, a thorn whose nature is perhaps *unknown* or not fully known but which is not or never *unfelt*.

# I

# The Experience of Hurt

In one sense, the expropriation of experience was implicit in the founding project of modern science. ... modern science has its origins in an unprecedented mistrust of experience as it was traditionally understood

---

[2] Derrida asks, what is a crypt? It is a kind of "false unconscious," an "artificial unconscious lodged like a prosthesis, a graft in the heart of an organ, within the divided self. A very specific and peculiar place, highly circumscribed, to which access can nevertheless

(Bacon defines it as a "forest" and a "maze" which has to be put in order). The view through Galileo's telescope produced not certainty and faith in experience but Descartes's doubt, and his famous hypothesis of a demon whose only preoccupation is to deceive our senses. (Agamben, 2007: 19–20)

Given the trivialization of the politics around hurt, the chapter foregrounds the need to attend to the question: what if one is[3] indeed hurt? We know 'indeed' is indeed a difficult claim to make. It is a claim that requires substantiation. What would be the level at which it will be substantiated? Would it be at a psychological level? Would it be at a historical plane? Would it gesture toward what Cornel West calls "ontological wounding?" However, the question of the *indeed* is indeed important in a contemporary milieu when 'politics (premised) on hurt' has lost much of its credibility; and we usually look at politics premised on hurt as primarily primordial or opportunistic politics. This is primarily because the indeed is perpetually in question in contemporary contexts. There is as if a secret consensus that politics premised on the deployment of hurt is not genuine or authentic politics; politics premised on exploitation, oppression, even humiliation is real(ly) politics.

Which is why, in this chapter we raise the question of the 'real *of* politics' as against 'real politics'. The politics of hurt perhaps shall not lend itself to the logic and language of what the official and the orthodox Left shall call 'real politics', the conventional Left has an equally

---

only be gained by following the routes of a different topography" (Derrida in Abraham and Torok, 1986: xiii). A crypt is as if this "monument of a lost object" preserved intact within the split ego. The "crypt is not unconscious although it functions as though it were, filtering all material bubbling up from this nether realm before any may submit to the secondary processes. When a *cryptophoric* subject speaks, then, it is only on behalf of the incorporated object. In place of words, a *cryptophoric* subject speaks *cryptonyms* or word-things whose relation to each other is determined less by laws of syntax or lexis than by their relation to the object itself" (see *I Wish to Dream and Other Impossible Effects of the Crypt* by Laurence Johnson; also see Abraham and Torok, 1986). Is the psyche then a "crypt effect" (Derrida in Abraham and Torok, 1986: xiii). Is it a repository of phantom effects? Is it *hauntological*?

[3] 'Is' can be temporal (setting the present off from past and future) or ontological; it can refer to essence or existence; it can be performative or constative; it can be mobilized to insist, declare, refute, or simply posit; and placed as an interrogative, it inverts its power of fixity and certainty; it undoes itself.

conventional scale of developing a secret nosology of politics—and judging which one is real politics and which one is not. We argue—against the Left's nosology—that it is at the level of the 'real *of* politics' that hurt shall make sense; where the 'real' of the 'real of politics' is different from the 'real' of 'real politics'. However, we shall have to explain what we mean by the 'real of politics'.

The Other approach (or what would also be an attempt at approaching the Other, the hurt Other, the hurt in the Other) would be to ask: what, if the hurt is 'real'? Not *really real*, necessarily. Not real in a realist sense. But 'real' in the sense that it is 'real for the subject'. 'Real' in the subject's somewhat non-symbolized pre-history. 'Real' in the sense that it has real subject effects–affects; affects that effect the response of the subject in future, in a time-to-come, somewhat in a manner that is marked as if by a kind of 'motivated irrationality' (what Lear calls *akrasia*, where "akrasia is one type of a more general form of irrationality which I shall call *reflexive breakdown*"; it is the "inability to give a full or coherent account of what one is doing" or why one is doing what one is doing [Lear, 1998: 81]).

This takes us to the Lacanian Real. One needs to mark the relationship between the experience of hurt and the Lacanian Real—how experiences of hurt find home in what Lacan calls the register of the Real, how such experiences remain secret or hidden in a somewhat non-symbolized manner. "What, if the hurt is Real" is gesturing toward such a (Lacanian) Real. This also takes us to the possibility of a 'politics of the real'. This chapter is in that sense a dialogue between the 'real of politics' and the 'politics of the real'. In other words, it is a dialogue between the 'inassimilable of (Left) politics' and the 'politics of the inassimilable'. It is a dialogue between an Other (kind of) politics—politics other than the politics of exploitation or oppression (in that sense, it is the 'real of [Left] politics') and the politics that gestures toward imagining the political around questions that have usually not qualified as legitimate political questions, say questions of exploitation and oppression (in that sense it is 'politics of the real'; it is politics of hurt or politics of humiliation). However, to set up the dialogue, we need to have a good sense of the Lacanian Real. The next section is a discussion on the Lacanian Real in its relation to the question of the experience and politics of hurt.

# II

# The Inassimilable Nature of Hurt

> ... whatever is refused in the symbolic order, in the sense of *Verwerfung*, reappears in the real. (Lacan, 1997a: 13)

> I always speak the truth. Not the whole truth, because there's no way, to say it all. Saying it all is literally impossible: words fail. Yet it's through this very impossibility that the truth holds onto the *real*.[4] (Lacan, 1990: 4)

It is through some kind of *impossibility* that the 'truth of hurt' holds onto the 'real'; one needs to make an effort; one needs to strain; not that we are surpassed eternally by an insurmountable impossibility; not that we do not know anything; not that we do not have any access to any truth; we know something; at times what we know we cannot explain for sure; but we feel it; we feel the hurt; and the hurt (of the demolition) is 'real'. We have felt it our entire lives. There is something wrong. One does not know for certain what it is but it's there, like a spur, a traumatic *pulsation* in our psyche, driving us mad. It is 'real'. One can also set up an encounter with the 'real'. Or perhaps, one can know with some certainty, one can at least touch upon some enabling perspective, however partial, even in this world and age of the "pragmatic-relativist New sophists and New Age obscurantists" (Badiou, 1989). Perhaps one needs to *read* hurt; and found a "theory of readability"[5] that does not just define the act of reading "but rather attempts to create avenues for reading where previously there were none" (Rand in Abraham and Torok, 1986: li). This is the world and age of the neo-sophists; and yet amid the sophistry that surrounds would it be too blasphemous to try and touch upon a political foothold with respect to

---

[4] Italics by Anup Dhar.

[5] Abraham and Torok's (1986) *Theory of Readability* suggests that "interpretation is possible even in the face of obvious obstruction. Such a theory is primarily concerned with converting obstructions into guides to understanding. Whereas most contemporary critical approaches deal with the perception and production of meaning, or alternatively with its potentially infinite deferral, the theory of readability implied in *The Wolf Man's Magic Word* proposes ways in which significance can be conjectured despite its apparent absence. Rather than analyze the vicissitudes of meaning (which may include its negation) within a signifying process, Abraham and Torok's theory of readability begins by addressing the problem of establishing a signifying process" (Rand in Abraham and Torok, 1986: lii).

the 'real of the hurt', instead of obsessing over whether the hurt is real or not, and whether the nature and quantum of (political) response is proportionate to the hurt or not. From the 'real of hurt', we move to 'politics of the real'. "Politics of the real" takes us in turn to the "real of politics." 'Politics of the real' is an attempt to rethink the traditional domain of politics by recognizing and acknowledging the dimension of the 'real', by setting up an encounter with the 'real'. It is an attempt at trying to retrieve to an extent the very thing excluded not just from the traditional field of epistemo-ontology but from the traditional field of politics as well and turn it, that is, the hitherto excluded, instead "into the legitimate territory of [politics]" (Zupancic, 2000: 3).

This work, thus, moves 'real politics' to a 'politics of the "real"' 'Politics of the "real"' is an *ab*original rendition of politics. Unabashedly *ab*original. *Ab*original politics is politics that refuses to be based and premised on the discourse and desire of the Master Left; it refuses to be based on what passes off as the left (categorical) imperative in politics.

The question, however, that could continue to trouble us in the context of 'politics of the real' and the 'real of politics' is: what is the 'real'? The real we are invoking here is not the real of real-ism; it is also not the real of the un-real. Perhaps there is something *irreal* about the real we are invoking; however, that does not make the real unreal. Let us now see how Lacan has tried to conceptualize the real. Let us also see whether a turn to the real shall help us turn to hurt. Would it in the process open up the social sciences to hurt, hurt as a legitimate object/site of enquiry?

The real has at times been seen in Lacanian psychoanalysis as that which is 'beyond Language'; here the real is seen as the *leftover* of the process of symbolization; the Real is as if the inassimilable *remainder* of the process of symbolization; it is the unspeakable limit of the process of symbolization (in the 1960s and the early 1970s, the second period of his teaching, Lacan defined the real as 'it' or *das Ding*. In this second period, Lacan described the real as the traumatic material of unassimilated memories and meanings that block the dialectical movement of symbolization). Perhaps there is something inassimilable about hurt; accruing possibly from the non-extimate, if not intimate nature of hurt. The real has at other times been seen as *'after* Language', as the by-product of the process of symbolization, as the *caputmortum*. Given the domination of legitimate discourses of politics, as also dominant political discourses of legitimacy, hurt is what remains as an afterthought; or perhaps that which does not find words, find language, given the domination of certain languages of politics. Or more radically, perhaps the question of hurt is what is *secreted out* by the very process of symbolization; the question of hurt is that which is *put outside, repudiated* in the process of the formation of the (Left secular) Symbolic—marked in turn by either the language of exploitation or oppression. In terms of the domination of such languages, experiences of hurt (as also of "humiliation" as Gopal Guru shows) get repudiated.

Does the experience of hurt—say, the hurt of the demolition of the mosque by a marauding big brother—then become a 'void space in being'? Is hurt at once impossible to possess and impossible to live without? Or what counts as hurt in the sense of the unsymbolizable is always relative to a linguistic domain that authorizes and produces that foreclosure, and achieves that effect by producing and policing a set of constitutive elements. Even if every discursive formation is produced through exclusion, that is not to claim that all exclusions are equivalent: what is needed is a way to assess politically how the production of cultural intelligibility is mobilized variably to regulate the political field, that is, who will count as a (political) 'subject', who will be required not to count (Butler, 1993: 207).

# III

# Response and Decipherment

To have pain is to have *certainty*; to hear about pain is to have *doubt*. (Scarry, 1985)

Our usual understanding of hurt is premised on a certain kind of 'action'; somebody has done something, say, written a text, painted a picture, or made a film on a revered "x". This follows from the fact that the response (say a protest against the text, painting, or film) determines what would count as hurt. However, hurt can be premised on non-action also; for example, the Indian state has not done anything substantive on the 2002 riots in Gujarat. Can someone be hurt by such non-action or inaction? Possibly. It is worth reflecting upon what effect–affect (and action perhaps) such non-action could generate? Is there a difference between hurt born out of action and hurt born out of non-action? Is hurt born out of non-action more authentic, more genuine? Hurt born out of non-action is also important because more often than not such hurt (unlike the question of 'hurt religious sentiments') does not generate an immediate (political) response. This is a kind of hurt that cannot be dismissed in terms of the response—through the invocation of hurt religious sentiments—hurt at times generates.

Some, however, continue to understand (and maybe assess the legitimacy of) hurt not through the truth of the experience but through the *response* of the one who is hurt. But how does one know that the response is in actuality not a delayed response, a displaced response to actual hurt? Interestingly, the experience of hurt in everyday individual life does not necessarily evoke action of a certain kind from the hurt subject. Stoicism, silence, or withdrawal at times becomes testimony to the fact that somebody is hurt. The symptom can be far more muted than the actual disease or the actual hurt that is harbored. Hurt perhaps cannot be assessed by the *response* to hurt; and the *politics* (at times, mobilization and consolidation) around hurt. While 'treatment' (that is akin to the response and the politics) may at times by far overtake the menace of the 'disease' (that is akin to the experience of hurt), the pain/suffering of disease can nevertheless be ignored. The ground of experience cannot be erased by the groundlessness (or the instrumental use of the rhetoric of hurt, or the irrational, at times 'politically incorrect' nature) of the response. One cannot disavow the "experience pole" through a denouncement of the 'response pole'. The chapter has, therefore, argued that if the 'phenomenology of pain/suffering' attends to one pole of the issue of hurt, the 'concept of the political' attends to the other; and the uncanny, perhaps politically perplexing response of those at the receiving end—the powerless—need to be understood not in terms of the accepted/conventional idioms of resistance.

Also, the response may not be a direct byproduct of the current evidence of hurt (say the cartoon or the film on the Prophet); it could be a delayed and displaced response to something deeper; it could be understood in terms of the psychoanalytic understanding of the *activated-afterness-of-hurt*; such an understanding would offer a deeper theorization of 'disadvantage'—a theorization that does not get reflected in the roll call register of disadvantage—and that cannot be addressed by mere reservation of seats for the disadvantaged. It would also offer a deeper understanding of the 'psychic life of hurt' that is not available in terms of what gets written on the 'transparent surface sheet' of the Mystic Writing Pad[6] but is retroactively recuperated with difficulty–patience–care from the somewhat illegible script, from the Other language inscribed–encrypted on the wax slab underneath.

Here the Mystic Writing Pad could be seen as a possible metaphor of the complexity of the human psyche (as against the rather simple notion of psyche with which much of Left politics works; the Frankfurt School and Althusser are of course exceptions). Freud invoked Mystic Writing Pad as a metaphor of the psyche to in turn foreground the importance of conceptualizing the psyche through the trope of *writing*. However, for Freud psychic writing was not ordinary or simple writing, not writing that was transparent or self-evident. Psychic writing was at least two layered; in fact it was *simultaneously* two layered; one layer was as if apparent, the other was, as if, beyond us; yet that which was beyond us was intimately tied to writing that was apparent. Freud, thus, cracks the commonsense understanding of writing and in the process the commonsense understanding of the psyche. The psyche was, as if, a two-layered writing apparatus; where the two layers were writing simultaneously; one constituting the other in ways not altogether known to us. To understand the psyche (here, the psychology of hurt), one needed to understand both layers and not just one layer; one also needed to understand the relation between the two layers. Of the two layers of writing, one is written on the surface and can be erased; the other layer is the sum-total of the wax impression of what has hitherto been written on the surface layer. According to Freud, human beings possess a system *Pcpt.-Cs.*, which receives perceptions but retains

---

[6] The Mystic (Writing) Pad, 1925, by Freud, is a slab of dark brown resin or wax with a work edging; over the slab is laid a thin transparent sheet; it itself consists of *two* layers which can be detached from each other except at their two ends. The upper layer is a transparent piece of celluloid; the lower layer is made of thin translucent waxed work. To make use of the Mystic (Writing) Pad one writes upon the celluloid portion of the covering sheet which rests upon the waxed slab. No pencil or chalk is necessary, since the writing does not depend on material being deposited upon the receptive surface. A pointed stylus scratches the surface, the depressions constitute the "writing." At the points which the stylus touches, it presses the lower surface of the waxed work on to the wax slab, and the grooves are visible as dark writing upon the otherwise smooth whitish gray surface of the celluloid. If one wishes to destroy what one has written, all that is necessary is to raise the double covering sheet from the wax slab; the close contact between the waxwork and the wax slab at the places, which have been scratched (upon which the visibility of the writing depended) is thus brought to an end. The Mystic Pad is now clear of writing and ready to receive fresh inscriptions.

no permanent trace of them so that it can react like a clean slate to every new perception; while the permanent traces of the excitations which have been received are preserved in 'mnemic systems' lying behind the perceptual systems. This *double system* contained in a single differentiated apparatus, a *perceptually available innocence* (an apparent innocence) and an *infinite resource of traces* (traces that cannot be erased) is reconciled with the Mystic Writing Pad which offers an ever ready receptive surface as also permanent traces of inscriptions that have been made on it; 'traces', thus, produce the space of their inscription only by acceding to the period of their erasure. Thus, received inscriptions *cannot be lost altogether*; and although such inscriptions would not qualify as a known script in the ordinary sense of the term, they would still constitute a language; constitute an altogether different language or a different structure of language. Traces of language remain, not on the surface, not on the writing surface, not on the given surface, but somewhere else, in another register, in an *Other* register, elsewhere, in another way:

> "… *it* [*ca*] thinks" in another way, *it* writes in another way. "*It* thinks rather badly, but *it* thinks steadily. It is in these terms that Freud announces the unconscious to us: thoughts that, while their laws are not exactly the same as those of our everyday thoughts … are certainly articulated. … Freud called the locus of the unconscious *ein anderer Schauplatz*, another scene" that "is found to subsist in an alterity with respect to the subject"… "the unconscious is the Other's discourse [*discourse de l'Autre*]." (Lacan, 2006: 458–459)

The experience of hurt is lodged somewhere *here*; in a certain inassimilability and illegibility. Decipherment, learning to read, or perhaps a 'theory of readability' interpretation in the face of obvious obstruction, a conjecturing of significance despite its apparent absence, establishing a cultural *Verbarium* of hurt (Abraham and Torok, 1986: 107) is perhaps the *grundrisse* for a 'politics of the real', which in turn gestures toward the 'real of politics'.

This is also because hurt will not lend itself to numbers, quantification, or an exact calculus of cause and action. Which is perhaps why the response to hurt looks strange, exaggerated, or out of place; all the more because even the protesting subject population cannot make a direct causal link between hurt and response. The sovereign solitude of the author subject in the Left is not available here. The punctual simplicity of the classical Left or even Right political subject is not to be found here. We would perhaps need to understand the response to hurt not as the work of a 'few shepherd subjects' and more as the work of a 'flock of subjectivities'— polymorphous, heterogeneous, disaggregated, conflict ridden, and contradictory. However, the distinction between violence and creative discursive rupture could still be maintained when one is discussing response to hurt.

Perhaps there is something uncanny (Scarry, 1985)[7] about being hurt. Hurt is either *before* language or *outside* language. Which is why, it is not anything that is really real. It is real in the Lacanian sense.[8] It is in effect ir-real. Which is why the foregrounding of hurt is happening through something that is somewhat like a 'substitute hurt'; a substitute for the everyday and the continuing experience of hurt; an experience, and because it is an experience of hurt (and not say violation or humiliation) has remained unaddressed; has been kept inordinately silent, and the response had been one of withdrawal. In the larger rhetoric of secular modernity and the impatience of it – the way it secretly bleeds subjects; the film on the Prophet becomes or emerges as the nodal point around which the politics of hurt suddenly takes shape. It is precisely because politics and the political—the first premised on substitute real-s and the second premised on the real—are two related yet different entities.

[7] Scarry showed how pain can neither be confirmed nor denied. While pain has no object of its own, its existence is undeniable. But so is the difficulty of expressing it for it "does not simply resist language but actively destroys it, bringing about an immediate reversion to a state *anterior* to language, to the sounds and cries a human being makes *before* language is learned ... its resistance to language is not simply one of its incidental or accidental attributes but is essential to what it is" (pp. 4–5). This is compounded by the fact that pain "unlike any other state of consciousness—has no referential content. It is not *of* or *for* anything. It is precisely because it takes no object that it, more than any other phenomenon, resists objectification in language" (p. 5). Pain requires us to "invent linguistic structures that will reach and accommodate this area of experience normally so inaccessible to language" (p. 6).

[8] Between the Imaginary of experience—between the ego and the alter ego—and the Symbolic—lies the Lacanian Real. The Real before language and the Real after language. The inassimilable *remainder*. The *reminder* that one has not symbolized all: there is a not-all; not-whole.

# IV
# Beyond 'Free Speech'/'Blasphemy'

Does the modern liberal aversion to the category of blasphemy derive from a suspicion of political religion?

Why is it that aggression in the name of God shocks secular liberal sensibilities, whereas the act of killing in the name of the secular nation, or of democracy, does not? (Asad, 2009)

I shall end this chapter with a short take on an established binary, 'free speech' versus 'blasphemy', that determines much of the politics around hurt and that according to me is a roadblock, a hindrance to developing an attentive listening to or an appreciation of hurt and an imagining of the political around hurt. One, the dominant argument around the 'threat to free speech'—if overdone—does not let us even access the register of hurt. Two, does the quick, rather hasty invocation of blasphemy—all too often for all kinds of hurt—also short-circuit access to the register of hurt? While I am not arguing for a hyper-separation of religion and politics, or a complete secularization of politics (which, as it is, is never the case in the Christian West), could there be forms of political imagination other than the ones marked by the trope of blasphemy? Was the Bhakti-Sufi movement in India such a pre-modern moment? Was Gandhian swaraj-satyagraha-swadeshi such a modern moment? Were both openings to the 'real of politics' and the 'real of religion'?

The opposition between free speech and blasphemy in turn translates into a discourse on democracy, secularism, liberty, and reason on one side (Talal Asad calls this a *presumed convergence*; and if this presumed convergence is questioned, Western culture may come up with a different self-description; it may not then be so difficult to relate to or understand the politics of hurt), and on the other the many opposites—religion (usually Islam in turn identified with aggression and death), intolerance, and violence. This dualism—used to the hilt by much of right wing Hindu politics in India—is represented in much of public discourse as a civilizational confrontation between Christianity (which automatically reconciles Greek reason [not Egyptian reason] with biblical faith and the doctrine of secular free speech), and Islam, which encourages 'violent conversion'. This, from time to time, can also become an East-West, Occident-Orient distinction; the West has managed to separate State and Church; the East has not; as if there is in the history of the Christian West the obvious *seed* or kernel of the secular which blossomed into a full-blown plant in European modernity. The above dualism is also representative of the debate between the liberal and the illiberal. The Orientalist nature of the division is of course apparent; also this reduction of a discursive space—liberalism—with its own history, vocabulary, idiom, and heuristic—to an identitarian ethic for the Christian West—is the master move on which the *hierarchy* (*not difference*) of Christianity and Islam can be marked; as if it is only the Christian West that is armed with 'secular critique'; and Islam (at times, other religions) is doomed to the 'repetition compulsion' of blasphemy. In this context, one can ask: is critique secular? What makes a critique and the secular align with such consummate ease? How did they become thoroughly bound to one another? Indeed, how has critique come to be defined as secular, and how has secularism come to be understood as both what animates critique and what critique yields? Would the transparency of appositionality evaporate if both terms are subjected to genealogical scrutiny? Does the very term 'critique' invite the *work* of further critique? Would this put to question the hyper-separation of Christianity and Islam (and by default of West and middle-East, modern and religious, capitalist and feudal) and the confluence of secular and critique?

A relationship with hurt and the political around hurt—both the politics of the real and the real of politics—could perhaps be possible once one has problematized such conceptual hyper-separation of religions and conceptual confluence of (somewhat illusory) liberal ideals. The relationship with hurt is further deepened once one has problematized the conceptual hyper-separation of religion and the (somewhat illusory) liberal ideals.

# References

Abraham, N. and M. Torok. 1986. *The Wolf Man's Magic Word: A Cryptonymy*. Trans. Nicholas Rand. Minneapolis: University of Minnesota Press.

Agamben, G. 2007. *Infancy and History: On the Destruction of Experience*. Trans. Liz Heron. London: Verso.

Asad, Talal, Brown, Wendy, Butler, Judith, and Mahmood, Saba. 2009. *Is Critique Secular? Blasphemy, Injury, and Free Speech.* UC Berkeley: Townsend Center for the Humanities. Retrieved from: http://escholarship.org/uc/item/84q9c6ft

Badiou, A. 2001. *Ethics: An Essay on the Understanding of Evil.* Verso: London.

Butler, J. 1993. *Bodies that Matter: On the Discursive Limits of "Sex."* New York and London: Routledge.

Lear, J. 1998. *Open Minded: Working Out the Logic of the Soul.* Harvard: Harvard University Press.

Scarry, E. 1985. *The Body in Pain: The Making and Unmaking of the World.* New York: Oxford University Press.

Zupancic, A. 2000. *Ethics of the Real: Kant, Lacan.* New York and London: Verso.

# 3

# Between Speech and Silence

*Dilip Simeon*

## I

I went to speak at a general assembly in the school playground. I wasn't afraid of anything. I was carried forward by the moment. After May '68 I've never again been able to speak at a public meeting. But then I could answer every argument, talk back to anybody.

In that month of talking you learnt more than in the whole of your five years of studying. Learnt because you could talk to anyone and everyone. It was really another world—a dream world perhaps—but that's what I'll always remember: the need and the right for everyone to speak.

It was fantastic. Everything we did immediately belonged to History.

—French students reminiscing about May 1968 (Marcus, 1997: 17)

If Aristotle's definition of humans as political animals (*zoon politikon*) is true, equally true is the proposition that politics is based on speech. Politics involves speech about common concerns—between equals, even if the equality lasts only for the duration of the communication. Where there is no speech, there is no politics. The advent of violence implies the end of speech. It also implies the weakness of the violent actors. The 'mass-mediated outrage' that the editors speak of is an apt description of the state of affairs as regards free speech and expression, and its implications deserve to be spelled out. These relate to the following:

- the degree of reasonableness of the basic statutes of the polity
- the degree to which these statutes are or may be implemented

- the institutions and spaces of political speech and the extent to which they are used, and by whom
- the existence of private armed groups and the degree of state complicity in their activities
- the functions of mob violence in the polity—its direction of flow
- the uses of ignorance

Assuming that we live in an era of mass democratic politics, we must recognize that all democracies face the requirement of legitimation, simply because the state is no longer grounded in the notion of divine right. Any state that appeals to a divine concept of sovereignty faces the problem of identifying the representative of divine law. Since such an agent must logically be above and beyond the control of the people, such a polity will be something less than a democracy. Its fundamental statutes will be of the kind that requires unconditional obedience, rather than dialogic consent and participation. Hence, states that invoke the sovereignty of God and revelation in their constituent statutes (such as Pakistan or Iran) must be adjudged as less than democratic.


# II

# Demos and Deity

However, even in the absence of divine legitimation, democratic politics may undergo perversion by means of an ideological subservience to a mythic ideal of the People or the Nation, which functions as a substitute for the absent deity. Nationalism here takes on the aspect of prayer. The more it assumes such an aspect, the more it moves away from democracy.[1] The dilemmas of the modern state arise both from certain essential features of the human condition, and from the specific aspects of a global system based on enmity (Mack, 1990). In such a system, ideologically enforced animus becomes an essential aspect of governance, not least because of the need to maintain armed forces as

---

[1] For a discussion of the emergence of the nation-state and its potentially anti-democratic impact, see Simeon (2013).

sentinels of sovereignty, both internally and externally. This dilemma was commented upon by Spinoza in his *Theologico-Political Treatise* (1670), a seminal text for early modern political theory that had to be written under an assumed name and in Latin rather than his native Dutch in order to escape censorship:

> All men are by nature subject to superstition ... nothing is as effective in ruling the masses as superstition ... the greatest care has been taken to invest religion, whether true or false, with pomp and circumstance to give it more weight than any other motive ... (Preface) Whoever has experienced the inconstant temperament of the multitude will be brought to despair by it. For it is governed not by reason but by the affects alone....[2]

Every state, therefore, needed to combine affective with rational means to maintain itself and public order. Analyzing history in terms pertinent to our own time, Spinoza railed against attempts by rulers to control the mind, and argued for the exclusion from political affairs of "ministers of religion":

> On the other hand, when the religious controversy ... began to be taken up by politicians and the States, it grew into a schism, and abundantly showed that laws dealing with religion and seeking to settle its controversies are much more calculated to irritate than to reform, and that they give rise to extreme licence: further, it was seen that schisms do not originate in a love of truth, which is a source of courtesy and gentleness, but rather in an inordinate desire for supremacy. From all these considerations it is clearer than the sun at noonday, that the true schismatics are those who condemn other men's writings, and seditiously stir up the quarrelsome masses against their authors, rather than those authors themselves, who generally write only for the learned, and appeal solely to reason. In fact, the real disturbers of the peace are those who, in a free state, seek to curtail the liberty of judgment which they are unable to tyrannize over. (Balibar, 1994: 13)

And in an earlier chapter,

> We may now clearly see from what I have said: How hurtful to religion and the state is the concession to ministers of religion of any power of issuing decrees or transacting the business of government: how, on the contrary, far greater stability is afforded, if the said ministers are only allowed to give answers to questions duly put to them, and are, as a rule, obliged to preach and practice the received and accepted doctrines. How dangerous it is to

---

[2] Cited in Balibar, 1994: 13.

refer to Divine right matters merely speculative and subject or liable to dispute. The most tyrannical governments are those which make crimes of opinions, for everyone has an inalienable right over his thoughts - nay, such a state of things leads to the rule of popular passion. Pontius Pilate made concession to the passion of the Pharisees in consenting to the crucifixion of Christ, whom he knew to be innocent. Again, the Pharisees, in order to shake the position of men richer than themselves, began to set on foot questions of religion, and accused the Sadducees of impiety, and, following their example, the vilest hypocrites, stirred, as they pretended, by the same holy wrath which they called zeal for the Lord, persecuted men whose unblemished character and distinguished virtue had excited the popular hatred, publicly denounced their opinions, and inflamed the fierce passions of the people against them.[3]

# III

# Nationalism and Animus

The institutionalization of patriotic hate was a powerful factor in strengthening political stability, because it was "stronger than any other feeling, a hate born of devotion, of piety, believed to be pious—the strongest and most persistent kind" (Balibar, 1994: 13). Here, then, is a clue to the functions of hate speech in our time. The French Revolution was an event that marked the arrival of the modern nation-state, as well as the advent of politicized militarism (the revolutionary armies were based on universal conscription and they fought for the ideals of the Republic). The severe internal conflicts of the time were cruelly put down for the sake of a united patriotic war effort against the monarchs of the absolutist Europe. The wars lasted a quarter of a century (1790–1815) and can be described as the first total war. Censorship and terror for the greater good of the People made their bloody appearance on the world stage. Nationalism was born as an enemy system, as an 'institutionalization of patriotic hate'.

The early modern Enlightenment was a campaign to reduce the power of religious dogma and authoritarian government and to assert the authority of human reason. All versions of the Enlightenment

---

[3] See the online version of the Treatise, available at http://www.yesselman.com/ttpelws4.htm#CXVIII(1), accessed on May 21, 2013.

attempted to eliminate restrictions upon intellectual inquiry. However two features of capitalist modernity have altered this pattern. The first is the sacralization of the Nation and, the second, the adaptation of science to nationalist ends. The first nullifies the rationalist challenge to religious dogma, by adapting traditional religiosity toward another sacred object, viz., the Nation. The second chanellizes scientific pursuits toward the militarist structure of modernity, contributing a new constraint to the pursuit of knowledge. Science and technology are impressive achievements of the human spirit. But they are ethically neutral, as is mathematics. As for religion, it has been transformed from a moral guide and source of ethical knowledge into a badge of political identity.

Given this predicament, the mind has also been nationalized, and undergone industrialization—there exists today a mind-making industry, along with all the others.[4] Modernity has discovered the uses of enforced ignorance, which along with the manipulation of the passions noted by Spinoza, today constitute an important weapon in the armory of governance. A crucial aspect of political speech today is the necessity of deceit, because of the need to mis-represent the sovereignty of capital as the sovereignty of the people—in other words, to dress up powerlessness as power. In such a situation, it is a lack of knowledge and an absence of the capacity to make reasonable judgments that the establishment seeks to foster among the populace. What remains of democracy is not power over life, but the freedom to vent the most base among human emotions. In these republics of hate, the only constraint is the need for modulation lest the tide of calibrated violence overrun the very interests whose purposes it serves. (This is as yet a tendency, albeit a powerful one. I do not wish to suggest that we inhabit a completely Orwellian universe.)

We are inundated, then, with a mixture of propaganda and censorship, each of which buttresses the other—it is clear that hate speech is accompanied by hateful silencing. In a clear-sighted analytical passage on the crucial place of dialogue in human existence, the philosopher Stanley Rosen argues (and I paraphrase him) that humans are by nature forever intermediate between speech and silence. Moderate speech may preserve their humanity, but it must not obscure the difference between the human and the divine. Speech

---

[4] See Enzensberger (1982).

that recognizes the difference is prayer, but the defect in the religious solution is the problem of the false prophet, and disagreement about the correct version of prayer. This may be enforced, but, says Rosen:

> … the appeal to force is an admission of the failure of interpretation, and so of speech. In admitting the insolubility of the meaning of the divine difference by speech, one admits the desirability not of a moderate speech, but of silence (and thus force is a silent immoderate speech which negates itself by excess). However this may preserve political stability in one sense, it cancels it in another and deeper sense; only human beings can dwell in political stability, but human beings are characterized by speech, not by silence. The stable city is no longer a city of men, but, to borrow a phrase from Plato, a city of pigs. The attempt to satisfy desire by recourse to prayer, if followed consistently, leads to the suppression of the difference it was designed to preserve. In order to safeguard their humanity, men must allow the false prophet to be heard; that is, they must dispute with him, thereby submitting and re-submitting the Holy Word to human interpretation. (Stanley, 1969: 209–211)

Our intellectual lives today are awash in a tide of ideologies (as distinct from contemplations of reality). As mixtures of reason and faith, ideologies restrict the pursuit of truth. Faith induces a theodicean element into politics (theodicy refers to God's plan to extract good from evil). This secularized religiosity propels its followers toward a belief in history with a capital H—a law-governed process redolent with visions of national glory, world domination, proletarian liberation, etc. Bent as it is toward futurity, the ideological experience of time erodes the sense of the Present. The mentality of the ideological cadre is characterized above all, by the desire and tendency to control the human intellect via deceit and intimidation. He does not understand, as we must, that the practice of violence signifies not an accretion, but contraction of power. Power can destroy but not replace truth. The repression by force of the freedom to speak and be creative must inevitably deprive humanity of its ability to attain wisdom via dialogue. Indeed, it is a moot point whether a citizenry under the tutelage of a politically enforced *Truth* (or what amounts to the same thing, a politically engendered stupidity) can even remember the ideal called wisdom.

When sentiment is used as a means to dominate the speech of others by way of force, then this mobilization of sentiment symbolizes tyranny, not democracy. It is also the enforcement of public deceit, because what is being stated is not that such-and-such persons are offended, and the reasons thereof, but that they propose to be violent and destructive unless their demands are accepted. The so-called hurt sentiment has now become the cutting edge of a campaign to replace democracy with mob rule. The degree to which we resist this will be the measure of our capacity to preserve the truest human capacity—the power to speak and to uphold truth.

# References

Balibar, Etienne. 1994. *Masses, Classes, Ideas: Studies on Politics and Philosophy Before and After Marx*. New York: Routledge.

Banaji, Jairus (Ed.). 2013. *Fascism: Essays on Europe and India*. Gurgaon: Three Essays Collective.

Enzensberger, Hans Magnus. 1982. "The Industrialization of the Mind," *Critical Essays*. New York: Continuum Press, available at http://faculty.washington.edu/cbehler/teaching/coursenotes/Texts/enzensbergindust.html (accessed on May 21, 2013).

Mack, John. 1990. *The Enemy System*, in Volkan, Julius and Montville, *The Psychodynamics of International Relationships, Vol. 1, Concepts and Theories*. Toronto: Lexington Books, available at http://johnemackinstitute.org/1988/08/the-enemy-system-short-version/, accessed on May 21, 2013.

Marcus, Greil. 1997. *The Dustbin of History*. London: Macmillan & Co.

Rosen, Stanley. 1969. *Nihilism: A Philosophical Essay*. London: Carthage Press, pp. 209–211.

Simeon, Dilip. 2013. "The Law of Killing: A Brief History of Indian Fascism," in *Fascism: Essays on Europe and India*, edited by Jairus Banaji. Gurgaon: Three Essays Collective.

# Forked Tongues of Hate

# 4

# The Harm in Hate Speech Laws: Examining the Origins of Hate Speech Legislation in India

*Siddharth Narrain*

I

## The English Common Law: Origins of Indian Hate Speech Law

Hate speech is often described as the fault line that divides advocates of free speech in India. In India, the substantive law on hate speech has been codified in the Indian Penal Code, 1860 and the Code of Criminal Procedure, 1872. This chapter attempts to look at the history and development of the category of 'hate speech' in the criminal law in India beginning at the time of the colonial encounter, a crucial moment that shapes the contours of the contemporary law on hate speech.

Hate speech provisions in India can be said to originate in the English common law principle of seditious and blasphemous libel. The British imported the common law principles of seditious libel and blasphemous libel into the criminal laws framed in India through specific provisions that were aimed at assuaging what they considered the peculiar religious sentiments and vulnerability to insult and offence (Holt, 1816). Blasphemous libel was seen to deal with material that affected the foundations of the Christian religion, the truth of the Holy Scriptures, and the acknowledged sacraments of the Church

(Holt, 1816). It was targeted at blasphemous material that was seen to be subverting all religion and morality, which were foundations of the government (Holt, 1816). Libels that tended to degrade and vilify the constitution, to promote insurrection, circulate discontent through its members, to asperse its justice and anywise impair the exercise of its functions, were termed "seditious libel" (Holt, 1816).

Macaulay, in his draft Indian Penal Code published by the Indian Law Commission, has one chapter titled "Of Offences Related to Religion." However, the provisions that we would consider hate speech today are distributed over three different chapters of the Code.

Table 4.1 illustrates this.

Note J of the First Indian Law Commission's Penal Code that was presented before the Governor General of India in Council in 1835 and formed the basis for the 1860 legislation throws light on Macaulay's thinking on this subject. The Note is directly relevant to Sections 298 and 295A both of which fall under this section.

> The principle on which this Chapter has been formed is a principle on which it would be desirable that all Governments should act, but from which the British Government in India cannot depart without risking the dissolution of society. It is this, that every man should be suffered to profess his own religion, and that no man should be suffered to insult the religion of another. (Indian Law Commissioners, 2002: 101)

It goes on to say

> ... There is perhaps no country in which the Government has so much to apprehend from religious excitement among the people.... (Indian Law Commissioners, 2002: 102)

These developments have been described by commentators as a strategy that "enabled the colonial state to assume the role of the rational and neutral arbiter of supposedly endemic and inevitable religious conflicts between what it presumed were its religiously and emotionally excitable subjects" (Ahmed, 2009: 173). Macaulay does attempt, however, to rationalize the law, and this was influenced by his opposition to religious fanaticism back home. In a parliamentary speech advocating the removal of civil disabilities against the Jewish community in England, Macaulay opposed England's existing blasphemy laws and specified the principle on which he would frame

**Table 4.1**

*Hate Speech Provisions in the Indian Penal Code*

| IPC section | 298 | 505 | 153(A) | 295(A) | 505(2) | 153(B) |
|---|---|---|---|---|---|---|
| **Chapter in IPC** | Of Offences Relating to Religion | Of Criminal Intimidation, Insult and Annoyance | Of Offences against the Public Tranquility | Of Offences Relating to Religion | Of Criminal Intimidation, Insult and Annoyance | Of Offences against the Public Tranquility |
| **Year of enactment, amendment** | 1860 (was section 282 in Draft Penal Code) | 1860(?), amended in 1898 | 1898 (separated from sec 124A), amended in 1961, 1969, 1972 | 1927, amended in 1961 | 1969 | 1972 |
| **Wording of section** | Uttering words, etc. with deliberate intent to wound religious feelings | Statements conducing to public mischief | Promoting enmity between different groups on grounds of religion, race, place of birth, residence, language etc. (Explanation dropped in 1961) | Deliberate and malicious acts intended to outrage religious feelings of any class by insulting its religion or religious beliefs | Statements creating or promoting hatred enmity or ill will between classes | Imputations, assertions prejudicial to national integration |

*(Table 4.1 Continued)*

(Table 4.1 Continued)

| IPC section | 298 | 505 | 153(A) | 295(A) | 505(2) | 153(B) |
|---|---|---|---|---|---|---|
| **Gravity of offence** | Non-cognizable, bailable, compoundable by the person whose religious feelings were intended to be wounded. Punishment may extend up to one year imprisonment. Triable by any Magistrate | Non-cognizable, non-bailable, non-compoundable, triable by any Magistrate | Cognizable, non-bailable, non-compoundable. Punishment may extend up to 3 years imprisonment. Triable by Magistrate of First Class | Cognizable, non-bailable, non-compoundable. Punishment may extend up to 3 years imprisonment. Triable by Magistrate of First Class. | Cognizable, non-bailable, non-compoundable. Punishment may extend up to 3 years imprisonment. Triable by any Magistrate. | Cognizable, non-bailable, non-compoundable. Punishment may extend up to 3 years imprisonment. Punishment may extend up to 5 years in cases where offence is committed in a place of worship or in an assembly engaged in the performance of religious worship or religious ceremonies. Triable by Magistrate of First Class. |

such a law. This principle, that everyone should be at liberty to discuss religion, but not so as to cause pain, disgust, or outrage and thereby infringe on the rights of others, is reflected in the Indian Penal Code (Pinney, 1974: 43–44).[1]

The other influential thinker of the time, writing on the role of criminal law was J.S. Mill. In his classic treatise on the subject, "On Liberty," Mill discusses at length how curbing speech would be deleterious to the development of new ideas. Mill, however, was aware that in certain circumstances, speech could be restricted. For instance, Mill warns against intemperate discussion when it is used against the comparatively defenseless.

> The worst offence of this kind which can be committed by a polemic, is to stigmatise those who hold the contrary opinion as bad and immoral men. To calumny of this sort, those who hold any unpopular opinion are peculiarly exposed because they are in general few and uninfluential, and nobody but themselves feels much interested in seeing justice done to them. (Mill, 2006: 62)

Mill's concern is not so much about insult to religion or blasphemy as unpopular thought. He goes on to say:

> In general, opinions contrary to those commonly received can only obtain a hearing by studied moderation of language, and the most cautious avoidance of unnecessary offence, from which they hardly ever deviate even in a slight degree from losing ground: while unmeasured vituperation employed on the side of prevailing opinion, really does deter people from professing contrary opinions, and from listening to people who profess them. For the interest, therefore, of truth and justice, it is far more important to restrain this employment of vituperative language than the other; and, for example, if it were necessary to choose, there would be much more need to discourage offensive attacks on infidelity, than on religion. (Mill, 2006: 62)

In the Indian Penal Code, there is a string of sections (see Table 4.1) that attempt to ensure that religious sentiments and hurt are protected by law. These have been added to the Code over a period of time and amended post-independence to expand their reach.

Of the three main provisions in the Indian Penal Code that deal with hate speech, only one existed in 1860 (see Table 4.1) Section 298 that

---

[1] Pinney (1974: 43–44) cited in Asad Ali Ahmed, p. 180.

dealt with "wounding religious feelings." Legal thinkers including Sir Lawrence Peel, Chief Justice of the Supreme Court in 1848, opposed this section arguing that 'wounding' religious feelings should not be criminalized unless it led to public disorder (Peel, 1848: 181).

# II

# History of Section 153A

Section 153A was born in 1898 when the sedition law was amended by the British Parliament after considering recommendations of a Select Committee. At the time, promoting class hatred was a part of the English law of sedition, but this offence was not included in the Indian law. The overall purpose of 1898 amendments was to bring Section 124A in line with English principles based on which Indian courts had interpreted the section and the law as it stood. This would ensure that the ambit of the law would be expanded and that the offence did not need an appeal to force, thus changing the strict requirement of direct incitement to violence or intention to commit rebellion. The British hoped that this would help tackle criticism of heavy-handedness by their government that was emerging from the vernacular press, the reasons for which were linked to the emergence of a class of English educated Indians (Donogh, 1911: 61–68).

British lawmakers like Mr Chalmers, Member of the Select Committee while introducing the Bill in Parliament on December 25, 1897, justified the introduction of Section 153A as a separate offence by saying that if such a provision was required in England with a relatively homogeneous population, it was even more important in India where different races and religions were in continual contact (Donogh, 1911: 163). The Report of the Select Committee on February 4, 1898 has a more detailed explanation for creating Section 153A as a separate offence.

> … It appears to us that the offence of stirring up class hatred differs in many important respects from the offences of sedition against the State. It comes more appropriately in the chapter relating to offences against the public tranquility. The offence only affects the Government or the State indirectly, and the essence of the offence is that it predisposes classes of people to

action which may disturb the public tranquility. The fact that this offence is punishable in England as seditious libel is probably due to historical causes, and has nothing to do with logical arrangement. But, in framing the clause we have altered the words "enmity or ill-will" into "enmity or hatred" and we have fixed the maximum punishment at two years imprisonment. The word ill-will was thought to be "too wide and vague" in its meaning and therefore unsuitable for either section. (Donogh, 1911: 164)

The deliberation of the Select Committee, when it met on February 18, 1898 for final consideration of the Bill, gives further insights into the reasons behind this section. These deliberations refer to "the persistent attacks on the officers and helpers engaged in plague operations," and a squabble over an alleged mosque that resulted in a riot and threatened to turn into a general attack on the European community in Calcutta, as examples of how accidental events can turn into explosions in India, and justify the law as a preventive measure "by taking power to punish people who foment class animosities to obviate the consequences of putting down the consequent disturbances with a high hand" (Donogh, 1911: 61–68).

There were, however, concerns raised about the possibility of abuse of a law that made a departure from English law. The safeguards cited by members were those that were common to Section 124A and 505 that prosecutions could not be commenced without the authority of the local government, the right of appeal and revision in the High Court and the addition of an Explanation to Section 153A. The explanation was added on the insistence of Sir Griffith Evans. It read:

> It does not amount to an offence within the meaning of this section to point out, without malicious intention, and in honest view to their removal, matters which are producing, or have the tendency to produce, feelings of enmity or hatred between different classes of Her Majesty's subjects. (Donogh, 1911: 165)

Thus, Section 124A remained on the statute book to deal with disaffection and disloyalty to the state, governing the relationship between the state and its citizens. Section 153A began to govern the relationship between various communities, a relationship that was mediated by the state.

The other section that was introduced along with Section 153A through the 1898 amendment was section 505. This section sought to change the existing provision dealing with circulating mischievous reports to shift the burden of proving the truth to the accused. The Select Committee, responding to concerns that the law would throw an impossible burden to require a person who published a statement to prove its actual truth, altered and enlarged the scope of the exception to the clause to allow for statements, rumors, or reports published without criminal intent (Donogh, 1911: 61–68). The Committee took into account the conditions under which journalism and the discussion of public questions were carried on at that time. The section was on the same footing as 153A except that it was a non-cognizable offence (Donogh, 1911: 61–68).

# III

# The Rangeela Rasool Episode

Of the hate speech laws I have highlighted, Section 295A has the most dramatic origin. In the 1920s, Punjab became a playground of competing religious interests—the Shuddhi movement founded by Swami Shraddhananda aimed at getting Hindus back into the fold. The Sangathan (Hindu Unity) movement had prominent members like Lala Lajpat Rai and Madan Mohan Malviya. The Tabligh-i-Islam and the Tanzim movement were founded to counter the influence of the Shuddhi movement. In 1926, the murder of Swami Shraddhananda by Abdur Rashid had given a major boost to the Shuddhi movement. The same year saw a major conflagration in Lahore over the alleged murder of a young Sikh girl by a Muslim (Jalal, 2000: 295). In this charged environment, those propagating these views often produced pamphlets and tracts that were critical of other religious viewpoints, often criticizing the personal lives of religious leaders and icons. Some of this material spilt into more public controversies, and legal battles that erupted into debates across the nation, and impacted religious tensions in various parts of the country.

The most prominent of these legal controversies that impacted the evolution of the law was the one around a pamphlet called "Rangeela Rasool" (The Colourful Prophet), a satire on the life of the Prophet Mohammad that had led to protests from the Muslim community. The pamphlet was put on sale by a proprietor of a Lahore bookstore,

Raj Pal (a follower of Shraddhananda) in May 1924. The pamphlet sold more than 1,000 copies and went into a second edition. After protests from the Muslim community, the Punjab government prosecuted Raj Pal under Section 153A (Thursby, 1975: 41–50). The case began to take on national dimensions with the well-publicized legal action against Raj Pal. The Arya Samaj claimed that Rangeela Rasool was a direct response to a work on Swami Dayanand called "Maharishi of the 19th Century" by a Muslim in Lahore.

Amid growing protests against the pamphlet, the case was tried before the Magistrate's court. The publisher argued that the publication of the work was intended to remove social evils such as concubinage and polygamy. This strategy was to see if it could be protected under the explanatory clause in 153A. His second defense was that the allegations were based on factual basis. Magistrate Phailbus said that though the truth of allegations was relevant, it was not decisive in determining guilt. The magistrate found Raj Pal guilty of creating enmity between classes and sentenced him to 18 months rigorous imprisonment and ₹1,000 fine. In his order, Judge Phailbus mentions that there were no mitigating factors and also mentions that communal relations were tense at the time.

The case then went up to the Lahore High Court. One of the arguments made by the government before the Lahore High Court was that in view of the tension between the Hindus and the Muslims, and the fact that the Mahommedan community is far more fanatical on the question of religion than other communities, a satire on the founder of the Muslim religion is more likely to promote hatred and enmity between the masses than a satire on the founder of another religion, for example, Christianity. On May 4, 1927, Justice Dalip Singh, the single judge deciding this case held that the accused could not be held to be guilty under Section 153A since the scope of the section did not include satiric writing about a deceased religious leader. In his order, the judge also recommended that a law be passed to take care of polemics against deceased religious leaders. Justice Singh wrote:

> I cannot consider that s. 153A was meant to be used in so wide a meaning. It seems to me that the section was intended to prevent persons from making attacks on a particular community as it exists at the present time and was not meant to stop polemics against deceased religious leaders however scurrilous and in bad taste such attacks might be. For instance, if the fact

that Mussalmans resent attacks on their Prophet, was to be the measure of whether s. 153A applied or not then an historical work in which the life of the prophet was considered and judgment passed on his character by a serious historian might come within the definition of section 153A.[2]

Dalip Singh's judgment created a furore amid the Muslim community. Radical elements within the community demanded that the judge resign. The *Muslim Outlook* carried an article on the front page targeted at Justice Dalip Singh on June 14, 1927 with the headline "Resign." The article demanded the judge's resignation and demanded an enquiry into how such a judgment was written. It also questioned the judge's credentials and competence.[3] The Lahore High Court initiated contempt proceedings against the magazine and sentenced the editor D.S. Bukhari to six months simple imprisonment and a fine of ₹750. The publisher Nur ul Haq was given three months simple imprisonment and ₹1,000 fine. This judgment led to further agitations against the *Raj Paul* decision. More newspapers joined in. The Qadian Ahmadiya Committee and Punjab Khilafat Committee observed High Court day on July 22, 1927 to ask for removal of J Dalip Singh from the Lahore High Court (Thursby, 1975: 41–50). The extraordinary events and intensity of public mobilization against the *Raj Paul* judgment qualify the event, in the eyes of historian Ayesha Jalal, as one of the factors that accelerated the formation of a Muslim public sphere in Punjab (Jalal, 2000: 295).

Around the same time, there were two other cases with very similar circumstances—one in the Lahore High Court and the other in the Allahabad High Court where, in very similar circumstances the judges took the opposite route, holding that the publishers of the material in question could be convicted under Section 153A. The Allahabad High Court case dealt with a ban of a book called *Vichitra Jivan* (Strange Life: Some Strange and Mysterious Incidents from the Life of Muhammad Sahib) by the United Provinces government. The book was proscribed and forfeited under Section 99A CrPC, and a case filed under 153A.

The Allahabad High Court in this case rejected the reasoning in the Raj Paul case. They said they could not appreciate the distinction between an attack on a system of religion and upon people who believe

---

[2] *Raj Paul* vs. *The Emperor*, AIR 1927 Lah 590, p. 592.
[3] *In the Matter of Muslim Outlook, Lahore*, AIR 1927 Lah 610, p. 611.

in it. The judges sentenced Kalicharan Sharma to one year rigorous imprisonment and ₹1,000 fine.

Justice Lindsay, with whom Justice Banerji and Chief Justice Walsh agreed, enunciated the law:

> If the language is of a nature calculated to produce or to promote feelings of enmity or hatred the writer must be presumed to intend that which his act was likely to produce. This was the principle laid down by Best, J. in Burdett's case in dealing with a case of seditious libel and the same principle clearly applies to the case of a publication punishable under Section 153A, I.P.C. Applying this test to the case before me I can only say that in my opinion the natural, indeed the inevitable, consequence of writing such as I find in this book is the excitement of enmity or hatred or both between the followers of the Hindu and Mahomedan religions.[4]

The judge went on to observe:

> It must of course be recognised that in countries where there is religious freedom a certain latitude must of necessity be conceded in respect of the free expression of religious opinions together with a certain measure of liberty to criticize the religious beliefs of others, but it is contrary to all reason to imagine that liberty to criticize includes a licence to resort to the vile and abusive language which characterizes the book now before me.[5]

In the other case, *Devi Sharan Sharma and Anr* vs. *King Emperor*[6] which was also decided within five weeks of the Raj Paul case, the Punjab government filed a case against an Amritsar Urdu journal *Risala-i-Vartman* for an article titled "Sair-i-Dozakh"—Trip to Hell. The May issue was proscribed and on June 6, 1927, prosecution began under 153A against the editor Gian Chand Pathak and author Devi Sharan Sharma, both of whom were members of the Arya Samaj. The government, keen on an early decision, transferred the case to a Special Division Bench heard by Justices Broadway and Skemp. The judges held that internal and external evidence showed that accused intended actual results of their actions. They referred to how Muslims in Amritsar were agitated after the article was published. The judges held that while a reasoned, critical, strong attack on a religion or its founder was permissible, the content here did not fit this description.

---

[4] *Kali Charan Sharma* vs. *Emperor*, AIR 1927 All 649.
[5] *Kali Charan Sharma* vs. *Emperor*.
[6] *Devi Sharan Sharma and Anr* v *King Emperor*, 1927, 14 AIR 594 [Lah].

Devi Sharan Sharma was sentenced to one year rigorous imprisonment and a fine of ₹5,000 and Gian Chand Pathak was sentenced to six months rigorous imprisonment and a fine of ₹250.

# IV

# Legislative Change

By this time, the situation had reached a stage where the British government at the Centre was alarmed. The Government of India's Home Department thought that the three judgments (Raj Pal, Kalicharan Sharma, and Devi Sharan Sharma) left an unanswered question: "Was it possible for a person to intend to insult the religion or religious feelings of another without thereby intending to promote hatred and enmity between classes?" (Thursby, 1975: 41–50)

The Government of India began the process of introducing legislation that would make it such that prosecution need not establish an intention to insult religion or outrage the religious feelings of a class, and need not prove that such insult was intended to produce feelings of enmity or hatred. In June 1926, the Government of India sent a letter to all local governments and administration asking whether the existing provisions of 153A IPC and 108 CrPC were adequate to deal with pamphlets, tracts, newspapers in question. (The government had repealed the Press Act in 1922.) The letter proposed amending Section 99A of the CrPC to empower local governments to search for and confiscate publications deemed to contain material punishable under 153A. Most local governments accepted these recommendations. Two notable exceptions were the governments of Punjab and Bengal. These governments said confiscating writing was not enough, the impact was when material reached subscribers and *trials offered further opportunity for scenes of communal disputes*. They asked for new legislation to restore executive authority lost during repeal of the Press Act (Thursby, 1975: 41–50).

The Criminal Procedure Code (Third Amendment) Bill was passed on August 25, 1926 in the Central Legislative Assembly after a lively debate. Lala Lajpat Rai, one of those who opposed the bill, said it would focus too much power in the hands of the executive and would not change hearts of people. Some people supported the move, for example,

Pandit Madan Mohan Malviya said that the only remedy was to empower the government to check circulation and that consideration outweighed the possibility of abuse by the executive. Section 99A of the Criminal Procedure Code was amended. This law was used often, as communal situation deteriorated (Thursby, 1975: 41–50).

Around a year later, the Government of India decided to introduce a Bill to amend Section 295 of the Indian Penal Code. On August 20, 1927, the Religious Insults Bill was introduced in the Legislative Assembly. This Bill would amend Section 295 of the Indian Penal Code. The Bill was referred to a Select Committee, which made recommendations. One such recommendation was that sanction of central government should be required for prosecution. Another was that cases should be triable at the level of Presidency, magistrate, or sessions court. In the debate in the Punjab Assembly, Hindu members generally saw the Bill as a concession to Muslims and Muslims saw it as not going far enough. Others argued that the Bill would prove to be ineffective, the government would fail to enforce it, and there was already remedy in law. Another view was that this was a panic legislation that would end freedom of the press and leave no room for rational criticism of religion. The Bill was passed on September 19, 1927 (Thursby, 1975: 41–50).

After the Bill was passed, local governments did prosecute under this section but found that prosecutions could lead to further tensions, and that many publications used dummy editors. So local governments often resorted to executive orders requiring press to put up security deposits, which they found more effective (Thursby, 1975: 41–50).

In a dramatic continuation of this saga, Raj Pal, the publisher acquitted in the Raj Paul case, was murdered in 1929 by one Ilim Din, who after his conviction and hanging by the British acquired the status of a *ghazi*, or a holy warrior in Pakistan.

# V

# Contemporary Developments

The law on hate speech has had diverse trajectories in the subcontinent. For instance, Section 295A has taken a virulent turn in Pakistan, after General Zia's government amended it to make punishment by death compulsory for violation of Section 295-C that criminalizes "defiling the sacred name of the Holy Prophet." The Chapter on "Offences against Religion" has been strengthened in Pakistan by a series of amendments from 1980 to 1986 that constitute Pakistan's blasphemy laws (Ahmed, 2009: 173). Criticized for being used to persecute religious minorities, this law has become a highly contested one between the liberal and more conservative sections of Pakistanis. Both Benazir Bhutto and General Musharraf's government had to back down from circumscribing these laws after severe opposition from fundamentalist groups in Pakistan (Ahmed, 2009: 173).

In India, the events at the time of Partition reflected in debates at the time of the framing of the Indian Constitution, and at the time of the First Amendment to the Indian Constitution, have ensured that hate speech law has remained on the statute books as reasonable restrictions permissible under the Indian Constitution. While this paper does not deal with these developments or subsequent court decisions in detail, it is important to note that appellate courts in India have generally dismissed accusations under hate speech laws when they have felt that procedural safeguards have not been followed or that these charges are frivolous. Court rulings post-independence have laid down specific guidelines on how these powers could be exercised. However, despite the court's record on these cases, the procedure that those accused have to go through and the process of trial itself become a huge deterrent to speech. This is similar to how provisions of law dealing with sedition, obscenity, defamation, and contempt are misused widely.

This paper shows that the debates around hate speech, especially around insult to, or offending sensibilities of religious groups and icons, are not new. These debates have transpired in courts and legislatures since the 1920s. What is new, however, is the government adapting, and sometimes expanding these laws gradually, at the expense of any genuine freedom to criticize or debate. The Internet has brought with it deep government suspicion and laws that are even broader than what existed, wide in their sweep, attempting to encompass any situation of religious, ethnic, or other tension.

This growing trend has resulted in severe restrictions on artistic freedom, freedom to criticize, creative freedoms that involve satire, intellectual, historic, and scientific thought. With new technologies ensuring a global reach of media, the provisions of the criminal law that allow for private complaints as well as for the accused to be tried in jurisdictions where the material circulates, make way for harassment through litigation.

Given this contemporary context, it is important to look at the historical evolution of the law, to situate how legal claims to hurt religious sentiments have shaped the reach and scope of the law today, helping form and solidify this notion of hurt religious sentiments. Veena Das, in a commentary on the M.F. Husain judgment, remarks that there is a contraction of the memory of the role of the colonial polity in putting in circulation such concepts as 'religious feelings' and the idea of a public order that needs to be protected from the eruptions of violence due to hurt (Das, 2011: 121–122).

> There is an uncanny way in which forms of writing from the late 19th and early 20th century (e.g., rhyming prose and to signal insult) combine with statements regarding what is natural and normal that result in positioning the idea of religious feelings as 'given', thereby hiding from view the mediation of law. The publics within which these forms of speech circulate are quite dispersed and heterogeneous but are homogenized by evoking numerical multitudes. Thus, for example the reference to 'crores of Hindus' in some legal briefs as well as in the propaganda literature acquires salience, not because these 'crores' have been counted but because they can mobilise affect. (Das, 2011: 120–121)

Not only do courts put in circulation these categories, but as Asad Ali Ahmed argues, legal contestations around hate speech perpetuate the discourse around hate speech as these are often based on exaggerated claims of hurt made by the parties before the judges. The nature of arguments in the courtroom and the judicial discourse that follows have further strengthened this discourse. In the *Rangeela Rasool* case,[7] one of the arguments that the government makes is that followers of Islam are more likely to be incited. This trend can be seen in contemporary cases too. For instance, an argument accepted in Indian courts is that saying that a section of Muslims is anti-national is permissible, but to say that all Muslims are anti-national is not acceptable. One of the most striking cases was the *Chandamal Chopra* case[8] filed in the Calcutta High Court where the petitioner asked the West Bengal government to forfeit all copies of the *Koran* printed in all languages. The petitioner argued that the *Koran* itself is in violation of 153A

---

[7] *Raj Paul vs. The Emperor*, AIR 1927 Lah 590.
[8] *Chandamal Chopra vs. State of West Bengal* 1988 CriLJ 739.

and 295A of the IPC. In this case, the judges refused to discuss these arguments in detail for fear of inciting hatred.

Thus, the harm in hate speech law is both in the way it is (mis)used and in the manner in which the law is itself implicated in the incitement of hatred. This forms one piece in the jigsaw puzzle of how the substantive law of hate speech in India has evolved.[9]

# References

Ali Ahmed, Asad. 2009. "Specters of Macaulay: Blasphemy, the Indian Penal Code, and Pakistan's Postcolonial Predicament," in Raminder Kaur and William Mazzarella (Eds.). *Censorship in South Asia: Cultural Regulation from Sedition to Seduction*. Indiana: Indiana University Press, 172–205 at p. 173.

Das, Veena. 2011. "Of M.F. Husain and an Impossible Love," in *Barefoot Across the Nation: Maqbool Fida Husain and the Idea of India,* edited by Sumathy Ramaswamy. New Delhi: Yoda Press, pp. 116, 121–22.

Donogh, W.R. 1911. *A Treatise on the Law of Sedition and Cognate Offences in British India.* Calcutta: Thakker, Spink and Co., pp. 61–68.

Indian Law Commissioners. 2002. *A Penal Code published by Command of the Governor General in Council.* New Jersey: Lawbook Exchange Ltd., p. 101.

Jalal, Ayesha. 2000. *Self and Sovereignty: Individual and Community in South Asian Islam since 1850.* London: Routledge, p. 295.

Ludlow Holt, Francis. 1816. *Law of Libel,* 2nd edition. London: Butterworth and Sons.

Mill, J.S. 2006. *On Liberty.* London: Penguin, p. 62.

Peel, Lawrence. 1848. *Observations on the Indian Penal Code.* Calcutta: Military Orphan Press, cited in Asad Ali Ahmed, p. 181.

Pinney, Thomas. 1974. *The Letters of Thomas Babington Macaulay* (Ed.), 6 vols. Cambridge: Cambridge University Press, pp. 43–44, cited in Asad Ali Ahmed, p. 180.

Thursby, Gene R. 1975. *Hindu Muslim Relations in British India: A Study of Controversy.* Leiden: E.J. Brill, pp. 41–50.

---

[9] For a more detailed account of the period that I have described in this paper see Neeti Nair. 2013. "Beyond the 'Communal' 1920s: The Problem of Intention, Communal Pragmatism, and the Making of Section 295A of the Indian Penal Code," *Indian Economic & Social History Review* July 2013 50: 317–340.

# 5

# The Alchemy of Hate and Hurt

## *Shohini Ghosh*

In South Asia, the debate on the legal regulation of hate speech acquired prominence over the last two decades with the rise of right-wing movements, all of which have fiercely targeted religious or ethnic minority communities. Internationally, hate speech is the generic term for speech attacks on race, ethnicity, caste, religion, gender, sexual orientation, or any other social grouping. Advocates for legal regulation claim that hate speech promotes discrimination and violence against those it describes. The debate about whether hate speech should be censored or protected has been a bitter bone of contention among those who are politically committed to safeguarding the rights of minorities.

In India, the recurring debate on censoring hate speech was shaped largely with the rise of the Hindu Right and the systematic targeting of Muslims during the Ramjanmabhoomi movement culminating in the demolition of Babri Masjid. The debate acquired greater urgency after the state-supported genocide of Muslims in Gujarat, 2002. Secular groups and individuals began debating the idea of a legislation that would prevent acts and omissions leading to the committing of communal crimes while taking immediate action to punish the guilty. Hate speech was seen to be instrumental in the creation of a hateful environment.[1] While the demand for a new law on hate speech is no longer a priority, there are recurring instances when the existing

---

[1] During this time, "Communalism Combat" attempted to push the state to prosecute hate speech by drafting a model FIR that concerned citizens could use to start criminal proceedings against hate speech. Similarly, the once proposed Communal Crimes Bill, 2004 had identified hate speech as a communal crime.

laws (or other methods) are mobilized to curtail 'hateful' speech or punish the 'hateful' speaker. Do restrictions on hate speech protect those who are deemed vulnerable to it?[2] This essay presents a series of reflections on the legal adjudication of 'hate speech' leading to a broader discussion about how we might understand the ideas of 'hate' and 'hurt' and the possibility of living with injury.

# Words that Wound

Within academia, the most influential arguments in favor of suppressing hate speech have come from critical race theorist Mari J. Matsuda and scholars like Kathleen Mahoney, Richard Delgado, Kimberley Crenshaw and others. In her book *Words That Wound: Critical Race Theory, Assaultive Speech, and the First Amendment* (1993), Matsuda argues that since words are powerful tools, racial vilification—the use of words to insult, ridicule, or incite violence against a group or individual because of their race or ethnicity—can have a devastating effect on the addressee leading to the creation of an environment where racist violence can flourish. Flagrant vilification with impunity not only acts upon the listener but also constitutes the addressee. Matsuda's formulation, as Judith Butler sums it up, "reinvokes and reinscribes a structural relation of domination, and constitutes the linguistic occasion for the reconstitution of that structural domination" (Butler, 1997: 18). In short, hate speech does not merely reflect a relation of social domination but enacts the domination thereby becoming a vehicle through which the social structure is reinstated. Hate speech, Matsuda contends, constitutes its addressee at the moment of utterance because the very speaking of it is the performance of the injury. Those who advocate the legal

---

[2] The Indian Constitution protects the right to Freedom of Speech and Expression under Article 19, while Article 19 (2) subjects this Fundamental Right to "reasonable restrictions" in the interests of the security of state, friendly relations with foreign states, public order, decency or morality, contempt of court, defamation or incitement to an offence. The "reasonable restrictions" constitute the basis for other statutory limitations on speech. We could say therefore that the Constitutional guarantee of Freedom of Speech is framed within a paradox. In addition, there are innumerable legal provisions that can be invoked for censoring purposes.

regulation of hate speech believe that since advantaged groups have a disproportionate share of freedom of expression by virtue of possessing greater power, privilege and wealth, it is their speech that is most likely to dominate and for this reason the state must speak on behalf of the historically disadvantaged and protect their interests. In combining the idea of a verbal slur with physical assault, Matsuda argues that words are just as capable of 'wounding' as physical violence. To this, I will return later.

Butler's rich and layered critique of Matsuda's position includes the provocation that far from being a neutral player, the state 'produces' hate speech. Since legal regulation requires the courts to be the final arbitrator to decide what constitutes hate speech, there is "no hate speech in the full sense of the term unless there is a court that decides there is" (Butler, 1997: 18). "In this sense," she argues, "it is the decision of the state, the sanctioned utterance of the state, which produces the act of hate speech—produces, but does not cause" (Butler, 1997: 96). Hate speech, as Butler correctly observes, cannot exist without the ratification of the state and, therefore, it is the power of the state's juridical language that actively produces the domain of the speakable and the unspeakable. This gives us pause to reflect, in the context of India, how the legal machinery adjudicated hate speech in the immediate aftermath of the Babri Masjid demolition.

The political rise of Hindutva was accompanied by a series of attacks on speech and cultural expression that were allegedly offensive to Hindu culture and sentiments. Ironically, Hindu Right parties which consistently targeted Muslims through communal and inflammatory speech never, or rarely, found themselves facing prosecution. Instead those who dissented with Hindutva politics frequently found themselves charged under hate speech provisions. In 1993, SAHMAT (The Safdar Hashmi Memorial Trust) held a multi-city exhibition titled "Hum Sab Ayodhya" which included a textual extract from the "Dasaratha Jātaka" describing Ram and Sita as siblings. The Bajrang Dal and VHP attacked and vandalized the exhibition in Ayodhya, while the BJP launched a vilification campaign against the show. In Faizabad, SAHMAT was charged under Section 153 (wantonly giving provocation with intent to cause riot); Section 153A (promoting enmity between different groups on account of religion); Section 125A (deliberate and malicious acts intended to raise religious feelings of any class by insulting its religion or religious beliefs); Section 298 (uttering words with deliberate intent to wound religious feelings); Section 505 (statements conducive to public mischief); and Section 120B (Criminal Conspiracy). Predictably, groups that had vandalized the SAHMAT exhibition went unpunished. On August 21, 1993, SAHMAT, now charged with practicing 'aggressive secularism' was compelled to withdraw the Ram Katha panel from Teen Murti Bhavan where the exhibition was being held. That same afternoon, police confiscated the text panel.[3]

Even more ironic was the 1995 Bombay High Court Judgment that dismissed a 1993 writ petition (filed by a journalist and a former Chief Secretary of Maharashtra) seeking to prosecute the Maharashtra Government for not initiating criminal proceedings against Bal Thackeray and Nitin Raut, editor of the Shiv Sena magazine *Saamna* and the contents it published during the pogrom against Muslims in Bombay after the Babri Masjid demolition.[4] Quoting Sections 153 and 153A of the Indian Penal Code (IPC), the petitioners drew attention to nine editorials that, apart from propagating hate against Muslims, brazenly took credit for the violence. In a shocking Judgment delivered over two days, Justice G.R. Majathia and Justice M.L. Dudhat upheld the contents of *Saamna* as protected speech providing elaborate justifications in their favor.[5] In exonerating a particularly malicious editorial, for instance, the judges favorably quoted the opening line that stated: "We respect all religions." The judicial condonement of the *Saamna* editorials illustrates Butler's argument that juridical language not only defines domains of un/speakability but also decides what does or does not constitute hate speech.

A similar 'inversion' recurred in the case of the famous painter M.F. Husain who at the instigation of Hindutva groups was charged by the Mumbai Police under Sections 153A and 295A. The 'hate speech' targeted in this instance was a painting of Saraswati made way back in 1976 and reproduced by a BJP-backed magazine to create precisely

---

[3] For detailed information on the controversy, see *Muktnaad Hum Sab Ayodhya: A Selection of Reports, Editorials, Discussion, Comments from the Press,* New Delhi: SAHMAT, January 1994.

[4] J.B. D'Souza vs. the State of Maharashtra.

[5] For a detailed discussion of the Judgment read Ghosh (1995).

this controversy, while the other artwork was a lithograph that had been titled "Sita Rescued" by Husain's curator. While an elderly Husain battled criminal charges, filed not just in Bombay, but across different states, those who ransacked his house and vandalized his art gallery enjoyed full impunity. Bal Thackeray proudly declared: "If Husain can enter Hindustan, why can't we barge into his house?" (Dhavan, 2007).

The inversion of the ostensible intent of hate speech laws is not unique to India. Studying the enforcement history of censorship laws across the world shows that speech on the margins is always the first to be censored. The first individuals prosecuted under the *British Race Relations Act of 1965*, which criminalized the intentional incitement of racial hatred, were black power leaders. The supreme irony of enacting hate speech laws is that the ultimate power to decide what constitutes hate speech rests, not with those targeted by that speech but the State that alone has the power to adjudicate. In her discussion of the Danish cartoon controversy, Saba Mehmood reminds us that laws are never neutral mechanisms equipped to mediate across a diversity of religious concepts and practices and are, therefore, most prone to reproducing normative notions of religion and religious subjectivity (Mehmood, 2009: 150). Regardless of social context, writes Mehmood, legal reasoning tends to privilege the cultural and religious subjectivities of the majority population (Mehmood, 2009a: 857).

## Uncertain States of Injury

So far I have used the word 'hate speech' in a way that might allow us to imagine that it is a self-evident category. On the contrary, it is one over which there is rarely any consensus. Equally, the proscription of this heterogeneous material is sought through a diversity of legal and extra-legal methods. While certain laws were enacted with the intention of combating hate speech and safeguarding the rights of the minorities, in practice a wide-ranging set of laws are deployed to censor material that is deemed to fall under this description. Moreover, the laws invoked are not always those that pertain to the regulation of speech. For instance, when the Congress government banned Salman Rushdie's *The Satanic Verses* in 1988, they prohibited the importation of the book under Section 11 of the "Indian Customs Act." In 2002, the Supreme Court charged writer Arundhati Roy with criminal contempt under the "Contempt of Court Act" for "scandalizing its authority with malafide intentions" by writing about her disagreement with the Judgement on the Sardar Sarovar Project.[6] In 2010, certain groups demanded that Roy be arrested under charges of sedition for speaking on Kashmir at a seminar in Delhi (Roy, 2010). In 2012, Ashis Nandy risked being arrested under the "SC/ST (Prevention of Atrocities Act), 1989", after his allegedly 'casteist' statement at the Jaipur Literary Festival.

Extra-legal measures are commonly deployed to silence material deemed hateful by certain groups. In 2010, the Vice Chancellor of Mumbai University, under pressure from the Bharatiya Vidyarthi Sena (the student wing of the Shiv Sena) hastily dropped Rohinton Mistry's acclaimed book *Such a Long Journey* from the BA English Literature Syllabus.[7] In 2011, the Academic Council headed by the Vice Chancellor of Delhi University unceremoniously dropped A.K. Ramanujan's erudite essay titled "Three Hundred Ramayanas: Five Examples and Three Thoughts on Translation", from an undergraduate course. The ABVP (the student wing of the BJP) had long been clamoring for its removal on grounds that the essay hurt 'Hindu sentiments' and misrepresented 'Hindu traditions' to young students.[8]

As is fairly evident, 'hate speech' is as broad and amorphous a category as hurt and elides any singular definition as it is made to stand for a range of emotions like outrage, anger, discomfort, humiliation, and insult, thereby eliding any singular definition or understanding. Hate speech controversies clearly demonstrate that hurt is not a

---

[6] Sentencing her to one day's imprisonment and "showing magnanimity of law by keeping in mind that the respondent is a woman," the two-judge bench court reprimanded the writer for having "drifted away from the path on which she was traversing by contributing to Art and Literature."

[7] Citizens Protest Dropping Book from Varsity Syllabus, *Hindustan Times*, October 11, 2010 http://www.hindustantimes.com/India-news/Mumbai/Citizens-protest-dropping-book-from-varsity-syllabus/Article1-611114.aspx and Mumbai University Drops Rohinton Mistry Book after Shiv Sena Student Wing Protest, http://www.dnaindia.com/mumbai/report_mumbai-varsity-drops-rohinton-mistry-book-after-shiv-sena-student-wing-protest_1446574 (both accessed on July 19, 2015).

[8] In this essay, Ramanujan speaks about the many versions of the Ramayana that challenge and contradict the two most popular versions attributed to Valmiki and Tulsidas including versions that depicted Rama and Sita as siblings.

monolithic emotion that sits uniformly or permanently on all members of the community. Needless to say, the claim of Hindutva groups that Husain had hurt the sentiments of Hindus was not shared by all Hindus; a large number of whom publicly defended Husain.[9] Similarly, the controversies over the Danish cartoons (published initially in 2005 and republished in 2008) and the "Innocence of Muslims" video showed how Muslims across the world interpreted hurt differently. While there is a tendency to assume that all members of a community are equally outraged and for exactly the same reasons, a careful study of hate speech controversies demonstrate that the reasons for feeling 'wounded' are as different as the degrees of outrage. John Cherian has pointed out that the loudest protests against the "Innocence of Muslims" video were staged under authoritarian pro-US governments (Cherian, 2012). Similarly, the Danish cartoons impacted differently on Danish Muslims than on, say, Indian and Pakistani Muslims. Regardless of intent therefore, the perception of hate and hurt is bound to differ from individual to individual, group to group. Location, identity, predisposition, collective and personal experiences all play a role in determining how injury is understood and experienced. There are always some more wounded than others and those whose 'states of injury' change with the passage of time. Perhaps for this reason, novelist Howard Jacobson remarked: "The very arbitrariness of offence – cruelly felt one day and not noticed the next – is reason itself to give it no quarter" (Jacobson, 2005).

While 'injury' is never universal across communities and social groups, hurt can indeed run very deep and has, therefore, to be understood against the larger context in which the provocation is extended. Hurt is always felt more acutely when a group or community is under attack or has been historically disadvantaged. Therefore, the response of Muslim communities to the Danish cartoons needs to be understood against the crisis of secularism and rampant Islamophobia in Euro-America. Most European commentators failed to make this link or understand the protests outside the binaries of free speech and

---

[9] Despite considerable support, why did Husain have to leave India and settle in Dubai? In his essay in "Barefoot Across the Nation" Ram Rehman provides a chilling account of a meeting with Home Minister Shivraj Patil who makes it clear that the Congress government was not willing to do much to protect Husain lest they be seen to be "appeasing" the minorities.

Islamic intolerance. Mahmood Mamdani wrote how every morning he would scan the newspapers and search the net hoping to discover significant European voices, "not from government but from the world of the intellect and the arts," that would refuse to promote Islamophobia as free speech. The search was futile. The same frustration found witty expression in a cartoon by Jordanian artist Emad Hajjaj. It shows a man pointing to a stereotypical drawing of a black person. "This is racism," he says with a frown. Still frowning, he points to a drawing that equates the Nazi swastika with the Jewish star and says: "This is anti-Semitic." Then pointing to the five Danish cartoons about Muhammad he breaks into a smile and says: "This is freedom of expression."[10]

When hate speech discussions are unshackled from the binaries of free speech and censorship, fascinating insights emerge. Saba Mehmood's essay on the Danish cartoon controversy, for instance, not only moves the discussion beyond the vocabulary of blasphemy and freedom of speech but illuminates the limits of 'secular law' as a site of neutrality and the conditions of intelligibility that render some moral claims legible and others mute. The hurt constituted by the cartoons of Muhammad, she explains, was not due to the contravention of a moral interdiction ("Thou shalt not make images of Muhammad"), but due to the violation of the personhood of the devout Muslim who, through assimilative gestures, wants to *ingest*, as it were, the exemplary persona of the Prophet. This relation of similitude, where the life of the Prophet presents not commandments, but virtues to emulate is what accounts for the deep sense of injury felt by the devout (Mehmood, 2009: 847). This line of discussion is useful, not to fight for a more even-handed dispensation of legal justice but to understand the many affective registers through which injuries are felt and articulated.

---

[10] The editorial policy of *Jyllands-Postens*, the Danish newspaper that carried the Prophet cartoons stood on contradictions. In April 2003, a Danish illustrator had submitted a series of unsolicited cartoons dealing with the resurrection of Christ to *Jyllands-Posten*, only to receive an email from the paper's Sunday editor: "I don't think Jyllands-Posten's readers will enjoy the drawings. As a matter of fact, I think that they will provoke an outcry. Therefore, I will not use them." In an interview to *Newsweek* (February 13, 2006), Flemming Rose, editor of *Jyllands-Posten* says, "My newspaper has its limits. In a pluralistic society where you do have freedom of speech, my limits should not be the limits of others. We do have laws against racism and blasphemy." During the Muhammad cartoon controversy, this newspaper was vaunted as the vanguard of free speech and expression.

# The Alchemy of Hate and Hurt

What purpose is served by removing words and images that are deemed to be hateful, offensive, or discriminatory? Or by punishing the hateful speaker whose words are out in the public domain? Matsuda contends that hateful comments directed against dominant group members do not require protection because harm and hurt is of a different degree when the abuse is not backed by a larger context of subordination and, therefore, lacks the same performative force (Matsuda, 1993: 36). While supporting the distinction she makes, I will still argue—and forcefully—that no speech (hate or sexual) directed at any group (dominant or marginal) should be subject to legal regulation. What needs relentless combating is the context of subordination that makes such speech possible and acceptable. Hate speech is merely symptomatic of a certain socioeconomic environment which would remain unchanged even if the offending speech was removed.

To this end, two subsequent controversies are particularly instructive. In May 2012, following protests in Parliament from a number of Dalit leaders, the Ministry of HRD ordered the removal from NCERT textbooks, an illustration by the cartoonist Shankar Pillai. The cartoon shows B.R. Ambedkar, Chairperson of the Constitution drafting committee, riding a snail with Nehru standing behind brandishing a whip. A furious debate over interpretations of the cartoon erupted within and outside the Parliament with proponents of its proscription arguing that the cartoon reinforced the stereotype of Dalits being lazy and inefficient, not to mention Ambedkar being shown in poor light. But if there is anything the public debate demonstrated clearly, it was the multiple ways in which the cartoon was being read and interpreted both within and outside the Dalit community. Most often it was the the self-identified pro-Dalit interlocutor who insisted on the stereotype-centered reading to the foreclosure of other interpretations. Disagreeing with the Ministry's decision to withdraw the cartoon, Ajay Skaria insists that it is imperative that the genuine hurt felt by the community needs redressal not through 'public reason' (which includes the processes of consultation through which the books came into existence) but by extending 'another civility' that may, on occasion, require some cartoons to be excised.[11] While the gesture of extending 'another civility' valuable, it is unclear how the possible excision is any different from extra-judicial speech restriction. If there is an anxiety that the cartoon would reinforce existing social prejudice around Dalits, then a better remedy to my mind would be to incorporate the debate and dissent into the contents of the textbook instead of removing the cartoon altogether on the basis of a singular interpretation.

In January 2012, a furious controversy was triggered by a statement made by academic Ashis Nandy at the Jaipur Literary Festival. During a panel discussion, Nandy said: "It will be an undignified even vulgar statement—but it is a fact that most of the corrupt come from the OBC, the Schedule Castes and increasingly the STs and as long as it's the case, the Indian Republic will survive." It is not hard to imagine how, disclaimer notwithstanding, this carelessly worded assertion could offend even though, as the public debate shows, there are many ways in which the provocation was heard and understood in the larger context of the debate.[12] Since, in the age of electronic and viral circulation a statement in the public domain cannot be excised, the speaker is required to be punished. Under pressure from several Dalit leaders an FIR was filed and a non-bailable arrest warrant was issued to Nandy under the Sections 506 and 3(1) of the SC/ST (Prevention of Atrocities Act).

This raises two questions. First, should we assume that this speech or any speech, however hateful, qualifies as 'atrocity' or a physical attack? When physical assaults are equated with assaultive words, then the injury that is inflicted is seen to be of equal value. This serves to legitimize a slippage that Hindutva groups have used to justify the conflation of speech and action. The physical attacks directed at Husain or the feature film *Fire*, or the shooting of *Water* are justified on grounds that speech is equal to action. I would like to persuade that legal intervention should be directed only at criminal acts and not speech, however hateful. Second, what happens when

[11] Violence and Laughter: Ajay Skaria on Ambedkar Cartoon Controversy. Available at http://kafila.org/2012/05/25/violence-and-laughter-ajay-skaria-on-the-ambedkar-cartoon-controversy/, accessed on July 19, 2015.

[12] The Last Word: Ashis Nandy's Statement on SCs OBCs on Corruption. Available at http://ibnlive.in.com/shows/The+Last+Word/318185.html, accessed on July 19, 2015. Also see debate on www.kafila.org, accessed on July 19, 2015.

a speaking subject is located as a site of responsibility, blame and punishment? Butler points out that by "locating the cause of our injury in a speaking subject and the power of that injury in the power of speech we imagine that by taking recourse to a "neutral" law, we will be able to control the onslaught of hateful words." Were we to imagine for a second that Nandy was a casteist man, making casteist utterances we would have to admit that no injury could possibly result if the offending statement was not reinforced through a history of social discrimination. In which case, we should ask whether or not punishing the 'hateful speaker' would successfully eliminate the hate and prejudice that exists in the social environment. Why political leaders would rush to restrict speech is understandable. Given the seemingly insurmountable task of removing hate, prejudice, and discrimination from the social environment, 'punishing' a public utterance provides the comfort of imagining that the problem has, at least partially, been solved. But those of us who have no such political stakes must seriously consider whether or not our purposes are better served through not reprisal but a sustained commitment to listening and speaking.

It is unlikely that those familiar with Nandy's work and views would conclude, though some certainly did, that his intention was to hurt and humiliate. But what of those whose stated intent is to offend, humiliate, and intimidate? Should such utterances be prosecuted? I would argue that if 'clear and present' danger was imminent, then the speaker should certainly be arrested but not under speech laws. For example, if a speaker whose instructions are likely to be carried out, says, "Set fire to those houses," the person must surely be arrested under provisions that prosecute abetment to murder. But what of hate speech that does not pose imminent danger but reiterates and re-enacts the existing prejudice? Such speech, no matter how disagreeable, should be protected because public utterances are merely amplifications of subterranean prejudice that have imploded onto the surface. Hate speech is 'rendered public' only after it has been produced and nurtured in spaces that lie beyond the pale of surveillance or legislation. Rumors, conversations, jokes, whispered speculations, and the sharing of fears and anxieties between individuals and small groups are possibly the most potent form of hate propaganda. Banishing hate speech from the public domain will only drive it underground where we can never hope to find it, leave alone fight it.

The "Central Board of Film Certification" (CBFC or the Indian Censor Board) frequently receives representations from minority groups who demand the removal of images deemed prejudicial and words that have historically functioned as slurs. While such interventions help to visibilize dissent and re-imagine the use of language, it does so by insisting on the process of removal. This strategy is fraught with danger not only because cinematic words and images lend themselves to multiple interpretations but because those very elements could be pressed to the service of resistance. Therefore, Satyajit Ray's realist film *Sadgati* (Deliverance, 1981) could be read, according to the predisposition and textual preferences of the viewer, as a statement against caste oppression or a re-enactment of the same.

The struggle for rights has shown that often a better strategy than removal is the grafting of slurs and epithets onto newer contexts. These "radical acts of misappropriation," argues Butler, allow the conventional bond between word and injury to be fractured (Butler, 1997: 100). Take, for instance, the complex history of the word 'queer' which first emerged as a term of social opprobrium and subcultural self-definition. The 1970s gay liberationists discarded it for its associations with self-loathing, but the 1990s reclaimed the word to suggest a diversity of non-heteronormative behavior. The discursive struggle around identity and rights has witnessed re-appropriations that evacuate the degradation implicit in the word while keeping it resonant with the history of both oppression and resistance.

## Living with Injury

Through a series of arguments, I have suggested that words and images can indeed inflict deep wounds and cause legitimate hurt even though notions of hate and hurt are not self-evident or categorical. Offensive speech and responses to them must be understood through interrogating the conditions that are generative of such speech with the hope that they can be transformed. Describing the dramatic changes in the new media ecology, Ravi Sundaram sees the mobile phone as the most ubiquitous producer and transmitter of media texts (Sundaram, 2012). Given the proliferation, speed and velocity of information exchange, older forms of control through legal regulation are destined to fail. In this new ecology, what is inevitable is the virality of hate speech and the resultant hurt. We can only be impelled to cultivate a new imagination around the idea of hurt. To this end is valuable Talal Asad, Saba Mehmood, and Ajay Skaria's insistence on an ethical engagement with the idea of hurt while moving away from the domain of legal regulation.

As older frameworks collapse and newer lines of inquiry emerge, certain philosophical questions about different states of injury will return. Do we give equal value to all types of hurt? Why are some kinds of hurt considered more injurious than others? How have religion and caste, at different points, acquired greater primacy over injury felt by other disadvantaged groups and minorities? Who can lay claim to the right to be hurt? Do only the religious have the right to define what constitutes religious hurt? Is it not curious that even those expected to value atheists and agnostics tend to privilege the "sentiments of the religious" to be more deserving of protection than that of those who are not? Does that not narrow considerably the scope for a robust debate on the idea of religion?

Yet there are other more compelling vectors that we may choose to pursue in our engagement with hate and hurt. Such a direction has been suggested by sociologist Veena Das who, in her essay on M.F. Husain, seeks to "understand better the political affects that have animated some of the controversy." Drawing attention to a longer history of intimate exchange and traffic of images between Hindus and Muslims, Das argues that perhaps it is Husain who has demonstrated "more intimacy with the ritual attitude to images than the Hindu believers." In an argument similar to those made by film scholars about spectatorial processes, Das argues that one's experience of a work of art "must draw on regions of the self that one is not fully awake to and thus the possibility of hurt is part of the contract to see." Let us extend that idea to suggest that the possibility of hurt may well be part of the contract to live.

# References

Butler, Judith. 1997. *Excitable Speech: A Politics of the Performative*. New York; London: Routledge.

Cherian, John. 2012. Roots of Discontent. *Frontline*.

Dhavan, Rajeev. 2007. *Harassing Husain: Uses and Abuses of the Laws of Hate Speech.* SAHMAT.

Ghosh, Shohini. 1995. "Challenge of Communalism: The Saamna Case," *Journal of Peace Studies,* II(8): 28–33.

Jacobson, Howard. 2005. "Art and Anathema," in *Free Expression Is No Offence,* edited by Lisa Appignanesi. An English PEN Book, London: Penguin Books.

Matsuda, Mari. 1993. "Public Response to Racist Speech," in *Words That Wound.* Boulder: Westview Press, pp. 36.

Mehmood, Saba. 2009. "Reply to Judith Butler, Is Critique Secular? Blasphemy, Injury and Free Speech," *The Townsend Papers in the Humanities* No. 2, Berkeley: University of California.

Roy, Arundhati. October 21, 2010. "Seditious Speech?" Transcript of speech delivered at a seminar titled "Azadi—The Only Way," in Delhi, available at http://www.dawn.com/news/587809/seditious-speech (accessed on July 18, 2015).

Sundaram, Ravi. 2012. "The Art of Rumour in the Age of Digital Reproduction," *The Hindu,* August 19, 2012.

# The Hurting State, Stating Hurt

# 6

# Strangers in the Land: Mapping the Muslim Hurt

*Mushirul Hasan*

## I

Islam is in its origins an Arab religion. Everyone not an Arab who is a Muslim is a convert. Islam is not simply a matter of conscience or private belief. It makes imperial demands. A convert's world view alters. His holy places are in Arab lands; his sacred language is Arabic. His idea of history alters. He rejects his own; he becomes, whether he likes it or not, a part of the Arab story. The convert has to turn away from everything that is his. The disturbance for societies is immense, and even after a thousand years can remain unresolved; the turning away has to be done again and again. People develop fantasies about who and what they are; and in the Islam of converted countries there is an element of neurosis and nihilism. These countries can be easily set on the boil. (Naipaul, 1998: 1)

Rabindranath Tagore (1861–1941), whose work and life were too closely interwoven with India's own life, began by noting that, "what is radically wrong with our rulers is this: they are fully aware that they do not know us, and yet they do not *care* to know us" (Thompson, 1926: 291). These words apply to Islam and the culture associated with it. Even though it is widely perceived and experienced as a dynamic way of life consisting of praxis and ideology and its followers in the subcontinent are regarded as a part of the repository of many events that make up its complex history, one is struck by the paucity of literature on Indian Islam. A book published a few years ago carries a chapter entitled "Islam matters to the West" (Tibi, 2001), but its author's 'understanding' and 'observance' are limited not only to West Asia but exclude the histories and contemporary predicaments of India's Muslims. This is a representative example of how the 21st century historian sees the 'Muslim world'.

My larger aim in this essay, then, is to put an end to the neglect that Barbara Metcalf, a renowned American historian on South Asia, calls 'too little', a phrase that runs as a motif throughout this narrative causing me to wonder, time and again, at both its reasons and its woeful consequences. If the place of Islam in the 21st century is permanent and that living with it as a political phenomenon is a certainty for the foreseeable future (Milton-Edwards, 2004: 217), we need to build a history that does not produce an *a priori* perception of "Islam"—the stereotypical thinking Barbara Metcalf calls 'too much' (Metcalf, 1995: 51–67; 2004: 210). Make no mistake, those who are unwilling to confront the past will be unable to understand the present and unfit to face the future (Lewis, 1993: 130).

To Jean Paul Sartre (1905–1980), French existentialist philosopher, dramatist, novelist and critic, writing in 1946, freedom of choice was axiomatic. But freedom to choose what sort of goal? To the argument that there seems to be no objective grounds for choosing anything in particular, the French novelist–philosopher replied that, "man finds himself in an organized situation in which he himself is involved: his choice involves mankind in its entirety, and he cannot avoid choosing" (Lichtheim, 1974: 43).[1] Taking my cue from these lines, I would argue that in a society where religion plays a dominant role in virtually every walk of life, it is the choices made by the historian that "involve mankind in its entirety" rather than writing into being one nation, one community, one time or one space. His is the choice to bring secularism into our public discussions and to affirm its validity as a principle guiding the nation's life. To renounce this claim is to surrender the nationalist project to the 'hurtful' protagonists of right-wing ideologies, be it Hindutva or pan-Islamism.

"The writing of history is a matter of conscience," wrote Leopold von Ranke (1795–1886) in one of his memorable phrases. "Remember your moral responsibility to our readers," admonished G.P. Gooch (1873–1968), a British historian. I hope that my approach and the

---

[1] Quoted in Lichtheim 1974.

purpose underpinning it will justify itself in terms of the aim outlined at the very outset.

# II

Every attempt at historical interpretation, wrote Alfred Cobban (1901–1968), the historian of the French Revolution, must stand or fall by its consistency with evidence (Cobban, 1964: 162). In terms of evidentiary potential, this essay shall begin by mapping the contours of collective hurt and identity politics through Nirad C. Chaudhuri, who, one presumes, converted a good many English and Bengali readers to his credo.

"Intellectually," Chaudhuri wrote in the mid-1960s, "the Hindus outraged the "European mind" precisely in those three principles which were fundamental to its approach to life, and which it had been applying with ever greater strictness since the Renaissance: that of reason, that of order, and that of measure." Discussing *A Passage to India* by E.M. Forster (1879–1970), one finds that Chaudhuri's Europeanism is most uncomfortable with Islamic identity, characterized through such figures as Aziz and the other supporting Indian Muslims in the novel. In his own view, Forster does this because he shares the liking the British had for the Muslims, and also shares the corresponding dislike for the Hindus. So much so that Dr Godbole, the chief Hindu character in the novel, turns out to be a clown rather than an exponent of Hinduism.

Gifted enough to distinguish between good and evil, Chaudhuri nonetheless disregards the commonly accepted social and cultural norms. He, therefore, finds himself in moral conflict with the existing institutions; and deeply unsettled by his own reason, he defends himself by his own convoluted logic. The noteworthy points are: why does Aziz fluster him? Is it not rather that he began with an *a priori* conviction and then sets out to prove it? More generally, it is worth asking: why did Muslim characters not figure, with some notable exceptions, in Bengali literary writings (outside the circle of Muslim writers) for well over a century? We seek answers to these questions in this chapter itself.

History can be made to supply the plot and the setting for the mind already made up. One of Chaudhuri's central arguments is that the Muslim intellectual tradition ran wholly independent of and without being influenced by the Hindus (Chaudhuri, 1967: 5). It is glaringly obvious that this proposition does not rest securely on the historical foundations he had otherwise built up so laboriously in his biographies of Robert Clive (1725–1774) and the Oxford-based German Orientalist Max Mueller (1823–1900); Bengal's *Census* reports and *Gazetteers* alone reveal the scale and depth of cultural and religious intermingling in rural as well as urban areas. The existence of the *Bauls* indicates a strong undercurrent of non-conformist popular materialism in the remote villages of Bengal (Ray, 1995: 14; Sarkar, 1973: 408–409). Reviewing Chaudhuri's *Autobiography*, Susobhan Sarkar (1900–1982) commented that the true determinants of medieval Indian civilization were not pure Islamic religion, language, or social practice, and that its author erred in dismissing the medieval coexistence of the Hindu and Muslim religions and their mutual influences, especially in rural Bengal. According to him, the way of life of the masses, the village organization, the social structure remained indeed largely the same throughout the ages (Sarkar, 1970: 192).

"Mahesh" by Sarat Chandra Chatterjee (1876–1938), Bengal's most popular novelist and short story writer, is a narrative of peasant life in Bengal as seen in the extent of deprivation in the life of the landless peasant, Gafoor. Within the span of a story, the author deftly weaves the web of inter-community life. The choice of the title "Mahesh", another name for Lord Shiva, brings out in stark terms his indictment of the Hindu priest–zamindar combination as against Gafoor's simple and unalloyed love and devotion for Mahesh. In the end, the zamindar's oppression compels Gafoor to leave the village and seek employment in the jute mills of Fulbere where he had refused to work earlier, because "there was no religion, no honour and privacy for women there." The story concludes:

> Gafoor set out holding the hand of his daughter in the darkness of the night. He had no one to call his own in the village; he had nothing to say to anyone. As he crossed the courtyard and reached the acacia tree, he stopped dead in his tracks and burst out crying loudly. Lifting up his head to the star studded black sky he said—Allah, punish me as much as you like... But Mahesh died with his thirst unquenched. They did not leave the tiniest patch of land for him to graze. Don't forgive the person who robbed him of the grass and the water that are your gifts to all creatures.[2]

[2] Introduction, Mushirul Hasan and Asaduddin (Eds.), *Image and Representation*, p. 9.

In *Gora*, Rabindranath's celebrated novel, the barber in the village lives in solidarity with the Muslims rather than with their Hindu oppressors (Nandy, 1994: 38). Chaudhuri knew this, but it suited him to disregard, first of all, the energy behind any form of cultural synthesis and the fact that such energy is derived not from any external, unintelligible force, but from the sheer experience of living together. Cultural synthesis is, in the words of Mujeeb, "an invitation to live and feel in a larger world, to see in love, suffering, beauty and indifference, grace and elusiveness a universalism that resents and rejects the bondage of time and space" (Mujeeb, 1972: 137). Chaudhuri, by contrast, resented such a synthesis with unruffled serenity. Evidence of fraternal living inspired him with distrust, and any hint of a composite culture incited his immediate rejection.

> In certain parts of India, notably the Punjab and Hindustan, the Hindus were so crushed by the Muslim conquest that they could just save their religion and social organization, but could not save their culture and its external features. Clothing, language, script were some of the things over which they had to accept compromises. So many Hindus took to wearing the Muslim costume, speaking Urdu, and writing in the Arabic script, and by doing all these things they gradually lost the sense, not only of the uncleanliness of these things from the Hindu point of view, but even of the unnaturalness. This was particularly true of the Punjab. I have seen Hindus belonging to such a strict sect as the Arya Samaj reading the Gita in an Urdu translation. It should also be recalled that the Rajputs, Marathas, and Jats, all of whom rose in revolt against Muslim rule, did not mind wearing the Muslim costume, even though they called the Muslim a Yavan in contempt. (Chaudhuri, 1976: 92)

The author of these views did not ever admit the falseness of his kind of argument. As much as any of the other works, *The Autobiography of an Unknown Indian* (1951) owed its inception as well as its tone and spirit to a fetishized impression of 'hurt' created by the partition of Bengal in 1905 and of India in 1947. Chaudhuri projected his interpretation, a mixture of fear and enmity, backwards and onwards. His literature of denunciation began with an appraisal of the Sultans and the Mughals and extended to a generalized hostility toward the Muslims. Even though Chaudhuri would have learnt of Muslim participation in virtually every aspect of the *swadeshi* movement (Sarkar, 1973: 426), he still nursed "a new kind of hatred" for Muslims at that time (Chaudhuri, 1979: 232). "We as children," he recalled, "held the tiny mustard in our hands and sowed it very diligently. In fact, this conflict was implicit in the very unfolding of our history, and could hardly be avoided" (Chaudhuri, 1951: 225).

Chaudhuri lambasted the Muslim clerics without reflecting on the role of those, notably Abul Kalam Azad (1888–1956), who had revolutionary links in their early days (Ray, 1985: 103–118). He should have known that a number of them also worked toward the overthrow of the British in the "Silk Letter Conspiracy" of 1915 (letters urging revolt against the British were wrapped in a piece of cloth), in which the students, teachers, and the head of Deoband's Dar al-ulum, proudly called "the Azhar of the East,"[3] took an active part.

> One day I saw a procession of Muslim divines trooping into Sarat Babu's house. I was quite familiar with the modern Muslim dress, but had no idea that these learned Muslims wore different clothes. They did, for they had green gowns on and big turbans on their heads .... We, the educated and urban Bengalis, with not a fraction of their Westernization in our manner of living, did not even imagine that such persons existed in Bengal. I with my knowledge of Islamic painting could only assume when I saw them that they were crude incarnations of the Muslim divines I had seen portrayed in Persian or Mughal miniatures. Their faces were grave, and even stern. One face struck me very forcibly. It was pinched and peevish, but of an incredible ferocity. The eyes were large, black, and burning, and in that emaciated face they looked even blacker and larger.... He looked like an ill-dressed Robespierre, the sea-green Incorruptible. Sarat Babu's house was not only crowded for the occasion with these survivals of Islam, but even reeked of them. (Chaudhuri, 1987: 469)

This was the man who claimed to have eagerly drunk in the message of 1789, the year of the French Revolution. In one of his much celebrated books, Chaudhuri wrote

> Muslims are now expiating for their short-sighted arrogance, which makes me observe that whatever clever people might say in defence of unscrupulousness in politics, and about its success, there is some power

---

[3] The most important *maktab*, which later developed into *Dar al-ulum* (an institution of high learning), was established by a group of *ulama* at Deoband soon after 1857. As a conservative theological seminary, this institution aimed at resisting social and religious changes introduced by the British and maintaining the cultural and religious identity of the Muslim community. Rashid Ahmad Gangohi (d. 1905), one of its founders, strongly opposed the introduction of Western education as advocated by Syed Ahmad Khan, and supported the Indian National Congress in order to counter the activities of the Aligarh reformer.

in the universe which sees to it that such cynicism does not pay, and that nothing but what is inherently right ever succeeds. Define it as you like, as theodicy or the justice of history, it is there, irrespective of any name. We see the operation of that power in the sad fate of the Muslims of India, both in the Hindu and in the Muslim state. What gave them victory in 1947 was not the opportunistic policy of their leaders, but their fanatical devotion to a cause which was a lost one in history. So, there is no escape for them today from that lost cause, and still less from the intolerable burden of fighting to the last for a lost cause. (Chaudhuri, 1965: 252)

Here, again, a scholar living on his emotions disconnects his commonsense to feed his own petty prejudices. Otherwise, why speak of 'victory' in 1947? Victory for whom? India's 'tryst with destiny' apart, that year brought tragedy rather than triumph.

Why demonize the Muslims (Chaudhuri, 1965: 128)? What is the cause of such pettiness and intellectual poverty? Are they intrinsic or are they resultants of a particular social and economic order? Bhudeb Mukhopadhyay (1827–1894), a thinker of stature, blamed British historiography and bureaucratic designs for the escalation of inter-community relations (Sen, 1993: 172; Raychaudhuri, 1988: 41–42). Chaudhuri would not admit that this was so. "Nothing was more natural for us," he answers, "than to feel about the Muslims in the way we did." His teachers in school impressed on his class that Islam spread by force, Muslims abducted women, and their rulers desecrated temples and forcibly converted Hindus to their faith. They also talked about the wars of the Rajputs, the Marathas, the Sikhs, and the oppression of Aurangzeb (Chaudhuri, 1987: 226). Later in life, Chaudhuri (and perhaps his classmates as well) was convinced of the enormity of destruction of places of worship. "It is impossible to judge," he speculated, "what Hindu temple architecture was like in its homeland in the greatest age of Hindu civilization" (Chaudhuri, 1979: 126). "During all those centuries all over northern India," he added a false note, "only *ruins* (emphasis mine) of the temples survived" (Chaudhuri, 1979).

What is to be done with people who will not give any reason for their assertions and, on the other, with people who cannot understand the implications of their views? Looking more closely, it will be seen that Chaudhuri's 'liberalism' was not only hollow but heavily laden with Bengali revivalist consciousness. But I have not yet mentioned the most astonishing example of his willful blindness.

Writing in *Thy Hand Great Anarch!* he recalled—without showing the slightest awareness of the resistance movements against the West in many parts of the world—celebrating Italy's attack on Tripoli in 1911, although his own father called it downright robbery, which indeed it was, and exulted at the victories of Serbia, Bulgaria, and the other Balkan states. After Turkey joined Germany at the end of 1914 (Chaudhuri, 1979), he felt that the Muslims would be taught a lesson. The British defeats in the Dardanelles and Mesopotamia upset him, "as strongly as any Englishman," whereas the Treaty of Sevres, despite being "unfair," did not (Chaudhuri, 1987: 37).[4]

At the time of the annulment of Bengal's partition in 1911, Maharaja Manindra Chunder Nundi lamented that in East Bengal "... the Muslim population will preponderate (and) the Bengali Hindu will be in a minority. *We shall be strangers in our own land*" (emphasis mine). Chaudhuri agreed. History for him meant celebrating British rule as an age of liberation from Muslim despotism; its key objective being the prevention of this 'despotism' from returning to Bengal when the British withdrew from its Indian Empire, and to deny that Muslims could be Bengalis, and by extension Indians (Chatterji, 1995: 268). 'Repelled' by the prospect of living in a Muslim-dominated Bengal (Chatterji, 1995: 466), he gave the impression of the Muslims growing in menace from minute to minute. The moral is simple enough: confront the devil now; for tomorrow it may be too late.

Bengal's partition unleashed the resentments of the poor, mainly the Muslim peasantry,[5] against the rich and the Hindu landlord–moneylender combine. After the swadeshi tremors subsided, the

---

[4] The Turkish peace terms (May 14, 1920) produced a blaze of resentment among every section of the Muslim community and gave a new dimension to the Khilafat agitation. Under the peace terms, Turkey was to be shorn of its Arab possessions—Syria, Palestine, Mesopotamia, and Hijaz, and other Turkish provinces in the Arab peninsula. The portion on the Asiatic and European shores of the Bosphorus was to be internationalized. The other half, extending from St. Stefano to Dalma Bagtche, was declared a port of international interest under a Commission on which Turkey was not even represented. In fact, the peace terms proposed to sever from Turkey provinces and districts predominantly inhabited by the Turks, and to impose suzerainty over the Turkish sovereign, which, according to the Indian Muslims, would affect his status and prestige as the religious head of the community. Finally, the terms were designed to retain the protectorate of the sacred cities of Islam in non-Muslim hands.

[5] The vast majority of Bengali Muslims were peasants. Among the ordinary cultivators, they were almost double the number of Hindus, but among the landlords there were nearly twice as many Hindus as Muslims. The Permanent Settlement had resulted in

landlords and their allies struck a deal with the government to bolster their influence in society and administration. Taking advantage of the benefits accruing from the Montagu–Chelmsford Reforms of 1918, they wrested control of the Bengal Congress, the party of the dominant classes, chiefly the Hindu *jotedars*. Soon enough, the 'Congress of the Poor' treated the other political formations, albeit weak, the parties of the masses, with a mixture of fear, contempt, and indifference. Of particular interest in all this was the defense of privileges and alliance with the landed classes, whose interests and aspirations were markedly different from the Hindu or Muslim peasantry.

More spectacular were the open collisions in the Bengal Legislative Council. In 1928 and 1937–1939, the lines of division were clear cut; whereas the Muslim members backed the motions against the landlords who cowed and browbeat the *raiyats*/sharecroppers, the Hindu members, especially Congressmen, tended to be pro-landlord (Chatterjee, 1982). Fazlul Haq (1873–1962), a product of Calcutta University, resigned from government service to join the Bar in 1912, entered the Bengal legislative council in 1912, and took a leading part in the Congress League negotiations of 1916. Starting public life as a nationalist, he served as secretary of the Congress from 1918 to 1919. One of those upwardly mobile commoners who reached the top of the social ladder, he found unacceptable the traditional image of the Muslims in which social mobility was an anomaly, and substituted a new image for it, that of a *community* as it came to be understood by the colonial government. As the founder of the Krishak Proja Party in 1927, he championed the interests of an oppressed and impoverished peasantry: and it was precisely because the peasants were becoming more conscious of their rights that the old feudal survivals and privileges appeared all the more vexatious and intolerable.

---

many families, mainly Muslims, losing their lands to a new class of Hindu landlords. The Resumption Proceedings between 1828 and 1846 not only further impoverished the few Muslim families which had survived the Permanent Settlement, but also destroyed the economic basis of Muslim educational institutions, which were almost entirely maintained by revenue-free grants. By the end of the nineteenth century, Hindus owned most of the land in Bengal. This was most strikingly evident in eastern Bengal, a Muslim-majority area. Muslims formed 80 per cent of the population in Bogra district, but there were only five Muslim zamindars. Muslims were 64.8 per cent of the population in Bakargunj district, but they owned less than 10 per cent of the estates and paid less than 9 per cent of the total land revenue.

Paradoxically, though, Fazlul Haq was derided, especially after becoming Bengal's chief minister from April 1, 1937 to March 1943, as 'communal' and 'separatist' whereas his detractors, who whipped up religious passions for personal gains, were exalted as 'nationalists'/'freedom fighters'. People like Chaudhuri categorized Fazlul Haq as communal and drew certain conclusions, mostly erroneous, from the growing polarization in Bengal's polity. "No one will grudge Mr Chaudhuri seeking his own consolation," observed Sarkar. "But," he added, "the path of history is indeed devious. And in all probability, his firm conclusions will break down in the process of its unfolding" (Chatterjee, 1982: 193).

Chaudhuri insisted that Muslims constituted a society of their own with a distinctive culture, and that they could not, therefore, be absorbed into a unified nation. This being the case, "no historical argument was too false or too foolish to be trotted out by the Hindus to contest the demand of the Indian Muslims to have their own way of life" (Chaudhuri, 1987: 38, 330). In projecting a communal 'hate' and 'hurt' as the basis of his exercise in history writing, Chaudhuri becomes the bearer of a wounding historical conscience.

# III

After Chaudhuri, I now turn to the more general reflections in the works of yet another overseas-based writer who routinely fulminates against the Muslims. He is none other than Sir Vidiadhar Surajprasad Naipaul. His ancestors left India in the early 1880s as indentured laborers for the sugar estates of Guyana and Trinidad. He returned to an area of darkness and chronicled the histories of a wounded civilization and a million mutinies in India. In between, he fired his shots at the world of Islam not once but twice, in labored projects. Samuel Huntington (b. 1927), a controversial American political scientist, earned his reputation by expounding the clash of civilizations theory; Naipaul by alerting his readers to the menace of Islam.

Snouck Hurgronje (1857–1936), a scholar at Leiden, wrote convincingly about Islam as a living and changing reality: what Muslims mean by it is constantly changing because of the particular circumstances of times and places. He insisted that if non-Muslims wish to understand Islam, they must study it in its historical reality, without judgment of value about what it ought to be (Hourani, 1991: 42–43). The sense of Islam as something more than words in texts, as something living in individual Muslims, is not known to many creative writers. Naipaul is only one of them.

Naipaul's disdain for the Muslims is based on a conviction that Islam is hurtful and aggressive toward the advanced and 'civilized' Western civilization, and that Muslim societies are, by comparison, rigid, authoritarian, and uncreative (Amin, 1998). So he writes in *Among the Believers: An Islamic Journey,* born out of his Islamic journey to Iran, Pakistan, Malaysia, and Indonesia. The whole of this book is permeated with these sentiments: "Islam sanctified rage, rage about the faith, political rage: one could be like the other. And more than once, on this journey I had met sensitive men who were ready to contemplate greater convulsions." *Beyond Belief: Islamic Excursions among the Converted Peoples,* published 18 years after *Among the Believers,* portrays "the same primitive, rudimentary, unsatisfactory and reductive thesis," that most Muslims, having been converted from Hinduism, must experience the ignominy of all converted people.[6]

In *India: A Million Mutinies Now* (1990), the 1857 revolt is regarded as the last flare-up of Muslim energy until the agitation, 80 years or so later, for a separate Muslim homeland. This is very fine as far as it goes. But, then, Naipaul's critical observation is that he found bazaars in Lucknow expressing the faith of the book and the mosque; whatever he saw in Aminabad, a crowded marketplace, served the faith (Naipaul, 1992: 356). Such notions we are not obliged to take seriously. As might be expected, they exhibit the cocksureness of the autodidact. The matter can be safely left to the growing army of Naipaul's critics.

Two years after *India: A Million Mutinies Now,* Naipaul defended the destruction of the Babri Masjid by calling it "an act of historical balance."[7] "Ayodhya," he rationalized, "was a sort of passion.... Any passion has to be encouraged. I always support actions coming out of passion as these reflect creativity." Whose passion? Is this passion a sentiment born of a misplaced feeling of 'collective hurt'? How

---

[6] Edward Said, in *Outlook*, October 30, 2001.

[7] "I would call it an act of historical balancing. The mosque built by Babur in Ayodhya was meant as an act of contempt. Babur was no lover of India. I think it is universally accepted that Babur despised India, the Indian people, and their faith." (Naipaul, "Hindu Revivalists are Mimicking Islamic Fundamentalists: V.S. Naipaul and Khushwant Singh in Conversation with Bhaichand Patel", in *Outlook*, May 08, 2000).

would Naipaul account for the passion of those Muslims who, despite the bitterness since December 1992, still weave the garlands used in the temple and produce everything necessary for dressing the icons preparatory to worship (Nandy, Trivedy, Mayaram, and Yagnik. 1995: 2)?

While Naipaul held forth on the calamitous effects of Islam,[8] Ali Sardar Jafri, an Urdu poet of considerable stature, used a secular rather than a religious vocabulary to delineate the tragic impact of the demolition of the Babri Masjid and the communal holocaust thereafter:

> Manaya jaayega jashn-i-masarrat soone khandaroan mein
> Andheri raat mein roshan charagh-e-chashme-e-tar honge.
> Jo yeh tabeer hogi Hind ke dereena khawabon ki
> To phir Hindustan hoga na uske deedawar honge.

> (Orgies of joy among desolate ruins
> Glimmer of tear-rimmed eyes in the black night
> If these be the meaning of our ancient dreams
> Then the land and its seers will be gone).

There is no place for such sentiments in Naipaul's jaundiced view of the Muslims. To him, Hindu militancy is a necessary corrective to the past,[9] a creative force. He therefore rejects the possibility of Islam, a religion of fixed laws, working out reconciliation with other religions on the subcontinent.[10] This is, in just a few crisp sentences, the clash of civilization theory. In sharp contrast, Mujeeb had written

Unless we have decided in our own minds that medieval Indian history is not the history of the Indian people, we must courageously examine our present criteria of judgment and develop a perspective on persons, policies

---

[8] *Outlook*, February 27, 2004. "Fractured past is too polite a way to describe India's calamitous millennium. The millennium began with the Muslim invasions and the grinding down of the Hindu-Buddhist culture of the north. This is such a big and bad event that people still have to find polite, destiny-defying ways of speaking about it. In art books and history books, people write of the Muslims 'arriving' in India, as though the Muslims came on a tourist bus and went away again." Again, the Muslim invasion had "a calamitous effect on converted peoples. To be converted you have to destroy your past, destroy your history. You have to stamp on it, you have to say 'my ancestral culture does not exist, it doesn't matter'." He claimed what he called "this abolition of the self demanded by Muslims' being 'worse than the similar colonial abolition of identity."

[9] Interview with Tarun Tejpal, in *Outlook*, March 23, 1998.

[10] Interview with Tarun Tejpal.

and events of the past that will enable us to understand and forgive and to obtain a clear vision of the past and the future. (Mujeeb, 2003: 3–4)

Given a choice, Naipaul would give voice to the 'defeated people', not the poor or the downtrodden, but the *Hindus* living in *Hindu India*. Among the many choices available in a country like India with its bewildering variety, he asserts cold-bloodedly, he focuses on the "grinding down of Hindu India" and the revival of memories of temples being destroyed, Hindus being forcibly converted to Islam, and Sikh *gurus* being mercilessly executed by the Mughal emperors.

If one has to build a modern India by invoking the brutal past, Naipaul's prescription is to rubbish what goes in the name of assimilation, and to drop Mahatma Gandhi (1869–1948) from the history syllabus. The hero of many a satyagraha against the British, Bapu—he feels—has no message today, even though Indians use the very idea of Mahatma to "turn dirt and backwardness into much-loved deities." *Hind Swaraj*, Gandhi's seminal work which he himself translated from Gujarati into English, is for Naipaul "so nonsensical that it would curl the hair of even the most devoted admirer"; the title especially moves him to scorn.[11] The fact is, as a social scientist points out

Hind Swaraj is the seed from which the tree of Gandhian thought has grown to its full stature. For those interested in Gandhi's thought in a general way, it is the right place to start, for it is here that he presents his basic ideas in their proper relationship to one another. (Gandhi, 2004 [reprint]: xiii)

Naipaul's exposition in contrast is clumsy, naïve, and, if taken seriously, potentially dangerous. He is as much ill-informed about India

[11] "Gandhi shouldn't be considered as laying down a prescription for anything. He was uneducated and never a thinker. He is a historical figure. He came at a particular moment; he turned all his drawbacks into religion; and he used religion to awaken the country in a way that none of the educated leaders could have done. He has absolutely no message today. People talk too much about Gandhi and study him too little. His first book, *Hind Swaraj*, written at white heat in two weeks in 1909, is so nonsensical it would curl the hair of even the most devoted admirer. I don't know Indians who actually read Gandhi. They take him some vague idea of a great redeeming holiness and they are free to ignore the practical side—Gandhi the hater of dirt, the hater of public defecation. That last is still very much an Indian sport. In fact, the Gandhian idea of piety and a very holy poverty is used now to excuse the dirt of the cities, the shoddiness of the architecture. By some inversion, Indians have used the very idea of Gandhi to turn dirt and backwardness into much-loved deities." (Interview with Tarun Tejpal, "Christianity Didn't Damage India Like Islam", in *Outlook*, November 15, 1999).

as Huntington is about the world outside the Western Hemisphere. He talks of a fractured past solely in terms of Muslim invasions and conveniently forgets the grinding down of the Buddhist–Jain culture during the period of Brahmanical revival. He fumes and frets regardless of the fact that only a fringe element celebrates the vandalism of the early Islamists who were driven more by establishing the might of evangelical Islam than having defacement of Hindus as a primary motive. With misplaced sentiments of hurt, anger, remorse, and bitterness being a substitute for study and analysis, Naipaul's plan for India's salvation collapses like a pack of cards. Hence, Edward Said's (1935–2003) devastating denunciation of *Beyond Belief*:

> Somewhere along the way Naipaul, in my opinion, himself suffered a serious intellectual accident. His obsession with Islam caused him somehow to stop thinking, to become instead a kind of mental suicide compelled to repeat the same formula over and over. This is what I would call an intellectual catastrophe of the first order.
>
> The pity of it is that so much is now lost on Naipaul. His writing has become repetitive and uninteresting. His gifts have been squandered. He can no longer make sense. He lives on his great reputation which has gulled his reviewers into thinking that they are still dealing with a great writer, whereas he has become a ghost. The greater pity is that Naipaul's latest book on Islam will be considered a major interpretation of a great religion, and more Muslims will suffer and be insulted. And the gap between them and the West will increase and deepen. No one will benefit except the publishers who will probably sell a lot of books, and Naipaul, who will make a lot of money. (Edward, October 30, 2001)

# References

Amin, Shahid. 1998. "Naipaul's Historical Baggage", *Outlook*, June 08, 1998 edition.

Chatterjee, Partha. 1982. "Agrarian Relations and Communalism in Bengal, 1926–1935," in *Subaltern Studies I: Writings on South Asian History and Society*, edited by Ranajit Guha. New Delhi: Oxford University Press.

Chatterji, Joya. 1995. *Bengal Divided: Hindu Communalism and Partition, 1932–1947*. Cambridge: Cambridge University Press, p. 268.

Chaudhuri, Nirad C. 1951. *The Autobiography of an Unknown Indian*. New York: NYRB Press, p. 225.

——— 1965. *The Continent of Circe*. London: Chatto & Windus.

——— 1967. *Intellectual in India*. New Delhi: Vir Publishing House.

——— 1976. *Culture in the Vanity Bag*. Bombay: Jaico Publishing House.

Chaudhuri, Nirad C. 1979. *Hinduism: A Religion to Live By*. New Delhi: Oxford University Press.

——— 1987. *Thy Hand Great Anarch! India, 1921–1952*. London: Addison-Wesley.

Cobban, Alfred. 1964. *The Social Interpretation of the French Revolution*. Cambridge: Cambridge University Press, p. 162.

Gandhi, M.K. 2004 (reprint). *Hind Swaraj and other Writings* (Ed.). Anthony J. Parel, p. xiii.

Hasan, Mushirul and Mohd. Asaduddin (Eds.). 2000. *Image and Representation*. New Delhi: Oxford University Press.

Hourani, Albert. 1991. *Islam in European Thought*. Cambridge: Cambridge University Press, pp. 42–43.

Lewis, Bernard. 1993. *Islam and the West*. New York and Oxford: Oxford University Press, p. 130.

Lichtheim, George. 1974. *Europe in the Twentieth Century*. London: Cardinal Books, p. 435.

Metcalf, Barbara. 1995. Presidential Address: "Too Little Too Much. Reflection on Muslims in the History of India," *Journal of Asian Studies*, 54(4): 51–67.

——— 2004. *Islamic Contestations: Essays on Muslim in India and Pakistan*. New Delhi: Oxford University Press, p. 210.

Milton-Edwards, Beverly. 2004. *Islam and Politics in the Contemporary World*. Cambridge: Polity Press, p. 217.

Mujeeb, Mohammad. 1972. *Islamic Influence on Indian Society*. Meerut: Meenakshi Prakashan, p. 137.

——— August–October 2003. "Approach to the Study of Medieval Indian History," in Special Issue on Professor Mohammad Mujeeb, *Islam and the Modern Age*, 34(3–4).

Naipaul, V.S. 2008. *Beyond Belief: Islamic Excursions among the Converted People*. New Delhi, p. 1.

——— 1992. *India: A Million Mutinies Now*. New York: Penguin Books, p. 356.

Nandy, Ashis. 1994. *The Illegitimacy of Nationalism*. New Delhi: Oxford University Press, p. 38.

Nandy, Ashis, Shikha Trivedy, Shail Mayaram, and Achyut Yagnik. 1995. *The Ramjanmabhumi Movement and Fear of the Self*. New Delhi: Oxford University Press, p. 2.

Ray, Rajat Kanta (Ed.). 1995. *Mind Body and Society: Life and Mentality in Colonial Bengal*. Calcutta: Oxford University Press, p. 14.

——— 1985. "Revolutionaries, Pan-Islamists and Bolsheviks: Maulana Abul Kalam Azad and the Political Underworld in Calcutta, 1905–1925," in *Communal and Pan-Islamic Trends*, edited by Mushirul Hasan. New Delhi: Manohar Publications, pp. 103–118.

Raychaudhuri, Tapan. 1988. *Europe Reconsidered: Perceptions of the West in Nineteenth Century Bengal*. New Delhi: Oxford University Press.

Said, Edward. 2001. "An Intellectual Catastrophe", Outlook, October 30, 2001 edition.

Sarkar, Sumit. 1973. *The Swadeshi Movement in Bengal, 1903–1908*. New Delhi: Orient Blackswan.

Sarkar, Susobhan. 1970. *Bengal Renaissance and Other Essays*. New Delhi: People's Publishing House.

Sen, Amiya P. 1993. *Hindu Revivalism in Bengal 1872: Some Essays in Interpretation*. New Delhi: Oxford University Press, p. 192.

Thompson, Edward. 1926. *Rabindranath Tagore: Poet and Dramatist*. Oxford, p. 291.

Tibi, Bassam. 2001. *Islam between Culture and Politics*. Harvard, Chapter 4.

# 7

# Commemorating Hurt: Memorializing Operation Bluestar*

*Radhika Chopra*

The orchestrated military assault on Sri Darbar Sahib, the Golden Temple complex in Amritsar, by the Indian Army during *Operation Bluestar* was executed in the first week of June 1984. The assault on the sacred site is most frequently spoken of as a deeply traumatic event evoking intense but uneasy remembrances. Residents of Amritsar confined to their homes during the course of a 32-hour curfew imposed on the walled city from June 1, 1984, recalled hearing the staccato gunfire of battle and feeling the ground shake beneath their feet, a memory that remains fresh in their minds. When curfew was finally lifted, many ran through the narrow gullies toward the Golden Temple, in frenzy akin to mourners hearing the news of death. Looking at the damaged dome, women broke out into spontaneous mourning laments. The first viewing of the destruction is a hurt remembered, and people come back again and again on successive anniversaries of Operation Bluestar to mourn the 'death' of the Takht.

Remembrance of things past[1] is a fundamental resource for actors and social groups living in the present. We do not leave our past behind; it is a palpable presence in our present and we actively commemorate

* Extract from *Militant and Migrant: The Politics and Social History of Punjab*. London, New York, and New Delhi: Routledge, 2011.

[1] The phrase is one of the translations of the title of Marcel Proust's seven volume work on involuntary memory.

and remember the past in monuments and memorials, in texts, images, songs, stories, rituals, art, and in evocations of the spirit of persons. Two classic scholars of memory Maurice Halbwachs and Paul Connerton speak of social memory as selective. Different groups, argued Halbwachs, have different collective memories that produce diverse forms of remembering (Halbwachs, 1992). Connerton put his finger on a central aspect of selective memory contending that social memory is a dimension of political power and "the control of a society's memory largely conditions the hierarchy of power ... (where) images of the past commonly legitimate a present social order" (Connerton, 1989: 3). Both authors addressed commemorations— physical monuments or enacted rituals—asserting that the past is preserved as a moral universe, sanctified, and homogenized by deleting disruptive counter memories. Commemorative monuments convey the illusion of reconciliation to a particular version of an authentic past, offering a façade of fixed and frozen memory, implying the successful transmission of messages of power and the submission to authorized memory. Others argue that remembering is an inherently generative process, selective, creative, and performative, mediated by material culture and ritual performances as well as by the written and spoken word (Williams, 2006: 2). Despite façades of permanence, commemorations are sites of creative remembering and strategic forgetting and remain deeply contested. Acts of remembering and forgetting create a paradox, for it is as important for people to remember what it is they must forget and continue to remember what they need to recall. Producing legitimated memory creates the context of strategically forgetting some elements of inherited memory, so that memory can be directed toward acceptable or 'usable pasts' through an editing in of what people need to remember and an editing out of what they need to remember to forget. The meanings of memorials shift over time and space reflecting strategic memory loss and recollection. William Blair's analysis of the metamorphoses of the Arlington Cemetery from the epitome of Civil War discord to a site of reconciliation (Blair, 2004) demonstrates the continuous process of construction and meaning making to which memorials and commemorations are subject.

Like monuments, rituals of commemoration are repositories of collective memory and expressive fields of power, sites at which hegemony and resistance are articulated, where officially authorized collective memories and contradictory counter memories exist in uncomfortable synchronicity. An uneasily remembered past is the subject of this essay, drawing on diverse writings on memory and disparate histories of violence. Cited most frequently as the source of 'hurt' for the Sikh community, the military assault on Sri Darbar Sahib, the Golden Temple complex is one in a series of prior and consequent political episodes[2] that is collectively referred to as the militancy period in Punjab of the movement for a separate state of Khalistan. But as an event, it also stands apart as an exemplar of hurt.

Punjabis use the English word 'hurt' to denote the feeling of being seized by pain, as well as to suggest intentionality—*hurt paunchya*—hurt reached, they say. Sometimes another English word is used: *feel hoya* a phrase that continually occurs among Punjabi speakers to suggest embodied emotion and distress, and the phrase *hurting the sentiment of community* is also frequently used. By profaning sacred space, the occupation of the Golden Temple complex was, and is, viewed as a deliberate hurt inflicted on the sentiments and standing of the Sikhs. Hurt is signified across different domains of experience. It is personal affront-numerous men interviewed during 2006–2007 (including those who fled Punjab and took refuge in Southall, UK) recounted stories of being accosted by police and Central Reserve Police Force (CRPF) personnel because they wore turbans, had long open beards,[3] or rode motorbikes.[4] A sense of political hurt is embedded in the demands of the Anandpur Sahib Resolution, a charter of demands championed by Bhindranwale

---

[2] Subsequent events include Operation Black Thunder One and Black Thunder Two (in 1986 and 1988, respectively) when the Golden Temple was again besieged and entered this time jointly by the Army and Police forces. These operations have been less well documented. (But see Singh, 2002.)

[3] Sikhs usually keep their beards groomed and tied. The tying of the beard in specific styles connotes difference within the community. For example, traders tie netting to keep their facial hair in place. Others tie special pieces of cloth over the beard, either tucking the cloth under the turban, or tied in a knot over a truncated turban. Matching turbans, beard cloth, and neckties are styles adopted by the urbane. Open beards, by contrast, and blue or saffron turbans, were a style adopted during the militant decades to assert an ascendant political identity.

[4] Motorbikes, a sign of male prowess and wealth among the Punjabi peasantry, were viewed with suspicion by the constabulary as swift get away vehicles during the entire period of militancy. At various points of time bans on adult males riding pillion were imposed (*The Tribune*, May 7, 1984, p. 5). This suspicion was perhaps heightened by the fact that the Punjab police were ill-equipped and feared for their safety. Almost 40 percent of the constabulary applied for leave during this period (*The Tribune*, May 14, 1984).

and other Sikh leaders at various points of time. The inclusion of Sikhs under the category Hindus under Article 25(b) of the Indian Constitution is resented and represented as 'hurting' the collective self. The sense of submergence of a distinct identity within the larger category of Hindu is represented as a deliberate attempt to obliterate the foundation of a political community. The Anandpur Sahib Resolution may perhaps be viewed as a constitution-in-the-making of a clearly theological state of Khalistan: the Nation of the Pure. On the one hand it demanded the right to carry religiously prescribed weapons like the *kirpan* (dagger) in public places; on the other it claimed the right over river waters of Punjab and the right to regulate the movement of food grain outside the state. Miming the Indian constitution, the Anandpur Sahib Resolution crucially drew away from the idea of the secular, envisioning a baptized community of faithful citizens. The imagined demography of Khalistan envisioned by the Resolution, effectively excluded non-believers as well as *patit*, or non-observing, Sikhs who did not conform to the code of Rehat Maryada (Sikh way of life enunciated in religious documents and pamphlets). Its provisions emphasized abstinence, observance of bodily symbols and cultural rejuvenation so that only those who were initiates could be citizens of Khalistan. Publicly enacted *amrit chakkna* initiations were performed throughout the early to mid-1980s as a form of renewal of faith and commitment to the emerging political community of Khalistan. Before he fled to take sanctuary in the Golden Temple, Bhindranwale toured the state and conducted initiation ceremonies. Subsequently, his father Jasbir Singh Rode also toured villages of Punjab actively encouraging people to re-enact the *amrit* ritual as a form of a personal pledge to defend the faith. The Anandpur Sahib Resolution seemed to suggest that citizenship was not an abstract identity conferred by the Indian state but rather a matter of language, ritual observance, and embodied spirit converging on a specific territory. The emotive language of disavowal drew simultaneously on scriptural tropes and political disaffection of dissent. From the Indian government's point of view, the Resolution and the claim to Khalistan were interpreted as an illegitimate political document of an unlawful nation which nevertheless had profound implications for the 'authentic' nation. The contest between nations was fought within the precincts of the Golden Temple, in June 1984.

The battle of Bluestar produced the monumental hurt—the architectural mutilation of the Akal Takht. The shattered shell of the

Takht destroyed by a rocket propelled grenade launcher was—and is—represented continually as the hurt that struck at the heart of sacred community and every individual member within it, reproduced in a series of different representations in poster art and in portraiture (Photograph 7.1). 'Hurt' moved from community to territory—the

**Photograph 7.1**

*Portrait of the Mutilated Akal Takht in the Museum within the Sacred Complex, June 2007*

*Source:* Author.

land of the imagined nation of Khalistan it was said, was being drained by a rapacious center, and only the control over its natural resources of water and food could make Punjab/Khalistan regain its sense of worth. The distribution of the *Ab*—river waters—of Punjab to other states was cited as hurting the rights to livelihood and territorial integrity.[5] The decimation of Takht and sapped territory of Punjab were widely spoken of together as a deliberate injury inflicted on Sikh *maryada* or sense of honour (Bourdieu, 1979).

The remembrance of the hurt of Operation Bluestar has a double tenor. The death of specific people is mourned as part of the rituals of remembrance. But the desecration of the sacred complex as a wellspring of hurt is powerfully stressed. The two sources of hurt are not evoked in the same way or with the same intent. I would argue in fact that among all the violent incidents that engulfed Punjab for almost three decades (Grover, 1995; Narayanan, 1996; Pettigrew, 1995; Puri et al., 1999; Singh, 2000) the siege and attack on the Golden Temple Complex and the shelling of its sacred buildings in June 1984 is remembered as pivotal,[6] especially hurtful because of the place of the Golden Temple in Sikh history and hagiography. In the sacred geography of Sikhism the Sri Darbar Sahib and the eponymous Golden Temple are the center of a moral and religious world.[7] So the army action was seen

[5] The forerunner to the Khalistan movement the Punjabi Suba movement of the 1960s also stressed the right of control over territory and water. The claim to territory has been interleaved with the demands for a substantive federal political structure.

[6] Operation Bluestar was not the only time the temple complex was entered and taken over by the state in the course of the period referred to as the *militancy period*. Its memory however is marked because of the simultaneous concurrence of events; it was the Gurpurab—Day of Remembrance—of Guru Arjan Dev and thousands of Sikh pilgrims had gathered in the Temple precincts to celebrate. Many killed in the army action on those two days included such pilgrims. The temple and its sacred buildings also suffered major damage.

[7] For Sikhs, pilgrimages to the Golden Temple on designated days of the ritual calendar or to mark personal life cycle events or for no special reason at all other than because someone *felt* like it, is a performance of membership of the *sangat* (religious collective). Visits are part of personal and collective memory, recounted and re-performed to produce a sense of community. Religious souvenirs—paintings, posters, books of religious discourses purchased from the surrounding bazaar shops layer memory with artefact. Bathing in the sacred pool around which the complex is structured, making offerings to the Book housed in the Harmandir, the symbolic center of the sacred complex, singing, listening to scriptural recitations and eating at the *langar*, the community kitchen of the complex, are all part of

not merely as a military occupation but a desecration, continuously cited in commemorations as an irreparable hurt.

The other interwoven event, in fact the explanation offered for the military operation, was the elimination of Jarnail Singh Bhindranwale and his militant cohorts. Though central to the entire event, there is a peculiar ambivalence surrounding the remembrance of Bhindranwale's death. His death is frequently fused with remembrances of other deaths,[8] many of ordinary people. One prominent death link, however, is between his death and the subsequent assassination of Indira Gandhi on October 31, 1984 (who, as Prime Minister, ordered the forcible takeover of the Temple Complex). The two deaths have been coupled as the revenge of the Indian state against militant violence unleashed against the legitimate nation by Bhindranwale and his followers, and Indira Gandhi's death by her Sikh bodyguards as a retaliation for violating and laying waste the sacred shrine and the massacre of

---

creating a sense of *sangat*, the gathered community of believers. Most of all the sense of community is created by the care of the complex through voluntary ritualized labor–*kar seva*–through which the monuments are maintained and quotidian tasks performed. Anything from regular sweeping, washing, cooking, to building and repair work in the Temple is done through *kar seva*. Building contractors give of their labour and expertise in a spirit of worship. Throughout the performance of *seva* (care of a superior being or site) some, though not all, workmen wear ritual clothing of blue turbans and *chogas* or long shirts denoting the practical as ceremonial, distinguished from the mundane.

[8] Two other major supporters of Khalistan were also killed during the Operation. Amrik Singh headed the militant All India Sikh Student Federation, while Shabeg Singh was a decorated Army general who resigned his commission in 1976. Shahbeg Singh was primarily responsible for the fortification of the Temple complex and planning the armed resistance. Houses in the narrow gullies surrounding the complex functioned as outposts connected by wireless to the command post within the Temple precinct. Soldiers of the Indian army were killed or wounded first by the sniper fire from these outposts, a situation reminiscent of the experience of the colonial British army entering the narrow gullies of Lucknow during the hot May days of the Mutiny of 1857 (Oldenberg, 1984). The exact day and time of Bhindranwale's death is unclear; he is said to have died either sometime on the night of 5th–6th of June or the night of 6th–7th of June. The *confusion* may reside in the different calculations of dates in Roman and vernacular calendars. However, June 6 is designated as the death anniversary of Bhindranwale and his closest followers (whose portraits are displayed in the Akal Takht Museum). June 6 has become an occasion for many to mourn those killed in the violence and is literally a death anniversary by extension of other deaths. In Amritsar, people who lost family members participate in the *Ghallughara Diwas* at the Golden Temple in June of every year. In London, placards with the photos of missing and dead kin are displayed in *Never Forget* rallies that mark public commemorations of Operation Bluestar.

Sikhs pilgrims.[9] Though the two deaths are equally mired in violence, remembrance and representation are wedged between forbidden and authorized memorials of two lives positioned as the antithesis of each other: Bhindranwale, the *Uggarvadi* (terrorist)[10] and a Threat to the Nation and Indira Gandhi, the putative Mother of modern India.

Performances of commemoration oscillate between allegories of sacrilege on the one hand and tropes of national identity, violence, and political personhood on the other. "Operation Bluestar" is an event at one site, but memory and rituals of remembrance move across space and time. Memorializations of Operation Bluestar metaphorically jettison the before and after, denoting the singularity of the event and its categorical, unsullied remembrance. Commemorations of the double deaths of Bhindranwale and Indira Gandhi are fragmented over a string of sites, including the newly created public spaces (Indira Gandhi's home where she was assassinated and her riverside *samadhi* or cremation site), familiar sacred places (the Golden Temple) and days of remembrance (June 6 and October 31),[11] even cities—the commemorations for Gandhi occur in Delhi, for Bhindranwale in Amritsar.[12] The invented styles of remembrance signal transformations

---

[9] The politics of aftermath is punctuated by assassinations that moved across national and global space from the assassination of Indira Gandhi in Delhi (1984), to Pune in western India of General Vaidya, in-charge of Operation Bluestar (1986), to Bucharest and the assassination attempt on Julio Ribeiro (1991) the Chief of Police in Punjab whose *bullet for bullet* policy created a new dimension of rule of the modern Indian state.

[10] *Uggarwadi* was the official term used freely in government statements and in the English language media, state television, and radio broadcasts. The official term stands in opposition to the more popular term *Khargu,* or freedom fighter. Both terms refer to masculine bodily styles—*ugar*—or ferocious, *kharg*—sword—embodying honed weaponry.

[11] There is a peculiar imprecision in the commemorations. October 31 is the anniversary of the assassination of Indira Gandhi who was gunned down at her residence; but most official *ceremonials* of remembrance are conducted at Shakti Sthal where she was cremated on November 4, 1984. The exact date of Bhindranwale's death is unclear (until very recently some of his supporters in the seminary refused to acknowledge that he had died at all declaring that he is *chardi kala*—in rising spirit). However, it is speculated that he was killed sometime on the night of 5th–6th June when the *storming* of the Temple complex began when some of the heaviest shelling of the Temple complex occurred. Surprisingly, *Ghallughara Diwas,* Genocide Day, is most fully memorialized on June 6, which may or may not be Bhindranwale's death anniversary. Imprecision argues against memorials as inextricably tied to both place and date—a point made by Lowenthal (1979: 121) in his discussions of IWW memorials.

[12] In the absence of a physical memorial to anchor collective memory, the commemoration of *Ghallughara Diwas* (Day of Genocide), and death anniversary of the militant, has *traveled* to become a transnational ritual, and a consequent shifting of meanings across space.

in the meanings of memorials and commemoration rituals and become locations to decipher memory and forgetting.

# Memorials, Spaces, and Commemoration Rituals

The army vacated the Golden Temple complex on September 28, 1984 and it was handed over to the five High Priests of the five Takhts on September 29, 1984. Within a day of its handover to the five priests,[13] the thanksgiving ceremonies were hijacked by a 300 strong *jatha* (band) of young men, who shouted pro-Bhindranwale slogans and mounted a Khalistan flag on the dome of the newly repaired Akal Takht. The gathered audience greeted these noisy interventions with approval and admiration.[14] When the rebuilt temple was finally handed over to the SGPC[15] (the body responsible for the maintenance of all sacred shrines), Gurcharan Singh Tohra, the President of the SGPC, decided that the entire building would be pulled down and rebuilt.[16] The demolition began on January 26, 1986[17] on another apparent coincidental twinning of memorials for recasting nations—India's Republic Day and the day of martyrdom of Baba Deep Singh,[18] who had been killed while

[13] Post Operation Bluestar, with Bhindranwale and other leaders dead, and major Akali party leaders jailed, the five High Priests of the major gurdwaras or Sikh shrines became the center of negotiations and conduct of affairs of the community.

[14] The handover of the Golden Temple did not mean army withdrawal from the state. In fact in the days just prior to and after the handover 68 young men between the ages 18 and 30 years were rounded up in adjoining Gurdaspur district. The police chief A.P. Pandey, when asked to clarify if they were militants, declared that most of them were *emotionally charged people who act impulsively* (*India Today,* October 31, 1984, p. 31).

[15] Shiromani Gurdwara Prabandhak Committee, the body that manages gurdwaras and the activities within them. Despite their centrality in the management of gurdwaras' affairs, the Temple complex was not handed over to the SGPC by the army on September 29, 1984 partly because the president of SGPC Gurcharan Singh Tohra was in jail and the SGPC was treated as a highly suspect organization for giving sanctuary to Bhindranwale within the Complex.

[16] Tohra's decision was disputed as unauthorized by the *sangat* and the *Panth* (Giani Kirpal Singh, 1999) unrepresentative of community opinion, a sign of the instability of the leadership within the community and divided opinions about the event itself.

[17] The re-built Akal Takht was opened for ritual prayers on Baisakhi, April 13, 1997.

[18] A shrine to Baba Deep Singh is built in one corner of the *parikrama* and forms part of the shrines of the complex.

defending the Akal Takht against Afghan invaders in 1757. The allusion to past destruction, invasion, and martyrdom in defence of political ideals and sacred spaces in the coincidence of dates was not lost on the contemporary audience of believers.

From the moment the complex was opened right up to the present, Operation Bluestar has been memorialized in some form within the precincts of the sacred complex though the tenor and style of the memorialization has altered dramatically over time. The most spectacular commemoration ritual is *Ghallughara Divas*, first observed officially by the Shiromani Gurdwara Prabandhak Committee in 1995. The naming of June 6 as *Ghallughara Divas* in 1995 harks back to the carnage of women and children by the Afghan invader Ahmed Shah Durrani and equates the Indian state's military desecration of the Darbar Sahib with the massacre inflicted by the Afghans. Rituals as repositories of memory enacted within mnemonic spaces combine to shape commemoration. The Golden Temple as a space haunted by diverse memories is a visceral site of emotion expressed in commemoration. Enacted within the site of destruction, the commemorative ritual of *Ghallughara* has become a storehouse of memory and emotional landscape that seeks to create an affective community of mourners.

On the morning of *Ghallughara Divas,* bands of pilgrims formally arrive in the sacred complex (Photograph 7.2), their spectacular presence conveying a sense of unity of the group as well as the singularity of the occasion when Sikh *maryada* or sense of honor was lost. The loss is continuously recouped through the presence of mainly male bands that arrive every year on the 6th of June dressed in saffron turbans, the color that came to symbolize politics of protest and white ensembles, the color of mourning. Their formal entry, ritual ensemble, and solemn demeanor segregate them from ordinary pilgrims and their cohesive presence imparts a depth of significance to the day and those who gather to restore *maryada.*

At the end of the day, the gathered assembly stands in attitudes of deep reverence in the forecourt before the Akal Takht and around the *sarovar* to recite the *Ardas*, the prayer that remembers martyrs (Photograph 7.3). Through the course of the full ritual day, people hang around in the complex for hours moving across and around the different spaces of the complex, a habitus of past and present. Under the shade of canopies in the forecourt of the Akal Takht groups gather

**Photograph 7.2**

*Groups of male mourners formally arrive at the Darbar Sahib during* Ghallughara Divas, *June 2007*

*Source:* Author.

**Photograph 7.3**

*Ardas in the Forecourt of the Akal Takht, June 2007*

*Source:* Author.

to listen to bards singing *vars*, ballads that hark back to a heroic history. They wander toward the community kitchens to eat together in an act of sharing bread. As the crowds swell, the kitchen volunteers seat pilgrims in the long verandas that run around the overcrowded halls. Pilgrims perform *kar sewa*, ritual labour of care, collecting steel buckets to fill with the water to wash the walkway around the sacred pool, and cool the marble of the uncovered path. As the June sun rises, some sit in quiet contemplation, resting against marble plaques donated in the memory of family members or comrades lost in battle (Photograph 7.4). Continuous recitations of the sacred scripture cast an aural canopy over the complex. It is at once a familiar ritual day, replicating many others,

**Photograph 7.4**

*Contemplation and Remembrance*

*Source:* Author.

seeming to restore normalcy through ritual commemoration. But the contemporary insertion of *Ghallughara Divas* into the ritual calendar of the Darbar Sahib, and the fact that its observance is still mired in controversy, disputes any assumption of a return to normality. This is not an event that can be forgotten, for the sense of hurt persists as a continually felt emotion.

Memory is deliberately evoked and fused in relics of 1984 preserved within the complex, including galleries and exhibition rooms of the newly restored museum of Sikh history. The series of memorials within and outside the museum, coupled with the rituals observed by the gathered assembly, confirm *ghallughara divas* as a day of remembrance of an emotive event that marked a sacred landscape with violence.

However, within the material, ritual, and aural commemorations for many years, there remained a remarkable absence—until 2007, Jarnail Singh Bhindranwale, a key leader of the Khalistan movement, seemed to be missing in commemorations. Commemorative rituals and absences acted in concert to underscore the destruction of the Takht as a key to remembrance, and Bhindranwale as 'troubling' memory. Memories of Bhindranwale are troubling for his legacy defies not just the Indian state, but the very concept of who and what is deemed central to Sikh history and political memory—the Takht, the *sangat*, and the Scripture.

# Globalization and the Commemoration of Hurt

One place where Bhindranwale is resurrected is in transnational commemorations of 'hurt' inscribed in "Never Forget" rallies and processions of the Diaspora. In the Punjabi dominated neighborhood of Southall, West London, for example, protests against Operation Bluestar that began in 1984 in Southall streets[19] and the local Havelock

---

[19] In an uncanny mimesis, 1984 street events in Southall replicated sorrow and celebration enacted in Delhi streets. Post Bluestar, Hindus at the Margaret Road temple offered sweets to passersby and wrote letters to the local newspapers in large numbers. On hearing the news of the assassination of Indira Gandhi, young Sikh men burst firecrackers and Southall sweet shops stayed open all night (*Southall Gazette*, July 20, 1984, p. 8; and November 2, 1984, p. 1), reflecting the deep fissures that the Punjab events had driven between the communities of Diaspora.

Road Gurudwara (Southall Gazette, July 6, 1984: 7) expanded to huge processions in 2007 that traversed Hyde Park and ended at Trafalgar Square.[20] The first anniversary of Operation Bluestar commemorated in the grounds of Hounslow College was named *Genocide Week* by friends and relatives of people who died in the Indian Army Action (Southall Gazette, June 14, 1985: 14), a term that traveled back in translation from Diaspora to Home.

In Diaspora commemorations enunciations of hurt intersect with human rights discourses to create new styles of memorializing. Objects of protest—placards, banners, armbands, and gags—drawn from modern art aesthetics and appropriations from exhibitions of human rights violations inserted within spectacular displays of *traditional* ritual performances reveal a fine understanding of maximizing international media attention. The *Nagara* (the huge drum) and the Panj Piyareh (ritual elect) dressed in turbans and *chogas* (long shirts) march barefoot leading the procession into Trafalgar Square; the *sangat* enters behind them bearing banners with photographs of the disappeared and bloodied corpses, demands for justice and slogan emblazoned T-shirts in ritually appropriate colours of blue, black and saffron. Placards and posters carried in procession are laid on the steps of India House (the Indian High Commission) after a candle lit vigil. Reaching outward to an international audience created through harnessing media, and the innovative deployment of modern technology is critical to Diaspora commemorations. In a modernized version of the Balinese cockfight, giant digital screens display the *sangat* to itself, while mammoth music systems transmitting sounds of the Nagara drum and recitations of *Ardas* cast an aural canopy over the "Sikhs in the Square."

The transnational evocation of hurt is a public ritual, dramatically displayed to international and migrant audiences. The theatrics of exhibition and display is a form of witnessing a past. But Diaspora commemorations go beyond bearing witness and sharing what is witnessed with the wider world via the visual word. Transnational commemorations are also purposive in a different way: assertions of

---

[20] In 1984, a week after the meetings in Southall, hundreds of coaches bringing Sikh protesters from all over Britain jammed Hyde Park. An estimated 50,000 Sikhs marched in procession. Bhindranwale was proclaimed a martyr by the protest marchers who carried a painting of him at the head of the procession (*Southall Gazette*, 1984, p. 5).

trauma express claims for political asylum and rights of residence of migrants who insert themselves into collective political memory as the embodiments of state inflicted hurt. Within the globally enacted event, Bhindranwale is *Zinda*—alive—in *Zindabad* (forever living) slogans and banners because he is both the exemplar victim of a repressive state and a symbol of the hurt.

# References

Bourdieu, P. 1979. *Algeria 1960: The Disenchantment of the World, the Sense of Honour, the Kabyle House or the World Reversed*. Cambridge: Cambridge University Press.

Chopra, R. *Militant and Migrant: The Politics and Social History of Punjab*. London, New York; New Delhi: Routledge.

Connerton, P. 1989. *How Societies Remember*. Cambridge and New York: Cambridge University Press.

Grover, V. (Ed.). 1995. *The Story of Punjab: Yesterday, Today and Tomorrow*. New Delhi: Deep and Deep Publications.

Halbwachs, M. 1992. *On Collective Memory*, Ed. and trans., and introduced by L.A. Coser. Chicago and London: University of Chicago Press.

Lowenthal, D. 1979. "Age and Artefact: Dilemmas of Appreciation," in *The Interpretation of Ordinary Landscapes*, edited by D.W. Meinig. Oxford and New York: Oxford University Press, pp. 103–128.

Narayanan, V.N. 1996. *Tryst with Terror: Punjab's Turbulent Decade*. New Delhi: Ajanta Publications.

Oldenberg, V.T. 1984. *Making of Colonial Lucknow*. Princeton: Princeton University Press.

Pettigrew, J. 1995. *The Sikhs of the Punjab: Unheard Voices of State and Guerrilla Violence*. London: Zed Books.

Puri, H.K., P.S. Judge, and J.S. Sekhon. 1999. *Terrorism in Punjab: Understanding Grassroots Reality*. New Delhi: Har Anand Publications.

Singh, Giani K. 1999. *Eye Witness Account of Operation Bluestar*. trans. and Ed. Anurag Singh. Amritsar: Chattar Singh Jiwan Singh Publishers.

Singh, G. 2000. *Ethnic Conflict in India: A Case Study of Punjab*. New York: St Martin's Press.

Singh, S.J. 2002. *Operation Black Thunder: An Eyewitness Account of Terrorism in Punjab*. New Delhi: SAGE.

Williams, H. 2006. *Death and Memory in Early Medieval Britain*. Cambridge: Cambridge University Press.

# 8

# The Reascription of Hurt: When Abu Gharaib Came to Kashmir

*Akhil Katyal*

## I

## The Political Case Study of Matilda

Hilaire Belloc (d. 1953), the Anglo-French writer of the last century, wrote about the particular relationship the concept of hurt has with its public recognition. He wrote about the shadow that necessarily falls between the experience of hurt and the act of its acknowledgment by others. His poem *Matilda, Who Told Lies, and Was Burned to Death* was apparently a cautionary tale meant for children but he laid within it an utterly adult political equation (Belloc, 1907). This equation helps us understand some links between the different branches of the Indian state and the experiences of hurt in Kashmir.

The best way to read a cautionary tale is to avoid the caution and to savor the drama. In sum, the poem is this: Matilda is a young girl with a particular character flaw—she lies a lot. The first time she lies and cries fire, all of London's fire brigades misinterpret her call to be real and come to her rescue, sousing a perfectly good house with gallons of water. The second time when her crisis call was actually real, the disreputed Matilda keeps on shouting from her house windows and no one on the streets buys her version of the story. "That night," Belloc writes, "a fire did break out," something did happen, but the onlookers purposely disbelieved it (Belloc, 1907). By the time her aunt came back, both Matilda and the house were burnt.

What is interesting in Belloc's poem is not so much that Matilda once lied about her hurt, but that the hurt itself is always subject to its recognition. All experiences of hurt are intimately tied in with the patterns in which they are recognized by people and institutions around you, whether the onlookers on the street or the fire-brigade of the state. And more notably, if you can play around with these patterns of recognition, that is, if you can disgrace a young girl as a perpetual liar, then you can effectively play around with the experience and consequences of her all too real hurt. The poem hangs more on how you recognize hurt than hurt itself.

In May 2004, by the time American television network CBS's *60 Minutes* and a Seymour Hersh article in *The New Yorker* had already broken out the story of the extensive torture in the Abu Gharaib prison, the American secretary of Defense Donald Rumsfeld managed to quibble a response not so much to the hurt of the Iraqi prisoners but, what was more important to him, to the patterns of recognizing that hurt (Rebecca, 2009; Hersh, 2004; Hochschild, 2004). What he did was quibbling over words and their technical meanings. "What has been charged so far," he said, "is abuse, which I believe technically is different from torture … I'm not going to address," he said point blank, "the 'torture' word" (Hochschild, 2004).

It is precisely this understanding that once you appropriate the perception of hurt, you can effectively control any political crisis it might trigger, that makes the Pentagon use the choicest of euphemisms, effectively hollowing out words, and censoring their actual content. This is the understanding that made Rumsfeld call 'torture', 'abuse'. And when the Iraqi prisoners were kept awake for more than a hundred hours, at which point any confession can be extracted from any one, which the medieval inquisitors called *tormentum insomniae* when they used it against suspected witches, this same practice Pentagon chose to christen with an inoffensive term used by doctors when they cure American suburbans of insomnia: "sleep management" (Hochschild, 2004). And it is again this understanding that made one American teenager—I suspect there are many more—think that "water-boarding" somehow involved water-skis.

However, there is another layer to Belloc's poem, which gives us an important clue about how different parts of the Indian state contend with the Kashmiri expression of hurt. And that clue is this: when Matilda faked the fire, the city responded, and when Matilda cried herself hoarse with the actual flames nearing her, the city was indifferent. What the poem really rests on, over and above Matilda's habit for lying, is the necessary mismatch between the call for help and the outlook of those to whom this call is directed, its drama lies in the space of this breach. It suggests that there is nothing intrinsic or natural in the experience of hurt that will lead to its public recognition, that reaching this recognition is actually a political process. That between feeling the hurt and its acknowledgement lies a vast space of political permutations.

It is in this space that my argument lies, a space given to distortion, to twisting of perceptions, to re-ascription of causes of the hurt, to the very misidentification of the hurting body, to finally obscuring the very category of "what did happen." It is because of this space that lies between hurt and its cognizance by others that in September 2010, one Kashmiri in the town of Tangmarg, while interrogating the habitual Indian claim of Kashmir being its integral part, asked the deputed Indian all-party delegation: "Why don't you feel our pain if we are a part of your body" (Rai, June 2011). His question substitutes the premise of a natural connection—*a part of your body*—with an enquiry that is unmistakably political in nature—*why don't you*. Hurt does not simply or naturally tend towards its identification. Between these two falls a shadow.

# II

# When Abu Gharaib Came to Kashmir

In the same month when the Kashmiri in Tangmarg asked that question, something else happened in Kashmir. In fact a cluster of virtual events happened. These evidenced how various limbs of the Indian state use censorship for managing political crises precipitated by the expression of hurt by Kashmiris. And integrated with the acts of censorship, they use a language of hurt that is re-choreographed for their own purposes.

On the night between September 8 and 9, 2010, a video, captured through a cell phone camera, started circulating on Facebook sites and YouTube channels that was tagged "Kashmir—India's Abu Gharib [*sic.*]." The video shows four Kashmiri boys being paraded naked by Indian policemen and paramilitary forces in a Kashmiri village. Step by step, this is confirmed. With every passing second, the video populates its own context, giving possible hooks to peg its veracity. You notice the khakis and the olive green fatigues of the escorting policemen who are abusing the boys in Hindi/Urdu. The policemen—their accents, abuses, and language—are north Indian. We take another step and soon discover from one of the policeman that the four boys have made the police chase them since the morning, so this enforced nakedness, this open parade to the police station or the camp is a humiliating retribution and over the three minutes or so of the video, it is this humiliation which expands and hangs over every second of the low-quality recording. They pass the freshly harvested village fields and toward the end of the video, the women of the village see the boys and can be heard lamenting. You take another step in giving a world to the contents of the video. The language of the lament is Kashmiri—*Hata Khodayo*, akin to *Oh God*. The video offers another marker: the site of this humiliating passage is Kashmir.

When the agents of hurt belong to a militarized state, the expression of that hurt by the people is not a simple opportunity of intervention *plus* self-legitimation for the state but instead a political crisis. This crisis is sought to be diffused by the subdivisions of the state by an array of at least three kinds of overlapping tactics—censorship, both covert and overt, denial, and finally the one which is the shrewdest, the very appropriation of the language of hurt in order to infinitely defer accountability. The rest of my work in this paper involves outlining these tactics through which the State and Central government ministries and Indian security forces manage political crises in Kashmir and which finally expose the ungainly and split life of the state, with its different branches—for example, the Home Ministry and the State Human Rights Commission—offering different versions of the same story and different desired ends.

Conversations with Kashmiri friends over the last few years have given a picture of how surfing the Internet in Kashmir is a particularly odd experience. One of them said it was always like opening a book with a few pages missing. At times, and these times come not infrequently, the whole book goes missing for a while. This simile of the book missing its pages elaborates the tactic of covert censorship. Within hours of the upload of the Kashmir's Abu Gharib video, it began its hide and seek with online viewers. Over the next few days, it would disappear arbitrarily from the YouTube channels which uploaded it. The Facebook posts that linked to the video vanished, even user discussions of the video which happened to mention the title faded away.

I remember it was the second year of my PhD and I was trying to access the video from my hostel room in London. Many times, the video link I would open would become defunct within a matter of hours. A Delhi-based writer, writing two days after this video came to light explained my problem. He wrote that this disappearing act "suggested what has been suspected for some time, that the Indian state—or some of its 'organs'—'lean' on platforms like Facebook and YouTube to ensure that content that is problematic for its image simply gets erased" (Sengupta, 2010). This suggestion was only confirmed with the suppressive Information Technology Act the year after. But that week, the collective effort of many users, Kashmiri and otherwise, ensured that, through repeated downloads and uploads, the video has an extended life despite it being followed by an invisible censor.

However, once it had dug its heels on the Internet, different elements in the Indian state adopted a second tactic. They, like the onlookers on Matilda's street, purposely disbelieved what they saw. In this headstrong tactic of denial, we come upon a concept of belief that is not so much an empirical exercise with the given text but instead a political investment in it, which always makes it yield its content selectively. The breach between seeing and believing was reopened into a space of political contestation.

"A senior police officer in the Valley," the *Indian Express* reported, said it looked like an "old video" as if the age of the recording tempered its content (*Indian Express*, 2010). Southward in Delhi, the then Union Home Minister P. Chidambaram immediately usurped the language of trust and potential trustworthiness, posing the specter of authentication. He said "No one has been able to authenticate the video so far," and that he had asked security agencies to find out whether anybody featuring in the video had spoken out (*Indian Express*, 2010). Chidambaram waits for the moving image to be confirmed by particular voices. The visual text itself is hollowed out. By itself it shows nothing at all, always needing external sanctification. This trait of the moving image is mined politically. "Until it is authenticated," Chidambaram said, resting on a deferral, "and the persons identified, I think it would be unsafe to rely on such a video" (*Indian Express*,

2010). The *Outlook* reported that the Union Home Minister "did not elaborate on what steps were being taken to ascertain the authenticity of the video" (*Outlook*, 2010). The idea of authenticity then is as much a political deployment as it is a laboratory process. This was confirmed when the CRPF spokesperson Prabhakar Tripathi was quoted as denying the authenticity of the video in all perpetuity, thus making the actual determination redundant—"Such a thing," he said, "is not possible in Kashmir," adding that "this video can never be proved to be genuine" (*Outlook*, 2010). Here, deferral shows what it is nesting within itself: denial.

However, the third and the final tactic that different parts of the Indian states adopt is the one which interests me the most because it is the most crafted, the most difficult to sieve out. This is when they appropriate the very language of hurt and transform it etiologically, that is, they play with the idea of what causes hurt. In the young graphic novelist Malik Sajad's short piece, "The Kashmir Intifada," he has an Indian army soldier address the media during the stone-pelting days earlier on the streets of downtown Srinagar in the summer of 2010 (Sajad, 2011: 120–131). The soldier's statement captures the form of the Indian security apparatus' tactic wonderfully whereby it re-ascribes the cause of the hurt, finding it somewhere else, and in doing so distances itself from it. "Our strategy," the soldier says speaking to the media, "is to shoot at legs so as to disperse the protesters. The trouble is kids there are short of height, so our bullets and tear-gas shells hit them on their heads" (Sajad, 2011: 120–131). In this statement, the cause of hurt takes flight. It bounces away from the fingers of the paramilitary forces who press the trigger on the stone-throwing and sometimes unarmed boys. It jumps far from the official policies of an excessively militarized state that facilitate such a strong reaction to stones. And where it comes to rest, oddly enough, is on the very bodies of the protestors and to their apparent divergence from the dictated norm of how tall or short young boys should be. What happens is that the cause of hurt is first delinked and then slotted elsewhere conveniently.

The word 'hurting' always means two things. The body that is in pain and also the entity that causes pain. Hurting both as a state to be in—for instance, my leg is hurting—and also a verb—hurting someone else. Linguistically, to be hurting is to be at once confusingly both the agent and the victim of hurt. When it comes to the militarized assortment that is the Indian state in Kashmir, it makes a life out of what could have been just a harmless duality of words. When the video of "Kashmir's Abu Gharaib" was being shared on social networking and video sharing websites, various branches of the Indian state found the cause of hurt in this instance not in the actions within the video but in the very sharing of it. The very next day of the circulation of the video, a police spokesperson told the PTI that this circulation can spread "disaffection among the people" (*Outlook*, 2010). "A formal case," he added, "is being registered against the YouTube and Facebook networks and investigation is on to locate the persons responsible for uploading this baseless and malicious clip" (*Outlook*, 2010). The tactic of denial here meets the more advanced tactic of shooting the messenger who carries that which you either deny or whose authenticity you place in the far future. Effectively replacing the hurt persons of the Kashmiris within the public domain, the state police offers its own wounded body of 'law and order', vulnerable to 'disaffection', vilifying by this account the sharing of the video as a cause by itself for spreading hostility among the Kashmiris. Sharing here is revised and spoken of as propagating, the emphasis shifts from the heinous content to the act of sharing, from the message to the medium—"Action shall also be taken," the same police spokesperson added, "against other organisations who tried to propagate it [the video]" (*Outlook*, 2010). In this etiological transformation, the cause of hurt becomes the very speaking of it. In the immediate aftermath of the Abu Gharaib pictures, Donald Rumsfeld similarly identified the sharing of pictures itself as illegal, as a process that by itself causes hurt, and went on, not denying their content but certainly their representativeness, to call them un-American. "In the information age," he rued: "where people are running around with digital cameras and taking these unbelievable photographs and then passing them off, against the law, to the media, to our surprise, when they had not even arrived in the Pentagon" (*The Washington Times*, 2004).

For the elements within the state, the hurt sentiment is a politically valuable entity or a self-legitimating device only if it comes from the right quarters. If not, then it is destabilizing and must immediately be contained. When the 2010 video started circulating, Chidambaram immediately asked for the persons in the video to speak up. He curtailed the wider implications of the video, directing himself toward even as he was obscuring its particularities. In September 2012, something similar happened. When the Home department of the J&K state government rejected the widespread testing of DNA from the mass graves identified by the state's own Human Rights Commission as possibly containing the dead bodies of disappeared non-combatant civilians, it asked again for this category of the impossible particular. "We can't go on digging all the graveyards," Secretary B.R. Sharma said, "if not pointedly specific, at least we need some clue, some direction from the relatives of the missing people where they think their disappeared kin might be buried" (Hussain, 2012). He is asking for information that is almost impossible to give. In fact this whole drive toward the particular is far from the intention of discovering it and instead defers this discovery. Which is what made the Secretary say one of the most paradoxical statements I have heard in recent times: "There is a need for closure to all this," he said, and then added, "we also want truth to come out" (Hussain, 2012).

The Home Department reasoned out its rejection of the HRC demand for DNA testing by the now familiar reascription of the cause of hurt. From the event to its sharing. From the act of injustice to the very process of asking for justice, so much so that the latter is seen as aggravating the hurt rather than being its salve. The random collection of the DNA from the graves would be, the report said, an "academic exercise" that would "hurt the local sentiments" of the people (Hussain, 2012). Continuing with this expedient appropriation of the vocabulary of hurt, it added that this testing would "attract undesired media attention, cause prolonged trauma to the people, and can also act as a trigger point/event for causing serious law and order disturbances" (Hussain, 2012). In this Home department's etiological experiment with hurt, the body of the dead Kashmiri civilian lying in the mass graves is eclipsed in favor of the body of the law and order that becomes the primary object of state protection. Here, the claim of being wronged rests with the latter. What should be evident to us is that the vocabulary of hurt is slippery. It passes through many hands making it mandatory for us to constantly sieve out one instance from the other, the vocabulary from its user. Rather than indifference to some instances of hurt and intervention in others, like that of Belloc's onlookers who let Matilda burn, we must keep an eye out for the premise of hurt each and every time it appears. This premise, as I have argued, is never simply obvious because it is a necessarily composite thing—never originating only from the hurt body but also from the way it is brought to cognizance by others.

# References

Belloc, Hilaire. 1907. "Matilda Who told Lies, and was Burned to Death," in *All Poetry*, available at http://allpoetry.com/poem/8493339-Matilda_Who_told_Lies__and_was_Burned_to_Death-by-Hilaire_Belloc (accessed in May 2012).

Hersh, Seymour M. May 10, 2004. "Torture at Abu Ghraib," in *The New Yorker*, available at http://www.newyorker.com/archive/2004/05/10/040510fa_fact (accessed in August 2012).

Hochschild, Adam. May 23, 2004. "What's in a Word? Torture," in *The New York Times*, available at http://www.nytimes.com/2004/05/23/opinion/23HOCH.html (accessed in September 2012).

Hussain, Aijaz. September 5, 2012. "AP NewsBreak: Kashmir won't DNA Test Mass Graves," in *The Big Story*, available at http://bigstory.ap.org/article/ap-newsbreak-kashmir-wont-dna-test-mass-graves (accessed in October 2012).

*Indian Express*. September 9, 2010. "Naked Parade: Centre to Look into Video Clip on Kashmir," available at http://expressindia.indianexpress.com/latest-news/Naked-parade-Centre-to-look-into-video-clip-on-Kashmir/679592/ (accessed in October 2012).

*Outlook*. September 9, 2010. "J&K Cops to Sue Facebook, Youtube," available at http://news.outlookindia.com/items.aspx?artid=692932 (accessed in October 2012).

Rai, Mridu. June 2011. "Making a Part Inalienable: Folding Kashmir into India's Imagination—III," in *Kashmir Dispatch*, available at http://www.kashmirdispatch.com/others/14063935-making-a-part-inalienable-folding-kashmir-into-indias-imagination-iii.htm (accessed in August 2012).

Rebecca, Leung. February 11, 2009. Video "Abuse of Iraqi POWs by GIs Probed," in *CBS News*, available at http://www.cbsnews.com/stories/2004/04/27/60ii/main614063.shtml (accessed in September 2012).

Sajad, Malik. 2011. "The Kashmir Intifada," in *Until My Freedom Has Come: The New Intifada in Kashmir*, edited by Sanjay Kak. Penguin Books: New Delhi and London, pp. 120–131.

Sengupta, Shuddhabrata. September, 2010. "Kashmir's Abu Gharaib?" in *Kafila*, available at http://kafila.org/2010/09/10/kashmirs-abu-gharaib/ (accessed in September 2012).

*The Washington Times*. May 7, 2004. "Iraq prisoner abuse 'un-American,' says Rumsfeld," available at http://www.washingtontimes.com/news/2004/may/7/20040507-115901-6736r/ (accessed in August 2012).

# Of Rights and Righteousness

# 9

# Anathema and Anachronism: A Contemporary Utilization of Ambedkar's Critique of Gandhism*

*Soumyabrata Choudhury*

What is to follow will comprise three sections. The first section will disaggregate and discuss some of the key points of the sum total of B.R. Ambedkar's critique of M.K. Gandhi's social and economic philosophy of what Ambedkar calls, Gandhism. Among these points will feature two parameters by which Ambedkar evaluates Gandhi's level and intensity of response to the caste system. These parameters are expressed by the two words Ambedkar employs: *anathema* and 'anachronism'. We will explain the meanings we think Ambedkar wants to give to these words in the context in which he uses them. This explanation becomes expedient because Ambedkar uses these words summarily, if not elliptically, toward the end of his essay.

The second section will partly dislocate the two parameters of Ambedkar's critique of Gandhism, toward what will be called

---

*We have chosen "utilization," not "use," deliberately. To utilize something is to instrumentalize it beyond its provenance for a very specific end. Which is what we intend to do with Ambedkar's critique. "Use" can have a much greater, and nobler, non-utilitarian amplitude and at the same time belong to the provenance of that which is used. We might say that the wide Dalit uses of Ambedkar's critical interventions in Indian history still belong to these critiques themselves. Ours is a more heteronomous relationship.

a "speculative philology" of their signifiers ("anathema" and "anachronism"). The philological exercise will be speculative in the sense that it will provide a certain conceptual depth to these signifiers, using resources extracted from contexts apparently remote from Ambedkar's own. Also, the speculative construction will relate the words Ambedkar addresses to the object at hand—Gandhi's social and economic philosophy in conjunction with Gandhi's explicit attitudes to the caste system over time, from the 1920s to 1945—with other signifiers and themes that, at least overtly, do not belong to Ambedkar's object and discourse. One set of such signifiers and themes will come from the domain of philosophy of language, which clearly, is not Ambedkar's preoccupation in the essay "Gandhism." But the real interest of what we have called a "speculative philology" is in reapplying the speculative lessons to the very context of the essay. And the wager underlying this attempt is the hypothesis that at the core of B.R. Ambedkar's critique of Gandhism, there exists an elusive yet insistent *speculative object.* And at the level of speculative unraveling, the critique and the debate between Ambedkar and Gandhi have pertinence beyond the tumults of their historical emergence.

The third and concluding section of this paper will be a contemporary utilization of the speculative possibilities opened up in the earlier sections but strictly re-insinuated in the following contemporary knot of experiences and problems: suppose we grant that in India at present there is a general tendency of social subjects and communities to 'feel' what could be roughly called 'symbolic violence' and 'perceive' threats of such violence from other subjects and communities. Then the question arises that does such experience of symbolic violence issue from one 'part' of the social totality, a part which can be suppressed, recognized, modified, assimilated, *re-symbolized*?[1] Or does the violence issue from the *totality* itself, which is society in the speculative sense? Conversely is the violence, or threat of violence, felt and perceived by some one part of the social assemblage, one which can be numerically classified as 'minority' or 'majority', and is identifiable and can be evaluated as a part which is *either essential or anachronistic*? Or, does

---

[1] Examples of such symbolic threat-perception and the retaliatory violence—often physical—in the wake of such perception abound today. We will refrain from citing any because that will interfere with our speculative approach. But the milieu is well known as is the rubric by which it is commonly called—'hurt sentiments'.

the violence and its perceived subjective threat arrive at the heart of society itself and open up a caesura, an anxiety, an *anathema* there? Referring back to the historical moment of Ambedkar's criticism of Gandhi and his critique of Gandhism, we can say that the dialectic of localization of violence in its historical as well as phenomenological site-specificity, and the universalization of the same as the very unsymbolizable caesura or 'anathema' of the *totality itself* that is society, concerned as much that tumult then as it provokes our ability to think amidst tumult(s) today.

# I

In the ninth volume of Ambedkar's collected works published by the Government of Maharashtra, the essay "Gandhism" is the last one (before the appendix). It also comes as the third chapter of a kind of trilogy accompanied by the other two pieces, "A Plea to the Foreigner" and "What do the Untouchables Say" (Ambedkar, 1991: 199–297). These two and "Gandhism" can be received as a trilogy with respect to at least the three following points: first, they are all written with an acute ear to the ground of an imminent national independence from British sovereignty. Along this imminence, its *vertigo*, as it were, arising out of the expectation of a new, collective, indigenous sovereignty, emerged these three texts but *against the grain* of this vertiginous imminence. One could ask, in what way? Well, the texts could be said to balance, nay, contrast, the stakes of national independence expressed in something like 'state sovereignty', with what Ambedkar called "self-government" (Ambedkar, 1991: 203). In that exercise, these texts clearly questioned the status of a 'national society' as the spontaneous subject of a new, imminent sovereignty—and tried to expose such a subject to be an ideological *decision*, silently naturalized, rather than a well-founded historical reality. Methodologically, this point also implied that the trilogy subjected the great—and true, why not!—political enthusiasm of the national movement in its imminent immediacy of sovereign victory to a rhythm of social and historical temporality that emanated from deeper long-standing structures, which beat with a seemingly eternal monotony impervious to the immediacy of events in the present.

The second point which united the three texts of volume nine pertained to the obvious question that *whose* ideological decision was it to present a 'national society' as if it was the natural protagonist of the political theatre of sovereign struggle. And how did the decision(s) actually produce their alleged effects of mystification on such a massive scale? To these questions the three essays, with variant addressees in mind, no doubt, answered with the name 'Congress' and with the technique "crypto-religious or crypto-Hindu majoritarian nationalization of an intractable multiplicity." But we must mention here—though it is not our topic for this paper—that the point of real concentration in Ambedkar's critique of 'Congressism' was not simply to drive deep doubt into the heart of the party's secular credentials, but to articulate the violent exclusions, and the silencing of this violence, of Congressist mass-ideology in its theoretical as well as programmatic aspects. Again, the articulation of the exclusion and its silent naturalization, in Ambedkar's view, resonated both in the immediate register of who gets to vitally express the political subjectivity of the national movement as well as in the *speculative eternity* of logical objects where a part of the object 'humanity' was foreclosed from actualizing the political capacity and transformation(s) it promised that, taken together, defined the consistency of that object. Thus, in these texts, the 'untouchable' was encoded as the common name of the exclusion in the time of history and the inconsistency in the eternity of logical humanity.[2]

But it is the third point of unification of these three essays that is of most interest here. And that is Ambedkar's analytical compression of a *greater* code and ideology than 'Congressism', and which subsumes the latter; greater because its power and mystery are its utter self-exposedness to stakes incalculable by historical measures and yet seamlessly flowing into the most granulated particles of historical existence and as if raising each particle to the life of eternity—the stakes

---

[2] This point resonates with Ambedkar's enquiry that does a particular doctrine, Gandhism, or any other, restore to the Untouchable her "title-deeds to humanity?" The appearance of legal language should not prevent us from entering the enquiry's fundamental *generic* and *logical* depth. And at this depth, the 'Untouchable' is both excluded and at the very centre of the caste relation. On the phenomenological level of course, the form of the last one at the periphery—*antyaja*—is valid. But a Gandhian or Ambedkarite phenomenology should not commit the error of ignoring the 'object' in depth where it exists with a kind of unbearable neutrality. See Ambedkar (1991: 269).

of *truth*. Of course the whole purpose of "Gandhism" is to analyze and expose that very mode of self-exposedness that characterizes Gandhi's technique of truth.[3] One would not be wrong in saying that among the three, the text of "Gandhism" draws the speculative battle-lines most clearly in the overall terrain of Ambedkar's polemic and logic. The speculative frankness of this polemic is in order because, with the analysis of Gandhism, Ambedkar is dealing with an object which is not anymore the duplicitous structure of Congressist secularity. Here, he is confronting an object openly declared to be permanent and *beyond* the locus of temporal and intra-worldly transformation that defines 'politics'. Call that object 'religion'—and Ambedkar often does so, no doubt—and one is immediately drawn into a plot of deception because the Gandhian frankness of uttering that word (at least in the English language), while intending speculative effectivity beyond historical intelligibility based on material experience (of which politics is an example), never confines 'religion' to speculative isolation. On the contrary, the entire Gandhian technique is to prescribe a life of worldly, minoritarian, *payable* spiritual—and material—debt albeit under the sign of an absolute debt which is *unpayable*.[4] In that sense, we could say that one payable part of the debt is "politics," according to Gandhi—the part which under his leadership, the Congress mobilized so exemplarily—and the unpayable, absolute speculative part is "religion"—or the hereditary caste system of Hinduism as a paradigm of the latter part (Ambedkar, 1991: 275).

> The genius of Mr. Gandhi is elvish, always and throughout. He has all the precocity of an elf with no little of its outward guise. Like an elf he can never grow up and grow out of the caste ideology. (Ambedkar, 1991: 290)

---

[3] We will not engage with the vast literature on Gandhi's philosophy and its practices of and experiments with truth. Off hand, let's say that Perry Anderson's recent essay on Gandhi in the *London Review of Books*, while very much on the lines of the Ambedkarite critique, fails to take the Gandhian stakes of truth seriously. It is primarily a philosophical failure.

[4] This interpretation, presented in a condensed form here, has been developed from a more political perspective on the Gandhian mass, militant, and minoritarian technique of Congress Party's transmutation from a petitioning organization to a party which imposes sanctions in the essay "Ambedkar contra Aristotle: On a Possible Contention about who is Capable of Politics." This essay was first presented by the author at Nehru Memorial Library, Teen Murti House, Delhi in August 2012 at the conference *Humanities in Ferment*. It is forthcoming for publication from the Centre for the Study of Developing Societies in Hindi translation.

Doesn't the superb imagery above in Ambedkar's text contradict our claim that Gandhi's is a technique of truth? Doesn't the imagery convey dissimulation and disguise rather than the frank exposure of a truth, however, contentious? Herein lies the real productivity of the imagery: in likening Gandhi to an elf, Ambedkar brings out the double character of 'Gandhism' such that the latter stands as much for an elvish ability to change, transmute, contradict one's position, and appearance in the course of espousing a worldly philosophy as it does for some fundamental, unverifiable, and axiomatic verity beyond the appearances of worlds. At once play-actor, mythical animal and precocious truth-declarer (or axiomatician), the 'genius' of Mr Gandhi is the one of a *speculative and dogmatic child*.

This is the psychology that Ambedkar sees enacted in the history of Gandhian positions on 'caste ideology' between 1920 and 1945, after which the essay is written. Very simply stated, this is a history, according to Ambedkar, of Gandhi's movement from wholesale defence of the hereditary caste system to speaking in favor of the *varna* system instead of caste to repudiating the caste structure which includes untouchability as "anachronism" in the year 1945. But the real force of Ambedkar's critique is that essentially, in all the frenetic movement and the detailed argumentation rationalizing it, Gandhi *stays exactly at the same place*. And it is his elvish genius that he is able to produce an *appearance* of such distinctive change that the very place of the object that is caste in Hinduism starts to lose its analytical markers (Ambedkar, 1991: 290). This, according to Ambedkar, is achieved by first moving from caste to *varna*, which is an occupational economy numerically compressing the multiplicity of caste hierarchy into an arrangement of three/four(?)/five(?) *varnas*, and subsequently re-collapsing the new arrangement into the erstwhile hereditary black-hole.[5] However, this violence is accomplished with the airy lightness of the elf, the imp—and other such delightful speculative equivalents of "Mr Gandhi!"

<hr/>

[5] In this context, Ambedkar does distinguish between Gandhi's peculiar conflations and the *Bhagwad Gita*'s basing of *varna* on innate qualities (*guna*). In other places he carries forward his critique from caste and *varna* to *guna*. Gandhi's numerical sentiment of reforming society from a teeming multiplicity to fewer *blocs* or corporations (from the 'Many' to the 'One' and the 'one' containing four blocs) is in evidence in 1925. But the collapse is imminent because the teeming multiplicity and the One of the bloc-society are perfectly consistent, as Ambedkar had shown very early in "Castes in India" (1916). See Dr. Babasaheb Ambedkar (1989).

Nevertheless, Ambedkar makes it his job to find the hard ground of these evanescent gestures of inegalitarian conservation. It seems to us that in the essay "Gandhism," Ambedkar finds that ground and measure of egalitarian thinking in economic equality. And by that measure, he judges Gandhian thought to have no "passion for economic equality" (Ambedkar, 1991: 282). It is as a result of this lack of passion that Gandhism substitutes for economic equality a prescriptive regime of *spiritual obligations* that 'corporations' owe to each other as part of a generalized alternative economy of spiritual or incorporeal debt (ibid.: 282). Nothing, in Ambedkar's critical view, fits better into this corporate philosophy of debt and obligation than the model of age-old Hindu caste. This is the *essence of Ambedkar's critique of Gandhism*. In speculative depth, the difficult but indispensible argument of this critique is the following: for the Gandhian doctrine of "spiritual obligations" between corporations— of which trusteeship is the famous economic example—to maintain itself and be unfettered by immanent historical transformations— which are inevitable in the material world—the status of the *totality* which encompasses and transcends these corporations must be conserved as unified, coherent, and permanent. In being these, the totality itself must not be a corporation and so must not be confused with any sovereign entity—but it must also not be open to any fundamental intra-worldly change of status even while the world changes rapidly through the forces of chance, thought and will.[6] This, in depth, is Ambedkar's critique of Gandhi's speculative status-quoism, which produces a social philosophy of immemorial or hereditary caste, *in some form or the other*.

Yet, we insist that the reason why Ambedkar finds Gandhism "interesting" at all is not because of its dissimulating genius but because of its serious *truth-effect*. And so, if the Gandhian doctrine of spiritual obligations must underlie the real defense of caste, then these obligations must be *truly* and subjectively lived in everyday worldly existence. The conservative power of Gandhi's defense of

---

[6] We indicated toward the end of the essay "Ambedkar contra Aristotle" how in Ambedkar's mention of the case of railways coming to India in *Annihilation of Caste*, we find the lineaments of a theory of "willing the chance that changes the world" as opposed to a Hindu (Gandhian?) technique of paying back the debt of chance (Railways disturbing social segregation in India) with *prayaschitta* (repenting conduct that transgresses codes of the world).

caste comes not from overt doctrinal violence but from the proposal that caste, in Hinduism, is the articulation of true *transformation* of the mere individual—which is the decadent 'modern' subject of Western economism—to a *caste-subject* who lives his (or her?) debt toward *other* corporations/subjects as *heartfelt* obligation on behalf of himself (herself?) and of the *totality* which secures, nay, *loves*, the caste-system but is *itself not a caste*. In the copious citations from Gandhi's several writings on caste from different historical junctures, the essay "Gandhism" manages to locate an unwavering speculative object—which is what Gandhism essentially is—with intensely damaging truth-effects. Of course nowhere is the damage more evident than when it is vividly brought out in these very citations how the *shudra* (or *ati-shudra* or Untouchable even more singularly) who is constitutively excluded from the truth of the totality and its highest stakes, contributes by service (without malice or resentment, according to the *Manu Smriti*, not part of Gandhi's texts cited) to the welfare of that totality.[7] Indeed, the truth becomes derisive when it is argued that the encoded Brahminical capacity for learning, from which the *shudra* is excluded, is a capacity obliged to realize itself also on behalf of the *shudra* as on behalf of the totality of which the *shudra* is the included exclusion.[8] Clearly according to the true complexity, delicacy, and duplicity of Gandhi's "elvish" philosophy, the *shudra* can be both excluded from the system of possible transformations that define caste-code (learning, warriordom, and trade) and be included in the *totality*, which is not a coded corporation/caste, on whose unmediated behalf the *shudra*, or the Untouchable (more singularly again) can serve all their mediate caste-masters. No surprise then that the Untouchables become the direct "children of God," the outcast-elves who are the speculative children dearest to Gandhi's heart!

[7] See Franco, Sarvar, and Chand, 2009. We would like to thank Sibaji Bandopadhyay for pointing out the alternative translation of "malice" with "resentment" (and its Nietzschean speculations in the *Manu Smriti*).

[8] This is a complicated point. In his 'reformed' texts, Gandhi will say that the encoded capacities are actually available to the other classes too. So the *shudra* can also be learned. *But*, the *shudra* must not use learning to earn a living (as must the 'higher' castes). It is as if, in one kind of 'free totality' of human enterprises, there is unlimited transaction, while in a 'bound totality' of social–economic organization there is a strict coding of conduct. In Ambedkar's critique what comes out vividly is (a) Gandhi's favor for the 'bound totality', (b) the spuriousness of the free totality when unbound from historical-material life.

# II

Gandhists may say that what I have stated is the old type of Gandhism. There is a new Gandhism, Gandhism without caste. This has reference to the recent statement [in *Hindustan Times*, 15th April 1945] of Mr. Gandhi that caste is an anachronism. Reformers were naturally gladdened by this declaration of Mr. Gandhi.... But is this really a matter of jubilation? Does it change the nature of Gandhism?... Those who are carried away by this recantation of Mr. Gandhi forget two things. In the first place, all that Mr. Gandhi has said is that caste is an anachronism. He does not say it is an evil. He does not say it is *anathema* [emphasis added]. Mr. Gandhi may be taken to be not in favour of caste. But Mr. Gandhi does not say that he is against *varna*-system. (Ambedkar, 1991: 297)

This verdict comes at the very end of Ambedkar's painstaking dismantling of Gandhism's reformist construction of a *varna* system based on the division, hierarchy, and articulation between either *varnas* (occupational categories) or/and *gunas* (innate qualities). We could say, combining our two key phrases from the earlier sections that Ambedkar wants to dismantle the theory and ideology of 'reformed' *spiritual corporations*, or to use Ambedkar's own more graphic term, spiritual "gangs" (ibid.: 285). This is a crucial invective because Gandhism, in this view, packs together two mutually resistant bundles. It articulates the apparent speculative generosity of avowing spiritual obligations toward other social groups on behalf of the immemorial totality of 'Hindu' society (which is also a kind of godly society, *ram-rajya*) and equally recommends the closed, 'anti-social' structure of each group's own immemorial place under the sun, which is what makes each group a 'gang'. The contradiction is resolved by a terrible paradox: Gandhism articulates the twisted prescription that each group/corporation/gang socializes its subject-group—the one under it in the hierarchy—into slavish acceptance of this "anti-society" that subjects it (ibid.: 285). Indeed the more powerful groups have a spiritual obligation to undertake this socialization of the dominated groups—and the process has a simple, "modern" name, which is, the "education" of the slaves into enslavement (ibid.: 282). This tautological prescription has its lurid anti-social reflection in the powerful gangs'/castes' own socialization. In Ambedkar's words, "It makes their culture sterile, their art showy, their wealth luminous and their manners fastidious" (ibid.: 282).

It is from this perspective that one must evaluate Ambedkar's dismissal of Gandhi's so-called "recantation." To say that caste is "anachronism," that is, a 'part' of the totality that has fallen into obsolescence and degenerated into a kind of temporal appendage of another *consistent* time of society, is to completely ignore the vital coupling of the caste-*relation* and the *inconsistent* and twisted subjective infrastructure of obligations that supports this relation and is absolutely contemporary with it. According to Ambedkar, this wound of inconsistency at the heart of the logical object that is caste-(anti) society can have only one name, which is "anathema."

Before we go on to the 'speculative philology' of Ambedkar's parameters, it is important to be clear about what is at issue here: it is not as if between 1921 when Gandhi was writing in *Young India* and other (Gujarati) journals about caste and 1945, when he would have Hindu society rid itself of hereditary caste, there were no significant change of historical conditions and Gandhi's responses did not reflect concrete changes of reformist program. What Ambedkar says here— which he also said after the publication of *Annihilation of Caste* in 1935—is that Gandhi is still not *thinking* of the logical object that is caste—and as long as he is not thinking that, he is also not thinking the logical object that is 'society', of which caste is not only a structural invariant but also the *subjective* locus of possible transformations that an individual could access as spiritual or corporeal possibilities within the modes of social existence. And that is why Gandhi is not able to grasp the *explosive* (which is Ambedkar's term again from *Krishna and his Gita*) potentiality of the Untouchables' limit position in the differential economy of caste. The Untouchable occupies that singular limit of a general space of increasing delimitation of subjective/ spiritual possibilities of every caste: she occupies the limit point of a delimitation of relative enslavements, including that of the most sovereign, that limit where *no one can bear to stay too long....*[9] And the Untouchable class had stayed there for at least two thousand years! And much as Gandhi would like that limit to be dissolved— and the explosion not to take place—he is powerless to do anything

---

[9] Here we remind ourselves of the Greek word *ate* in Sophocles' tragedy *Antigone*, the limit-(non)space where, as the chorus says, Antigone has reached. And yet as shown by Jacques Lacan in his Ethics seminar, *ate* is not a place outside Antigone—she does not reach a place (*ate*) where no one can bear to stay too long. She *is ate*.

about it until he starts thinking the *anathema* of Untouchability at the heart of caste.

***

Here are two short exercises in what we have called 'speculative philology' somewhat at a distance from the historical tumult of Ambedkar's critique of Gandhism:

(a) In the Hellenist Stoic philosophy of language, there occurs an interesting notion that the Greeks expressed by the word *lekhton*. *Lekhton* was to be distinguished from the statements of language—sounds, words, and propositions—and the object's linguistic utterances were supposed to refer to. It rather directed attention toward incorporeal events of transformations that language-use effectuated (Deleuze, 1990). So, for instance, if I made the simple assertion, "the knife cuts the butter," apart from the bodies (or corporations) of the world (the knife and the butter) and the acts immediately attributable to bodies ('cutting' attributable to the knife, or implicitly, the human agent who uses the knife, the butter which is being cut, and so on), there also comes into the world, with the assertion, a pure 'cutting in itself' as an incorporeal transformation. This is the *lekhton* of the utterance, its 'pure expressed' that, as if, is an incorporeal body, immaculate and thinkable as such, which gets reimplanted into the world's pre-existent corporeal bodies in the very movement of its effectuation (so 'cutting' as re-attributed to knife, agent, butter, and so on). But, once brought into the world and remixed with it to become indiscernible, it could carry on existing as a possibility of transformation in the form of *codes of the world*.[10] Or, it could be resisted, suppressed, and foreclosed from every code of the world.

---

[10] When we use the subject-form 'Dalit', we can construe it in at least three ways in light of our speculative parameter: 'Dalit' can mean a subject born of an incorporeal transformation in history but now entered into the 'codes of the world' such as constitutional rights-bearing collective; or 'Dalit' can mean that incandescent event of transformation that is sought to be extinguished by dominant spiritual corporations. Or, it can also mean the struggle to *force* these corporations to incorporate the new subject as it is the passionate search for a new body of the event itself.

To briefly illustrate this slightly elusive point from the Ambedkar–Gandhi archives: one of the most 'explosive' points of contention between Ambedkar and Gandhi is the one of conversion. We could say that the speculative battle lines are drawn in the real historical sites of this contention between Ambedkar's call for the existential openness of pre-coded corporations to the incorporeal *event* of conversion and Gandhi's paradoxical prescription toward the *codification of hearts*, where no such incorporeal event of conversion could possibly arise. This is a peculiar situation of the two interlocutors' seeming to talk past each other, and yet producing striking speculative effects.[11] For Gandhi, conversion can never be true in its purported change of being because it is only an external change from corporation to corporation, nominal religion to another, symbolic form to symbolic form. "True-real"[12] change must pertain to a change of *heart*—and if the grievance is only regarding an 'anachronistic' albeit great wounding part of the totality, then that part can be *purified*, or the totality can be purified of that part. Now this is precisely the logic which is built on the silent assumption—axiom—of the immemorial "true-reality" of the totality and any change of heart must already be coded by the demands of this axiom. Now it is the unique genius of Gandhi's philosophy to never corporatize the transcendence of the totality and instead to give it the mobility and minority of the elf that travels fluently between the sovereignty of Ram in *ram-rajya* and the granulation (or minority) of the "swa" in *swarajya*. And it is this speculative subtlety that effectively secures the 'heart' of the historically situated social individual from experiencing a real incorporeal event of transformation yielding the pure expressed, the *lekhton*, of a 'converting in itself' in the putative utterance, 'I convert'.

It seems to us that between 1935, when in *Annihilation of Caste*, Ambedkar declared that it was the last time that he

---

[11] This counterposition was suggested by Partha Chatterjee following an improvised presentation of these points by the author at the Centre for Study of Social Sciences, Kolkata.

[12] We will not cite the document here but simply recall from the 1980s feminist psychoanalytic conceptual creations, Julia Kristeva's coinage.

was addressing the public as a Hindu, and his conversion to Buddhism nearly 20 years later, his was the *duration of the instant* of an incorporeal event of transformation, a 'converting in itself' in intense and canny search of a new spiritual corporation. Indeed this could be called the duration of not Ambedkar's minority position—because as we have seen, Gandhism is precisely the encoding of the majority's minoritarian program—but his caesural existence, that had dared to grow out of the elvish shadow of Gandhi's speculative totality. So, the step beyond the unbearable limit-position of the Untouchable was into a caesura, which, unlike the Gandhian totality, marked the passion of a historical existence, through and through, which believed a *new immemorial* was possible in history; which, when the time came, was unafraid to write a new Book of Buddhism. And while this caesural courage drove Ambedkar on, it only also made him articulate even more sharply his 'logical revolt' against Gandhi's cathartic (or purificatory) understanding of caste as anachronism; it made him articulate the *anathema* of caste society as its 'Untouchable' truth.

(b) In St Paul's *Letter to the Romans* (9–11), it is written: "I am speaking the truth in Christ.... I have great sorrow and unceasing anguish in my heart. For I could wish that I myself were accused and cut-off [*anathema*] from Christ" (Taubes, 2004: 27).

Paul clearly exacerbates the function of the anathema beyond its ready roles as *feature*—caste as a feature which is the scourge of the system called 'Hinduism'—and as *act*—the declaring of something as anathema in an act of cursing—into a gesture of being itself. Paul would self-anathematize himself as an act of spiritual deprivation of Christ's love for the sake of Christ's love. It is a tortuous, involuted gesture of bearing the incorporeal wound of being-anathema on one's own corporeal body. Granted the difference of the Pauline context, which is a redemptive one and not an annihilative, doesn't there, in Ambedkar's 'logical revolt', also lurk an ontological appeal to Gandhi to *be* anathema of Hindu (non)society, be its self-separative truth? Wasn't there always such an appeal

in the question of Gandhi's fasting for temple-entry, vis-à-vis
the mode of egalitarian participation of the lower castes in
the management of the Harijan Sevak Sangh and in many
other occasions?[13] And always frustrated, nay, infuriated in
its outcome? The reason to pose these obviously speculative
questions is the following concrete historical exigency: it was
the indubitable exigency of that time which real individual and
collective bodies, in the ephemeral instance(s) of historical
time, bear and incorporate the structural *permanence* of
an anathema and not pretend they can dispense with their
anachronistic habits of caste. And it is also doubtless the case that
no one occupied that individual as well as collective place
better than Gandhi, Gandhi's hyper-invested yet ungraspable
'child-like' historical body.[14] But the logic is inexorable here:
If Gandhi was the incorporeal transformation, the *event* of
Indian history at a certain juncture, then by definition that
transformation couldn't be coded beforehand, couldn't be
mastered—not even by the master-logician of the historical
process, B.R. Ambedkar.

# III

If the challenge, "Let Gandhi *be* the annihilation of caste, if he can!"
mixed with the appeal, "because only he can!" was reduced to utter,
well-demonstrated scorn, "As far as caste is concerned, he is just not
thinking!" It was on another terrain that Ambedkar could take much
better control of an instrument that he himself substantially created with
an intensity that is today considered messianic. Ambedkar wants the

---

[13] See Ambedkar (1991: 268), on the issue of equal participation of Harijans in the
management of the Sevak Sangh and the argument about the upper caste Hindu obligation
to active penance granting them a *superior* incorporation of their debt as the only managers
of the Sangh.

[14] This tremendous insight we owe to George Verghese, who in a talk in Jawaharlal Nehru
University on the philosopher Alain Badiou, sweepingly declared that Gandhi created the
"void-point" (Alain Badiou's critical concept) in modern Indian history, which was the
condition for an unforeseen, hazardous and courageous *decision* on who/what was to
be the *true* subject to animate that void.

Constitution of India, in the making by the new Constituent Assembly after 1947, to inscribe in the world a new incorporeal transformation called 'citizenship'. And the excluded castes, the Untouchables, to be the new incorporeal 'citizens'. It seems to us that *this* is Ambedkar's rigorous desire and he does not want the incorporeal of citizenship to be created in the image of a corporation among corporations. In a strange syncopation with Gandhi's speculative totality, Ambedkar wants the form, or should one say the *figura/persona*, of the citizen to be *universal* and *indiscernible*. But unlike Gandhi's totality, which, in all its subtlety, remains rooted to a kind of hereditary immemorial soil, to an autochthony, Ambedkar is the architect here of a 'new immemorial'. How to forge this new immemorial that is the Constitution of India to actualize the goal we have tried to highlight? Simply the document and linguistic statement of the Constitution are not enough. The statement must effectuate the *event* of an incorporeal transformation, must create an 'eventative' body of the citizen. To achieve this truly emancipated *political* body, according to Ambedkar, the Constitution must, briefly but resolutely, undertake the peril of passing through the *anathema* of society, its structural wound; its universality must be entirely localized to its most fragmented particularity, its most 'Untouchable' extremity. The brevity of this passage must be measured not only by the external parameter of number of years (10 years of legislative reservations) but as much by the coefficient of its intensity. In that sense, the Constitution, for all its universality, must be the intense space of a partisan enforcement of the event of generic equality—without depleting into the Gandhian cathartic treatment of purification of anachronisms.

*But*, by definition, the event, which is an exception without the coded bodies/corporations of the world to support it, cannot be enforced. And a Constitution, by definition, must be capable of encompassing all the bodies and codes in its jurisdiction. It cannot be, however briefly, its own exception and separation, its own anathema and abandonment; it can *have* exceptions by coding them, as Ambedkar knew better than most, as temporally and spatially delimited within 'reservations'. In his own words, if constitutional rule was not to be "swallowed up"[15] by its exceptions, it must codify the latter as socio-legal *anachronisms*.

---

[15] See Sen (2007: 110).

SCs, STs, and minorities as such are constituted as anachronistic corporations, always and permanently on the way out.... This seems to us to be the central meaning of B.R. Ambedkar's much-mentioned remark on India entering a life of contradiction in the new Republic to be lived out between political equality and social oppression, constitutional power for the 'form' of the nation and persistent disarmament of the contents of its society.

By way of concluding remarks, it could be said that between the making of the Constitution and now, a deeply fissured social consensus has been on the existence of *permanent anachronisms*. Where "anathema" consisted of a rigorous (and in the logical sense, permanent) structural potential of the most explosive kind, searching for its *true* realization or pacification in new incorporeal bodies—true *Dalit* bodies—"anachronism" consisted of a terrible but dispensable historical wrong seeking a purified, loving, catholic (!) heart. On the other hand, "permanent anachronism" secretes a totally circumstantial existential irritation and yet permanently "tends to" and is repelled by other such "anachronisms" with an *identical* existential irritability, with a permanent propensity to hurt....[16]

Now, at the very end, we must state point-blank, just in case there is confusion about the matter, that the "permanent anachronisms" are *not* the minorities for whom Ambedkar (and many others) argued in favor of constitutional safeguards. "Permanent anachronism" denotes society's neurotic disavowal of its structural violence. It is a compromise manipulated by the majoritarian part of society with the minority that instead of transforming to a state of generic equality, the majority will henceforth see its own self in the image of a generalized minority, a more numerous bundle of anachronisms. Like all compromise-formations, it carries deep unhappiness and delicate sensitivities. Most crucially, it is a badly unstable compromise and, so often, lapses into *episodic anathemas* incarnated with more than symbolic violence. But even then we seem to rush to re-negotiate the compromise instead of renewing Ambedkar's critical exhortation to Gandhi: "At least *think* the anathema even if you can't *be* it!"

---

[16] Two caveats: First, when we say "permanent propensity to hurt," we intend the verb to serve both functions, the active one of hurting and the passive one of being hurt; second, the "tending to" of bodies to each other which is also their tendency to be mutually repulsed, is an admittedly perverse utilization of the Spinozist notion of *conatus*.

# References

Ambedkar, Babasaheb. 1991. *Writings and Speeches*, Vol. 9 (Ed.). Vasant Moon. Bombay: Government of Maharashtra, pp. 199–297.

———. 1989. *Writings and Speeches*, Vol. 1. (Ed.) Vasant Moon. Bombay: Government of Maharashtra, pp. 5–22.

Franco, F., V. Sarvar, and Sherry Chand. 2009. *Varna: Ideology as Social Practice*. New Delhi: Critical Quest, p. 13.

Gilles Deleuze. 1990. *The Logic of Sense*, trans. Mark Lester and Charles Sitvale, New York: Columbia University Press.

Sen, Sarbani. 2007. *The Constitution of India: Popular Sovereignty and Democratic Transformation*, New Delhi: Oxford University Press, p. 110.

Taubes, Jacob. 2004. *The Political Theology of Paul*, trans. Dana Hollander, Stanford, California: Stanford University Press, p. 27.

# 10

# The Cartoon Controversy: Crafty Politicos, Impatient Pedagogues

*Manas Ray*

## I

Hegel, said the German playwright Bertolt Brecht, had the makings of one of the greatest humorists among the philosophers. He had such a sense of humor that he could not think, for example, of order without disorder. For Brecht, no one without an appreciation of humor can understand dialectics. But what kind of dialectical grasp over the nature of things would it require, one wonders, to appreciate that what seems an 'innocuous' object of humor to someone might not seem exactly so to someone else of a different history and location—as a matter of fact, it might even seem a pugnacious continuation of old social wounds, now picked up from the archival past and given a fresh lease of life? What kind of dialectics can convert my obduracy into someone else's intolerance? Commitment to what politics can make the country's well-known academics ignore charges of cultural insensitivity and community resentment against a schoolbook cartoon in the name of pedagogic advances?

In the way the so-called cartoon controversy has shaped up over the past weeks, what was not all that surprising is the bonhomie of players in the Parliament across party lines in support of a Dalit cause. For anyone with some idea of how our Parliament works in this era of allies and identity politics, it was the all too familiar repetition of transforming a socially contentious issue into a filmy item number.

What was genuinely surprising, though, is the resolute support the country's learned class, some of its best known academics, showed in defense of the inclusion of a cartoon in a National Council of Educational Research and Training (NCERT) Class XI Political Science textbook on the Constitution and how it works. They had reasons for their anger, their repugnance mixed with a degree of helplessness as a protest against a particular cartoon was allowed to snowball over the next few days into a downright demand for exclusion of any cartoon involving political figures and more: criminal prosecution for those responsible for putting this cartoon in the textbook. This was bizarre. But the height of the show was left for Ram Vilas Paswan of the Lok Janshakti Party who wanted the government to disband the NCERT itself!

There can be little doubt that over the years NCERT has done a commendable job and some of its textbooks are very good, lucid and clear, certainly much better than the average textbook of the past or those available even today through other channels. Politically speaking, they also represent a necessary corrective to the ones brought out during the earlier NDA regimes.

But this does not mean whatever gets included in any of those books need to be defended, that the commendable efforts of the academics responsible for producing them are above any blemish, and that the controversy over the particular cartoon was either motivated or the result of not being trained in the politics of reading a visual— in other words, poor reading skills. I get the feeling, what hurt this class of committed intellectuals the most is what they see as Dalit injudiciousness (if not impudence)—people to whom they provided the language to understand themselves and to demand their rightful place in the world, are now pointing their fingers at them. Even if for one cartoon, this cannot be tolerated. The Dalits should know that they are 'pulling up the ladder' that helped them to climb in the first place.

What was surprising also, and sad, is to find the famed academics in their defense of the cartoon going back on some of the recent advances of social-human studies. After all these years with Foucault, after all this talk about the imbrication of power-knowledge, our faith in the sacrosanct nature of 'experts' knowledge—and of committees, institutions, adornments and affiliations—seemed to have remained intact. It was interesting also to see how after all that was written on the volatile, fissiparous nature of representation and the inevitable spilling over constructed boundaries, on the unruly truth of image that respects no guarded separations and constituencies, commentator after commentator kept asserting that the Ambedkar present in the cartoon was not the Ambedkar the Dalit leader but Ambedkar the law minister and framer of our Constitution.

Pressure group politics, the ruling party bending over backwards to woo one vote bank or the other (even if at times notional), the culture of ban: with increasing rapidity these now have become the order of the day. The determined ruthlessness with which A.K. Ramanujan's essay on the Ramayana was taken out from the Delhi University undergraduate syllabus under Hindutva pressure is an instance. It was like pulling out a steadfast screw with pliers alone, ignoring the recommendations of the committee set-up by the Supreme Court, and the protests of the students and the teaching community nationwide. The frequency of such happenings is making them seem banal. If not from the same book then at least of the same genre is another recent episode of alleged textual blasphemy—the one involving Mamata Banerjee. The other day our Mother Courage of a different brand defended her decision to arrest a university professor for circulating in the net-land a cartoon on her. She sees in it an assassination threat—otherwise, she wondered, why 'vanish'? Her life being so precious, it has been targeted innumerable times; one hopes (against hope) that the trend is coming to an end.

But closer to the interest of this article is the question: Can the furore over the cartoon on her be conflated with the one on Ambedkar? Can one instance of protest be seen as equal to another? What is lost in such conflation, all the drama of the parliamentarians over a "*sarkari kitab*" and the threat on freedom of intellection that looms large, regardless?

# II

# Of Takes and Mistakes

In a recent edit page essay in *The Hindu*, the veteran journalist Akhileswari observes that the cartoon pithily summarized the delay in Constitution-making but is now outdated (Akhileswari, 2012). Her piece is excellent, one of the few that came out in mainstream newspapers in support of the withdrawal of the cartoon. However, I find it difficult to agree on either of the two points she makes here. First, I don't think the cartoon summarizes the delay well, for it gives no idea of what primarily caused the delay. Ambedkar started with six other members nominated by the President to draft the Constitution. Soon it became a matter of his lone effort; others were not available due to a variety of reasons and one member had expired (and was not replaced). It was a Herculean task but Ambedkar performed it meticulously, caringly. In retrospect, what seems more important than the delay in the making of the Constitution is the fact of its being at all completed and that too, so marvelously. The delay was apparently due to Ambedkar's fussy obsession with questions of social inclusion, or this is how the issue is made out to be by a few commentators on the ongoing controversy. The main source of delay very clearly, however, was not any fastidiousness on Ambedkar's part but obstructions caused by retro-grade social and political perspectives of those at the helm of affairs against which the Dalit leader took a firm stand. As Akhileshwari herself points out in that piece:

> There are more important things that need to be foregrounded to understand the process of the making of the Constitution such as how the then President Rajendra Prasad, a confirmed conservative, opposed equal property rights for women, and how a modernist Nehru caved in to him and how when an outraged Ambedkar threatened to quit the team they agreed to it. (Akhileswari, 2012)

The textbook at best makes a vague gesture to such constitutive tensions of the politics of that time. I presume it chose to ignore such issues because it was written for students with an average age of 16 and, hence, too young to be exposed to the power-play that politics is and also because as a (government sponsored) textbook, it had to operate within the zones of sanctioned freedom, never too large and always vulnerable.

Be it as it may, and this brings me to the second point, I don't think the cartoon is by any means outdated, a spent-force piece of illustration dug out from dusty oblivion. It would have been so had there been a radical shift in the position of the Dalits in society at large in the last so many decades and a change in upper caste attitudes towards them or, to talk of the other side, had there happened no consolidation of the Dalits, politically. The intervening decades—especially from the late 1970s—have witnessed an emergence of

Dalit power while the scenario of social ostracization and economic marginalization remain quite the same for the vast majority of them. Hence, it is quite logical that a visualization of the so-called 'delay' showing Nehru cracking his whip from behind as Ambedkar, hunched on an inflated snail, inertly holds on to something that looks more like a diminutive fishing stick than a whip proper, will cause consternation. Given the peculiar combination of continuing socio-economic marginalization and recent political consolidation in a multiparty polity, it is easy to see that even though the cartoon is about the Constitution in the offing, the figure sitting on the snail will be viewed by Dalits less as the framer of the Indian Constitution and more as their icon of liberation. Perhaps it is the nature of the political conjuncture we are in, far from being passé, the cartoon in its textbook life has quickly become the sign of what Benjamin once called (later Foucault would elaborate on it), the history of the present—not the sanitized idea of history written from the standpoint of the present, but history as the sudden constellation of a moment of the past and a moment of the present in a language of crisis. So unanimous and overwhelming has been the defense of the cartoon among colleagues and friends in the academia that I too was initially mistaken, till I actually saw it with my eyes. Nehru's over-lordship is beyond question, irrespective of whether he is shown whipping Ambedkar (which, I think, may not be what it is). Irrespective of any variations, the fact that I consider the cartoon pejorative will be taken as part of the 'mischievous' attempts to present its content by "overlooking the positive symbolism (that Ambedkar holds the reins to the Constitution and holds a whip) and over-playing a possible negative symbolism (Nehru holding a whip behind Ambedkar has been presented as Nehru whipping Ambedkar)" (Yadav, 2012).

I also fail to read the whips as figures of art.[1] Instead what comes across as more pertinent to me are the possible difficulties to accept the cartoon for someone who considers Ambedkar, and not Nehru, as the country's best democratic icon. The load of memory and the charged nature of the present being what they are, the signs of the cartoon will far exceed the text-supplied guidelines for its reading (seldom a docile

[1] See petition submitted to Prof Sukhadeo Thorat, Chairperson, NCERT textbooks review committee for a discussion on the significance of the whip in history of marginalized groups (reproduced in *The Hindu*, June 8, 2012).

act). And once a controversy erupts, all the more so. No amount of talk about the games the 'frothy' mouthed parliamentarians play can hide the cultural and political insensitivity of the cartoon.

The cartoons of Shankar (and, subsequently, Laxman)—along with that missing element in today's visual culture: the newsreel—were among those that made up for a pedagogic exercise in developing the right democratic comportment of the fledging nation state. They tried to train the citizen in different liberal verities and thus performed an important function of governmentality. Unlike the newsreel (a wholly government sponsored medium), Shankar placed special importance on being vigilant about the politicians, their indifference, frailties and corruption, their mendacity and cunning, thus offering, in each instance, an advice or two for the new government and the imagined community of citizens. Nehru adored Shankar. He defined a time, a texture of civil life, a climate of rule, the dreams of the urban middle class in an era marked by boom in salaried jobs, particularly *sarkari*. Shankar in all his mellow humanism did not think it necessary to have a cartoon or two against casteism. His was the theater of urban upper castes—those present as peons, *khansamas*, *chaprasis*, *safai karamcharis*, and the like were there merely as sideshows. No one cared, no one so much noticed—such were the days of halcyon hegemony of the upper castes. Shankar had no intention of being a casteist. Casteism was too pervasive, too insidious to be in any need of intention.

The other day I suggested to an anthropologist friend a thought experiment. Let's try to visualize, I told her, the cartoon with Nehru replaced by Lord Mountbatten and Ambedkar by Gandhi, and see what it does to us. The proposal must seem patently absurd to us because by no stretch of imagination can these two figures be placed on the same side of the divide.

If that is true, then going by the same argument, the sanity or otherwise of the cartoon would depend on whether its two characters— Nehru and Ambedkar—can be seen as part of the same social-political bloc. As the law minister and the person responsible for the writing of the Constitution, and a law graduate of Columbia, Ambedkar was for all practical purposes included in the same cultural-social bloc as Nehru's. But as himself a Dalit and a champion of the Dalit cause, in the perception of fellow Dalits, this other identity of his is primordial, now or then. To the extent real participation of the Dalits has been achieved in society, the aesthetic luxury of having a laugh at oneself was open to us. But is there a 'one-self', an 'us'? It seems to me, sadly but surely, we are still laughing at them.

If we are interested in the social cartography of this primordiality, as an example let us ask: What was the ratio of Dalits and non-Dalits doing manual scavenging jobs in the Indian Railways in 1949—that is, the year the cartoon was done—and what is that ratio today, that is, after years of Dalit power (and when in its new life in the textbook, the cartoon is taken as an archival witness to time past)? There would hardly be any change, for such jobs, now as then, are meant almost exclusively for the so-called designated 'scavenger castes'. Manual scavenging, we are told, is the only option for the railways since there is not enough money available to modernize the trains and stations. Yet as the then Railways Minister, Laloo Prasad Yadav had announced plans to smarten up 18 railway stations for the 2010 Commonwealth Games with budgetary allocations from the Prime Minister's Committee on Infrastructure in the vicinity of ₹4,000 crores (he is so good with huge funds!). For the decent class, as long as the quotas are in place and as long as homage to the contributions of Ambedkar in the life of the nation is regularly and uninhibitedly paid, it need not be anything else than Business as Usual.

# III

# Obdurate Solidarity

The position of the HRD minister that "cartoons on the political class should not find a place in textbooks" is a demand that needs to be contested by all means. I hope the panel of academics set up to examine the new NCERT textbooks will not bow down to such draconian and palpably motivated demands. The issue therefore is not that certain prominent members of the country's academic community are protesting the intervention of the government in the writing of textbooks. The issue is the (almost obligatory) way the concerns about a particular cartoon are translated into a lack of appreciation of humorous visuals and—taking an unbelievably huge leap—of the productive power of laughter as such in 'movements for social justice'. Additionally, it is charged that given the context, to create consternation about a particular inclusion is a willful ignorance of the pioneering role the NCERT textbooks (especially in their new version) have been playing in school pedagogy (this second aspect, in combination with the wiliness of politicians, manages to give the demand for abolition of the cartoon a dangerous hue).

At issue also is the attitude displayed by the protesting academics—a kind of holier-than-thou infallibility working in tandem with a governmentalized defense of the visual which would suggest that nothing could be wrong in its inclusion because the text has gone through all the prescribed bureaucratic procedures: the different committees through which it had to pass, the different authorities in those committees with venerable track records, 'the extensive consultations', 'the leading political scientists and educationists' involved, 'the collective wisdom', 'the best known academics,' and so on. I presume, it is part of the governmentalized mode to draw anyone who participates in it, however tangentially, into its groove of language and mode of justification. This, however, is not an argument favoring hermetic non-participation.

There is something incestuous in writing about one's own profession. Quite a few of the participants in the debate are friends, academic colleagues, people one meets from time to time in different academic gatherings; with some, one is in regular email correspondence. All that I can say is that the critique intended here is partly also a self-critique. The issue is not of intention but of collective silence, in which I too could be a party in another instance. Call it silence, call it blindness: naming does not matter here—basically, it is a sign of belonging, even if loosely (and flexibly), to the wide ruling class hegemony.

The sanctimonious tone displayed by some commentators is well-nigh disturbing. As a commentator puts it forcefully:

> Is it even thinkable that these two individuals, Yadav and Palshikar, who have spent their entire lives studying and teaching about democracy, elections, affirmative action, state, society, politics and nation in India, would want to desecrate the legacy of B.R. Ambedkar through some insidious form of insult and mockery? That they deliberately chose an offensive cartoon and slipped it into schoolbooks decades after the fact, just to put Ambedkar down? (Vajpeyi, 2012)

Does it have to be deliberate? What basically is being said is this: how can you have problems about a cartoon the authors chose to include when they are very much part of *us*? Some of *us* have written pioneeringly against casteism; how could *we* possibly have gone wrong? "In the on-going Shankar cartoon controversy," says Ananya Vajpeyi:

> (t)he real issue is not whether Ambedkar or Nehru are mocked in this particular case, but what kind of understanding of social inequality we want our children to have; what history of India's founding principles, efforts at nation-building and Constitutional democracy we want to impart to the younger generation. (Vajpeyi, 2012)

I am generally appreciative of Vajpeyi's writings; they carry a sense of nuanced conviction. Nonetheless, in this instance, I cannot help thinking that only those whose own participation in the societal process is beyond doubt can display such evangelical urgency. It is the cosmopolitan, imperative voice of the nation-builder. (Incidentally, has anyone even by default suggested that Nehru has been mocked in this particular case? Or is it a case of easy equivalence?) "The argument that the cartoon could be misconstrued by the 11th standard schoolchildren who read the textbook is bogus and an insult to their intelligence," opines a newspaper editorial.[2] What it perhaps overlooks is that casteism is not about lack of intelligence (which would have made rectification, if that is the word, much easier) but willful (willed?) suspension of intelligence. It is a matter of culturally facilitated cognition. The argument that the cartoon in question—a student, Ishaan Sharma, puts it cogently and with a great deal of honesty—hurts Dalits is neither true nor false. He wrote the Class XII CBSE Board exam in 2012, with political science as one of his subjects. The cartoons in the textbook used to provide him with comic relief in the grinding drudgery of exam preparation. His take on the controversy is somewhat like this: India is a vast smorgasbord of ideas and opinion. Some will hurt one section of people, some others might hurt another. It is all about the relative strength of an argument and about commitment to democratic values and respect for diversity (Sharma, 2012). There is so much for preparing students "to enter into a complex world with multiple received and achieved hierarchies" (Nair, 2012). Pedagogues, interested as they are in the public life of ideas and lessons, should take such readings seriously, indicative as these are of politics of culture and vice versa, of an assumed equality, of sanctioned amnesia and knowledge

---

[2] "The Comic Republic," *The Hindu*, May 14, 2012.

that guide the process of meaning making. More than any *sui generis* of whether or not—or, to what extent—high school students have impressionable, vulnerable minds, it is about the truths that operate in society to which adults and adolescents alike, those with impressionable minds and those presumably otherwise, are equally game.

Going by the writings or comments that appeared in the newspapers, circulated on the Internet and broadcast on television—from promising historians, high profile academics to a young student just out of school—one senses a reverberative continuity. This is the advanced, positive class that seeks to eradicate poverty and inequality, establish effective rule of law, and make Dalits (particularly, Dalit children) part of this drive. This also implies a reciprocal obligation on the part of Dalits: they on their part should not scout around for signs of insult and humiliation. In the cartoon, we are told affirmatively, Ambedkar has not been mocked; to protest in this context necessarily has to mean exercising the most frequently asserted of rights: "the right to be offended." In other words, if Dalit children hear in the cartoon resonances of the snickers, spits, and yells they confront every day, they should learn to ignore such distractions and keep the bigger picture intact. Whatever causes unease from a lingering past will be eradicated, as long as we fight unitedly and do not get unnecessarily distracted. Conviction is temporality—a certain temporality, that is. I cannot help thinking that this is one India talking to another. It is an India that is global, thoroughly professional, networked, confident, and has no room for opacities. These qualities are not necessarily bad on their own (and their opposites surely do not deserve valorization), but they do indicate a certain location and comportment.

In this positive project of the nation, Ambedkar, understandably, has the presence of a luminary: "one of the greatest scholars, intellectuals and political thinkers that India produced in the 20th century, *in addition to* being the leader of the Dalits" (Vajpeyi, 2012 [emphasis mine]). There is nothing that is not honest in such outpourings of admiration. Nonetheless, it would not be entirely cynical to take pause and ask (if not for anything else then for the sake of the nation's political biography), when did this lionizing of Ambedkar begin, at least as widely as one finds now? When did the inclusion of his photograph, for instance, become a must in the galleries of the nation's pantheon, even in the barest, trimmed down version of just a Gandhi and a Nehru (and, almost always, a Tagore)? Would it be too cynical to presume that once the man acquired a certain canonical status, one can endlessly bestow praise on him without causing any damage to the mushy continuation of casteism in our academic life (as in all other departments of life), even in the highest echelons? The clue to this lies perhaps in the secured duality we have attributed to his existence: the scholar-leader *extraordinaire* of modern India and *also* the leader of the Dalits.

# IV

# Reading Lessons

It is so vastly wrong to hold that it is Ambedkar the law maker, and not Ambedkar the Dalit (the wretched of the law), who is represented in the cartoon. (For those in support of the cartoon, this division is absolutely central, the bulwark of their defense.) Even Nehru, dependent as he was on Ambedkar's chiselled knowledge of Western law, wanted to make an announcement to the whole world by appointing a Dalit to write the Constitution of the independent country. For the Dalit, he has remained, then as now, someone their very own and also purely magical. For a myriad of reasons, he has to have an in-between existence, a contested location, irrespective of the context in which he is placed: a leader of the most oppressed sections of society *as well as* the nation's hero (belatedly recognized and, for many even now, only formally, grudgingly). This fuzziness attributes the politics of reading the cartoon a particular tension—the aleatory nature that characterizes signs, their nefarious slippages and alliances come especially alive.

The German word for image is *Bild*. It means fabrication. Fabrication is at the heart of the image. Cartoons exaggerate this basic trait of image making. It is all about inhabiting the limits of verisimilitude. The cartoon is a political being. It violates to attain its truth. Therefore, its history is one of valorization and censorship. Janaki Nair uses contemporary insights about the prodigious nature of making meaning and how a text is caught in other larger texts to ultimately make an argument in favor of binding the text (an image, in this case) to its prescribed context—a necessary docility, I would presume, to avoid the otherwise "intolerable burden on the production of knowledge." She seems to be suggesting two things together: (a) that the cartoons are there to give the students some idea of how they always exceed the text; and (b) that the cartoon(s) should be read in terms of the written text that has been provided for it. Such a position displays the historian's at once excitement and anxiety of the manifold: the traces from which evidences are to be constructed are also caught in a multitude of other traces. I am not a historian, so undue speculation on my part won't hurt the discipline. I wonder if it would be much too wrong to presume that part of the joy of writing the past is to be telling stories about the difficulties of telling stories in the ruffled context of the past. A textbook on the Constitution—that too, for high school students—is not supposed to go into such issues. But alas, this is no guarantee that such issues would not invade what gets written and represented there. And if that is the case, then one should be even more careful about what gets included (particularly, since as a state sponsored textbook the space of freedom is never huge). Regarding whether more caution would reduce the whole exercise to banality, I am not convinced that the non-inclusion (and replacement) of one particular cartoon would have made learning a dull affair, any more than what it is in its present format. The critical pedagogues compare their efforts with what used to be: "a sanitized, pious, celebratory account of our past and present" (Nair, 2012, 2015). While much better than what used to pass as textbooks for higher classes, the academics concerned might have awarded themselves a shade too radical self-portrait too easily. What has gone into the text is pretty useful stuff to produce a dutiful, rights-bearing hegemonic citizenry in keeping with the contemporary conjuncture of a globalized nation state, a type of training in the right political taste of the future urban middle class. Students of science at the Class XI level are challenged with really difficult conceptual problems. Why can't students of humanities and social sciences be similarly challenged too?

The Constitution gives a collective identity to the people, says the textbook. But it is left as a statement without any probing into its possible implications. What does the abstraction "we, the people"—an ever-receding center—have for the society that was achieved through the Constitution? Apart from the explication of the

Constitution and the various ways in which it works, there is also the other aspect—in a way secondary but crucial: What kind of political imagination does the book invite the students to participate in? To give an elementary notion of the kind of dissonance that inheres in modern law would have done no harm. The tension between legal determination and broader justice, the coded nature of law and the endlessness of context, or the fact that it is transgression that brings law into being (thus, each owing its life to the other) and similar other issues could have made for an interesting read, provided explained in lucid language and enriched by innovative everyday examples (and cartoons). One of the primary distractions of school level human-social studies textbooks is that they offer so little as intellectual challenge to the students.

If the demands for the withdrawal of the cartoon "spell long-term danger to the processes of reflection on and critique of the past, and even the present" (Nair, 2012), then what sort of opening (or otherwise) does the smug assertion that the cartoon *does not mock* the Dalit sentiment create for these Enlightenment values? Is not the complete refusal to reconsider the question of social justice (which one might not have happened to see earlier) also a danger to the process of reflection and critique? That there could be any life to this protest outside the parliamentary drama, that there could be individuals and constituencies genuinely hurt, is squarely denied. What makes this situation at all possible, we are told, is the lack of proper citizenship training that disables the protesting Dalits from seeing beyond their own community. The extent of narcissistic endorsement of one's own community by the group of committed scholars is truly remarkable. Therefore such protest, we are reminded, "produces a great vulnerability among those engaged in such knowledge production, who may find it impossible to anticipate which future (politicised) group or community will object to representations in visual or linguistic forms" (Nair, 2012). To maintain that any 'dissidence and dissonance' to any inclusion that I/we might have decided on will necessarily 'fatally damage' 'the possibility of generating critical knowledge', is to define oneself *a priori* as the fountainhead of critical knowledge. While everybody else has a determined location, the small community of scholars engaged in such knowledge production is truly a community of free-floating intellectuals. Their commitment is their location; they are the realization of critique itself.

# V

# Critical Pedagogy

For Satish Deshpande, one of the most revered sociologists of the country with a rich record of research and writing on democracy and the caste system, the real issue is not the cartoon in question and the controversy it has caused, but something that is much larger in scope—namely, the reality of Dalit assertion. His resort to the language of assertion and 'veto power' manages to give a special spin to the whole issue, as the question of pejorative representation of a specific visual is transformed into a tussle, a tug-of-war of sorts, between rival interest groups in a fractious liberal polity—and not so much whether it has hurt and offended Dalit sensibility (Deshpande, 2012).

In a remarkable display of fairness, he says that the Dalit community has a "strong entitlement" to demand a presumptive ban on the cartoon and stall debate. But it soon turns out to be a heuristic pronouncement in an argument aimed basically to make the Dalits understand the importance of critical pedagogy in their fight for justice and how mistaken they are in taking position against their genuine allies, the initiators of that pedagogy, which has over the years served as "the very conditions of a possibility" of Dalit power.

In the ongoing controversy, what troubles and pains the critical pedagogues is how to create the right space for a critical and engaged pedagogy in a system prone to craven conformity and how to make the textbooks and the years of collective labor that has gone into their making safe from the wielders of power bent on reaping gains by exploiting vulnerable Dalit sentiments. The prospect is magnanimous as is the picture it evokes: in the face of Dalit clamor, the calm of committed wisdom. Such stance also puts the class of critical pedagogues above flaws, especially political flaws.

The conclusion is nothing much short of a giveaway: let the Dalits, says Deshpande, not make the mistake of pulling up the ladders of social mobility provided by critical pedagogy. The concern for the plight of the Dalit is unmistakable and genuine. But so is another concern: the prospect of a rupture with the order of filiation, and a streak of (uncharacteristic) conceit. And it is such gesture that makes room for a Hindutva ideologue, used to viewing Dalit power as how far India has moved away from its ideals of equality, to read the whole issue as the result of left-secular scholars' long history of Dalit appeasement and gross self-aggrandizement (Dasgupta, 2012). The fact of the matter is, the easy alliance of left-liberal intellectuals with the Dalit cause is in crisis today as Dalits have started questioning the right of these intellectuals to decide on their own matters that affect the interest of their community. I am bent on reading the course of events optimistically, since such alliances in future will not be with the political *idea* of the Dalit but with Dalits as political partners of equal rights and say, and both of whom have means of knowing each other in their respective ways.

With casteism being under attack in academic discourse, there are attempts to formalize Dalit hurt and desensitize one to what it means to be a Dalit by constructing spurious equivalences. For instance, in Maharashtra where the desecration of Ambedkar's statue is even now a regular practice (leading to cloistered silences from the community as well as different forms of resistances), it is claimed—even by left-liberal academics with broad anti-casteist pronouncements—that the narratives of pride around Shivaji and of Ambedkar are, though not identical, similar in nature and certainly of the same genre, thus brushing away their vastly dissimilar histories and presents (especially, of affect) simply on the operative category of assertion. The broader question is: Can assertion take care of humiliation and pain? Are they indicative of the same trajectory? Can statuaries speak the silences of the tears?

# VI

# Democracy and the Parliament

The fear that if the government can change the content of a textbook every time it is under pressure, then no self-respecting scholar will in future agree to write for NCERT is not unfounded, but the demand that the classroom must be insulated from the Parliament and that under no circumstance the government intervene into the autonomy of an organization like NCERT cannot be a valid one. Prabhat Patnaik is right in arguing that even though normally school textbooks, or curricula, are affairs of academics in which the government should have only minimal say, if a strong objection is raised by certain sections of society—especially, the underprivileged—against the contents of a textbook (a public good), then the government is obliged to appoint a team of scholars to look into the matter. The government's commitment to principles of fairness is determined not by the fact that it appoints a committee but by the composition of the committee. I think it is important that the concerned authors are not left out of the process of deliberations. However, to suggest that the maximum that the committee set up by the government can do is to make recommendations for alterations to the authors and it is up to the authors to implement those is too patently consensual.

Thinking adventurously, I am suggesting that the cartoon in question should not be banished but made into an appendix—in this textbook or some other deemed more relevant—accompanied by a synopsis of the debates that took place around it. The two authors of the book will have the right to choose a particular member from the new committee set up by the government on whom would be vested the responsibility of writing the synopsis. The write-up needs to be endorsed by a majority of members (including the two authors). In its new life, the cartoon becomes a supplement and not part of the regular text from which questions are set. Its function would be to initiate a discussion on how a visual can give rise to sharply opposed readings in a politically divided community. Thus, it serves as material for 'compilation, critique, and study' and not simply as an illustration of the text. In other words, it would foreground its own life as a cartoon to be read in its relation with the text.

This said, I find Patnaik's endorsement of the Parliament as having the last say in a democracy whose jurisdiction no one can cede—a kind of 'determination in the last instance' logic—even if not formally wrong, at best displays only a rudimentary understanding of how a democratic system functions. Elected on the basis of one-person-one-vote, the MPs, he argues, are an embodiment of one aspect of the principle of equality. They enjoy the mandate of the people which no other institution in the country has. The fact that those who qualify through the process of one-person-one-vote 'allegedly' have "crooks, criminals and corrupt persons" in their midst (by Patnaik's own admission) does indicate that the kind of representation he valorizes as having the overriding power in democracy is premised on large and crucial alienations. Representational equality, French philosopher Jacques Ranciere has indicated in a number of places, is the equality already there at the core of inequality.

Rule by consent is a complex technology with a long history. But there are good democratic reasons for not equating parliamentary numbers with democracy. What happens if people consent to the demolition of democracy by voting away their own rights and their say, not an altogether unfamiliar phenomenon in history? At a much more quotidian level, and leaving out the predicament of the proverbial 49 per cent in the mandating process, minority groups are systematically defeated in the legislature, even in proportional representation. The reality of representation is that it is nothing more than a workaday approximation of democracy, while in actuality and in spirit as well as in its architectonics, democracy works in multiple sites, coeval and simultaneous: the Constitution, the Parliament, forms of government, institutions and different spheres of activities. It would be wrong to assume that they would all follow the same language game.

There are other problems in any easy to-and-fro between the MPs and the so-called 'people out there'. Our commitment to democracy and equality must not make us oblivious to the metonymic role of 'the people' in a democratic state. The people, which comes into being only on its citing by the Constitution ("In the name of the people …") and which attributes a sacredness to the Parliament's transactions, is a trope par excellence of modern polity. It is a crucial but unknown presence, forever a possible impossibility, a complete subject of transcendence and autonomy, a quasi-deific center of a professedly groundless, post-theocratic order. The members of the Parliament are at best 'approximate successive representatives'—equivocations—of the people, churned out by a particular machinery called the *election*. In a democracy, popular sovereignty and the government are held in a peculiar mesh, each having its own rationality and each undergoing its own mutations in its bid to articulate with the other.

More and more in modern democracy, popular sovereignty's 'self-generating supremacy' hinges on its ability to incorporate and put to its advantage 'the multitude of disparate forces' that the fractured polity keeps generating (Fitzpatrick 2008). In other words, sovereignty is crucially dependent on the art of the government. A neat compartment between decisions in the Parliament and protests on the streets not only allows a limited conception of how a democratic polity works, it is erroneous too. Democracy is at once all and nothing, full and empty, grounded and groundless—a restlessness, an alterity, that actually helps in its ceaseless renewal. The reality of democracy is the phenomenology of a promise of democracy to come. If democracy seems an 'unsurpassable principle or horizon' of political formations, observes the French historian and philosopher of democracy, Pierre Rosanvallon, it is because it manages even now to retain its early poser of an experiment (Rosanvallon, 2007).

In other words, its strength lies in offering solutions that are provisional, opening spaces for agonistic contest. In the process, democracy becomes even more embedded and inevitable.

Ambedkar's immaculate training in liberal law came in handy for Nehru. On his part, Ambedkar made strategic use of liberalism's promises and cherished virtues and initiated the first effective moves toward the equality of the Dalits, people absurdly wronged. Over the years, the legacy acquired its own dynamics. As a creature of power, politics of identity quite often tends to get entangled in the logic of rule, not all the results of which would have gratified Ambedkar, the great visionary and equity seeker of Indian politics.

In electoral democracy with a large Dalit constituency, establishing real equalities had always to be far more difficult than achieving the reservations. In moments of despondency, Ambedkar looks like a Sisyphus in our tryst with democracy.

Regardless of what hullabaloo the parliamentarians are engaged in, let us not give up on the best that such a conflict of perspectives can offer: its agonal quality, the dialogical encounters as part of the broader struggle over citizenship. Is it possible that in the process of such encounters, identities, instead of becoming more cocooned, actually start waking up to their heterogeneities? Is it possible to imagine a politics where, in the very process of taking up positions, inventing, and assembling strategies in a field necessarily fractured, one also strives, perhaps absurdly, for a certain kind of recognition of others that comes from waking up to one's own opacity to oneself? The understanding of suffering from the standpoint of a subject of self-presence and autonomy can seek solution only in a politics of assertion and rights, and express itself in the changing distribution of space in a liberal polity. While this mode of negotiation cannot be denied, we need to think beyond the psychological subject of interest and create within the political (and as part of the political) a space for disinterested compassion, and an attachment to the "quiddity of suffering" (Levinas) as a mode of being.

Why do the Dalits have to claim monopoly over Ambedkar, it has been asked, when he belongs to every Indian? Perhaps there is a point in remembering the terrible insularity that violence creates through its excess. Violence knows nothing of what it violates, while it makes the violated recognize its essence only as a being violated (Jean-Luc, 2005). To maintain that the cartoon causes no insult to Dalit psyche is to occasion interpretative violence. People who are praising the Ambedkar cartoon would not have possibly praised the Muhammad cartoons that caused protest from Islamic people in Denmark and Europe at large. To resemble, a cartoon assembles itself from a singular perspective. But this singularity is a strange one, since it is also an invocation to the restless multitude of disparate forces. The tussle between these two registers is a cartoon's opening to the real. Let this not be read as an argument against the inclusion of cartoons in school textbooks. By all means, they should be included. But with a keener eye and, when a controversy breaks out, patient ears to listen.

# References

Akhileswari, R. May 15, 2012. "Hardly Funny," *The Hindu*.
Dasgupta, Swapan. May 20, 2012. "Unfunny, Literally," *The Times of India*.
Deshpande, Satish. May 18, 2012. "Schooled In Sanctimony," *The Hindu*.
Fitzpatrick, Peter. 2008. *Law as Resistance: Modernism, Imperialism, Legalism*, Ashgate, pp. 21–22.
Nair, Janaki. May 15, 2012. "Reading Politics, and the Politics of Reading," *The Hindu*.
Rosanvallon, Pierre. 2007. *Democracy Past and Future*, Columbia University Press, pp. 36–37.
Sharma, Ishaan. May 18, 2012. "Lesson for Life: Shankar Made Me Smile as I Slogged," *The Hindu*.
Vajpeyi, Ananya. May 16, 2012. "Critical Struggle," *The Telegraph*.
Yadav, Yogendra. May 14, 2012. "Dangers of Deletion," *The Indian Express*.

# 11

# Writing Humiliation, Righting Humiliation: Marking the Dalit Moment in the History of India's Untouchables and Beyond

*Tapan Basu*

Middle class (that is upper caste middle class) opinion in our country has been notoriously unsympathetic, if not totally hostile, toward Dalit social aspirations. From the crass lionization in the media and on other public fora of the self-immolating 'martyrs' of the anti-Mandal, anti-caste-based reservations agitation of 1990 to the endless jibes at the expense of Mayawati's megalomaniacal tendencies, Dalit achievements, whether realized or promised, are always sought to be underplayed as being the underserved rewards of vote-bank-oriented political engineering.

It is against this background that I wish to examine the phenomenon of Dalit hurt, most recently foregrounded through protests on the issue of the 'whipping of Ambedkar' cartoon which featured in an NCERT (the state-administered National Council of Educational Research and Training)–published Political Science textbook. The fact that the indignation aroused among large sections of the Dalit intelligentsia by the cartoon was vociferous and sustained (resulting in the government decision to withdraw the offending cartoon from the textbook) is an indication of heightened Dalit sensitivity to humiliation (intended or otherwise) in contemporary times. I use the word humiliation, in the sense that Gopal Guru understands it, as a claim to a feeling of devaluation or degradation. This claim, according to Guru, makes resistance an intrinsic component of a hurt experienced as a hurt. To quote Guru:

> Resistance is internal to humiliation, since humiliation does not get defined unless it is claimed, it naturally involves the capacity to protest. A society or a group with socially dead people would not offer any space for resistance against humiliation. In such cases, people lack the minimum moral capacity to take risk. Risk is motivational and leads a person to make sacrifices in favour of higher goods like the right to appear in public without a sense of shame. Those who seek to exercise this civil right would always run the risk of inciting opposition from those who want to push these people to the margins. (Guru, 2009)

The articulation of humiliation, therefore, I would argue, following Guru, is symptomatic of the arrival of the Dalit moment in the history of India's 'untouchables', a moment in which the 'untouchable' ceases to be an object of maltreatment and becomes instead the subject of negotiation of her/his historically downtrodden condition. I would like to invoke here the dualistic connotations of the term 'Dalit' as remarked upon by Eleanor Zelliot in the "Introduction" to the third edition of her book, *From Untouchable to Dalit: Essays on the Ambedkar Movement*:

> Just last year I was asked by some highly educated followers of Dr. Ambedkar if I was going to do a book called "From Untouchable to Buddhist," since this group resented the term Dalit as negative, even demeaning. I replied that I could not, since not all Dalits were Buddhist, and that the term Dalit was not only to be interpreted as "the oppressed," but also as "the proud, the defiant." (Zelliot, 2001)

In my paper, I will begin with an analysis of two pieces of writing, one each by a so-called upper caste and a so-called lower caste writer, in which the two contrary, even contradictory, configurations of the Dalit self (highlighted by Eleanor Zelliot) are respectively projected—the latter an extract from *Joothan,* the celebrated autobiography of Dalit author, Om Prakash Valmiki, and the former the equally celebrated short story, "Sadgati," by the progressive author Premchand. I shall read these two texts as illustration, by turn, of what I shall designate as the pre-humiliation and the post-humiliation modes of representation of the untouchable as protagonist in Indian literature.

Written in the 1930s, before free India's enactment of a 'modern' constitution for itself, "Sadgati" is an eminent example of what Sisir Kumar Das has described as "narratives of suffering," through which phrase he alluded to all discursive engagements with the miseries of India's outcastes undertaken from a liberal, benevolent, upper-caste point of view. The protagonist, appropriately called Dukhi, is a hapless victim of caste laws which inscribe his everyday existence as a poor tanner. His sense of self (or rather the lack of it) is constituted by the observance of these laws as are the selfhoods of his oppressors, the Pandit and the Panditayin. On opposite sides of the great divide of pollution norms which enforce a mandate of segregation upon them, the Brahmans and the *Chamar* are nevertheless united by their shared subjection to the dictates of caste, evident, most of all, in their deep dread of caste violation. Their mutual resistance to proximity is recorded in the story through an exaggerated body language of fear articulated by both Dukhi and the Pandit and the Panditayin. As Premchand portrays their plight neither operates through free agency and are equally hostages to the inflexible caste codes which they stringently uphold.

But try as they might to steer clear of each other's path, they are inevitably drawn to each other by the requirement of particular services which only particular castes can provide within the framework of caste—founded demarcation of labor in their society. In this respect, needless to state, as per the structure of 'graded inequality' that caste erects, the Brahmans have an undoubted advantage over the untouchable because of the specialized dispensation at their command, the exquisite gift of grace, and therefore extract a heavy price for agreeing to oblige the 'worthless' Dukhi.

Dukhi's 'worthlessness' is, indeed, dinned into his consciousness not only by the strenuous tasks he is made to perform, which finally lead to his inhuman end, but also by the extremely derogatory conversation about himself between the Brahmans which he is forced to overhear.

Panditji was eating and his wife said, "Who's that man asking for a light?"

"It's only that damned little Dukhi, the tanner. I told him to cut some wood. The fires' lit, so give him his light."

Frowning, the Panditayain said, "You've become so wrapped up in your books and astrological charts that you've forgotten all about caste rules. If there's a tanner or a washerman or a birdcatcher, why he can just come walking right into the house as though he owned it. You'd think it was an inn and not a decent Hindu's house. Tell that good-for-nothing to get out or I'll scorch his face with a firebrand."

Trying to calm her down, Panditji said,

"He's come inside—so what? Nothing that belongs to you has been stolen. The floor is clean, it hasn't been desecrated. Why not just let him have his light?—he's doing our work, isn't he? You'd have to pay at least four annas if you hired some labourer to split it."

Losing her temper, the Panditayin said, "What does he mean coming into this house?"

"It was the son of a bitch's bad luck, what else?" the Pandit said.

"It's all right," she said. "This time I'll give him his fire, but if he ever comes into the house again like that I'll give him the coals in his face." (Premchand, 2006)

Fragments of this conversation reach Dukhi's ears. Yet he does not retaliate.

... He repented: It was a mistake to come. She was speaking the truth –how could a tanner ever come into a Brahman's house? These people were clean and holy, that was why the whole world worshipped and respected them. A mere tanner was absolutely nothing. He had all his life lived in the village without understanding this before. (Premchand, 2006)

Dukhi's utter servility towards the Brahmans forecloses any occasion for his humiliation at their hands. To cite Gopal Guru once again, a servile person cannot be humiliated because "servility necessarily postpones the possibility of an insight into humiliation; it exists because ... the servile person lacks the capacity to aspire for self-respect." In other words, "a person who lacks self-respect, and does not aspire to attain it, cannot be humiliated" (Guru, 2009).

From this perspective, no humiliation registers on Dukhi, but the many ways in which his oppressors attempt to undermine his human dignity are noted by his ally, the Gond, who is an ubiquitous spectator of the entire episode of the ruthless abuse of Dukhi by the Pandit and the Panditayin. The Gond is a most interesting subsidiary character in the plot, a disembodied presence, unlike the Brahmans and the tanner, whose detailed body maps unambiguously pronounce their caste standings. Outraged by the persecution of the tanner, the Gond sympathizes with him, and again and again instigates him to rebel.

> In the meantime, the Gond came. He said, "Why are you wearing yourself out, old friend? You can whack it all you like but you won't split this trunk. You're killing yourself for nothing."
>
> Wiping the sweat from his forehead, Dukhi said. "I've still got to cart off a whole wagon of hay, brother."
>
> "Have you had anything to eat? Or are they just making you work without feeding you? Why don't you ask them for something?"
>
> "How can you expect me to digest a Brahman's food, Chikuri?"
>
> "Digesting it is no problem, you have to get it first. He sits in there and eats like a king and then has a nice little nap after he tells you that you have to split his wood. The government officials may force you to work for them but they pay you something for it, no matter how little. This fellow's gone one better, calling himself a holy man." (Premchand, 2006)

The Gond's confidence evidently derives from the fact that he is one of the adivasis. To refer to Susan Bayly's statement in her monograph, *Caste, Society, and Politics in India,* such a figure would be an outsider to the framework of Hinduism's varnavyavastha (Bayly, 1999). It is his location "outside the fold" (to borrow B.R. Ambedkar's phrase from another context) which allows for his bold opposition to the atrocities committed upon Dukhi. Quite obviously, the Gond remains a significant excess over the Gandhian world—a view usually applauded in Premchand's writings.

The subversive interrogator of caste hierarchies, the person who inhabits the peripheries of the narrative in "Sadgati" is, in *Joothan,* at the narrative's centre, and is the downtrodden—the Dalit—person himself. Here the interrogation stems from the Dalit's own realization of the exploitativeness of the equations between himself and his traditionally decreed superiors in society. I refer, specifically, to the incident within this record of "A Dalit's life" in which the Dalit protagonist finds his aspirations to an education baulked by intentional intimidation from a prejudiced headmaster. Kaliram, the headmaster of the village school which the child Om Prakash Valmiki attends, time and time again tries to debase the child in front of his peers by forcing him to 'live up' to his caste—decreed calling as a sweeper.

> "Chuhre ka?" Headmaster threw his question at me.
>
> "Ji"

"All right.... See that teak tree there? Go climb that tree. Break some twigs and make a broom and sweep the whole school clean as a mirror. It is, after all, your family occupation."

"Go ... get to it."

Obeying Headmaster's orders, I cleaned all the rooms and the verandas. Just as I was about to finish, he came to me and said. "After you have swept the rooms, go and sweep the playground."

The playground was way larger than my small physique could handle and in cleaning it my back began to ache.... (Valmiki, 2006)

It is on the third day of his daily ordeal that Om Prakash is spotted at his ignominious toils by his father. His father turns out to be an exemplary figure of humiliation on this occasion, encoding both defiance and pride in his response to oppression.

Pitaji snatched the broom from my hand and threw it away. His eyes were blazing. Pitaji who was always taut as a bowstring in front of others was so angry that his dense moustache was fluttering. He began to scream.

"Who is that teacher, that progeny of Dronacharya, who forces my son to sweep?"

Pitaji's voice had echoed through the whole school. All the teachers, along with the headmaster, came out. Kaliram, the headmaster, threatened my father and called him names. But his threats had no effect on Pitaji....

The headmaster had roared, "Take him away from here.... The Chuhra wants him educated.... Go, go.... Otherwise I will have your bones broken."

Pitaji took my hand and started walking towards our home. As he walked away, he said, loudly enough for the headmaster to hear, "You are a teacher.... So I am leaving now. But remember this much, Master.... This Chuhre Ka will study right here in the school. And not just him, but there will be more coming after him." (Valmiki, 2006)

Pitaji's audacity in speaking back to the headmaster enfranchizes Omprakash from the awe in which he has thus far held the man. Henceforth for him, the incarnation of Dronacharya is no more than the replica of a "snorting wild boar with his snout up in the air" (Valmiki, 2006).

The emergence of the Dalit as a political subject, signaled by the dramatic outburst of Pitaji in *Joothan*, though a relatively novel development in the literary scene of India (perhaps no older than the Dalit Panthers movement in Maharashtra of the 1970s), was by no means a late 20th century occurrence in the Indian public domain. Its lineage stretches back to the century's early decades, especially to the arrival of Ambedkar on to an arena of contending pre-nationalist and nationalist ideologies, and his efforts to construct an axis of Dalit solidarity, to begin with in Maharashtra, out of collective violation of the strictures and structures of caste.

The *Mahad Satyagraha*, staged in the precincts of the Chavadar Lake at Mahad in December, 1927, was a pilot project in this direction. An outline of the project was plotted by Ambedkar before a substantial gathering of members of several 'untouchable' castes, dominated of course by the Mahars, his own caste fellows. The ostensible aim of the project was to win for the 'untouchables' the hitherto forbidden right to draw water from the Chavadar Lake. But its actual purpose was what Gopal Guru has denominated as the "rejection of rejection" (Guru, 2009) or the foregrounding of self-respect of the Dalits.

> It is not as if drinking the water of the Chavadar Lake will make us immortal. We have survived well enough all these days without drinking it. We are not going to the Chavadar Lake merely to drink its water. We are going to the Lake to assert that we too are human beings like others. It must be clear that this meeting has been called to set up the norm of equality. (Ambedkar, 2009)

Ambedkar was clear, however, even at that somewhat triumphalist moment for his nascent movement of the insufficiency of a Dalit agenda limited to the issue of self-respect or the "rejection of rejection." For was not the sense of hurt which proceeded out of reduction or denial of the humanity of the Dalit to be assuaged by removal of the cause of hurt itself rather than just of its symptoms?

> Some of you may feel that since we are untouchables, it is enough if we are set free from the prohibition of inter drinking and social intercourse. That we need not concern ourselves with the caste system; how does it matter if it remains? In my opinion this is a total error. If we adopt only the removal of untouchability as our policy, people will say we have chosen a low aim. To raise men, aspiration is needed as much as outward efforts. Indeed it is to be doubted whether efforts are possible without aspiration. Hence, if a great effort is to be made, a great aspiration must be nursed. In adopting an aspiration, one need not be abashed or deterred by doubts about one's power to satisfy it. One should be ashamed only of mean aspirations; not of failure that may result because one's aspiration is high. If untouchability alone is removed, we may change from ati-shudras to shudras; but can we say that this radically removes untouchability? If such puny reforms as the removal of restrictions on social intercourse, etc. were enough for the

eradication of untouchability, I would not have suggested that the caste system itself must go. (Ambedkar, 2009)

In other words, according to Ambedkar, nothing short of the "annihilation of caste" would eliminate the persistence of casteism, the everyday rehearsal of the script of asymmetrical associations between the non-Dalits and the Dalits. It is, therefore, essential for the Dalit to think beyond the epistemology of humiliation in order to rescue herself/himself from a perpetual futurity of Dalithood.

The invocation of the idea behind the French National Assembly, convened in 1789, was meant to offer his audience a profile of a democratic community founded on the ideals of liberty, equality, and fraternity. He presented this to his followers as a model social order which Dalits could aspire to inhabit.

But acutely aware as he was of adverse social realities, he nevertheless spent the years between 1927 and 1936, the year in which he published the tract entitled, "Annihilation of Caste", struggling to ensure enactment of legislative/administrative measures for the rectification of Dalit disabilities. It was a difficult mission at the best of times, but the worst of hours, no doubt, was the hour in September, 1932, at which he was forced to withdraw his demand for Separate (Dalit) Electorates in favor of Joint Electorates proposed by the Congress leadership. Gandhi, who had accorded the matter of the electorates a life-and-death dimension by going on an indefinite fast against Separate Electorates, remained famously obdurate in his stance of condescension.

> The possible consequences of separate electorates for Harijans fill me with horror. Separate electorates for all other communities will still leave room for me to deal with them, but I have no other means to deal with the untouchables. These poor fellows will ask why I who claim to be their friend should offer *satyagraha* simply because they were granted some privileges: they would vote separately but vote with me. They do not realize that the separate electorates will create division among Hindus so much as it will lead to bloodshed. Untouchable hooligans will make common cause with Muslim hooligans and kill Caste Hindus. Has the British Government no idea of all this? (Zelliot, 1922)

The hurt was palpable in Ambedkar's rejoinder to Gandhi.

> It would have been justifiable if Mr. Gandhi had resorted to this extreme step [the indefinite fast] for obtaining independence for the country on which

he was so insistent all through the Round Table Conference debates.... It is also a painful surprise that Mr. Gandhi should have singled out special representation of the Depressed Classes in the Communal Award as an excuse for self-immolation. The Mahatma is not an immortal person, nor the Congress.... Mahatmas have come and Mahatmas have gone. But the untouchables have remained as untouchables. (Ambedkar, 2009)

And it is because he believed that the untouchables would remain untouchables, notwithstanding all reform within Hinduism, he announced with great sorrow at a Depressed Classes Conference held at Yeola, in October, 1935.

[the] indignities we had to put up with, were the result of our being the members of the Hindu community. Will it not be better for us to leave that fold and embrace a new faith that would give us equal status, a secure position and rightful treatment? I advise you to sever your connection with Hinduism and to embrace any other religion. But, in doing so, be careful in choosing the new faith and see that equality of treatment, status and opportunities will be guaranteed to you unreservedly.... Unfortunately for me I was born a Hindu Untouchable. It was beyond my power to prevent that, but I declare that it is within my power to refuse to live under ignoble and humiliating conditions. I solemnly assure you that I will not die a Hindu.[1]

In the "Annihilation of Caste", his last address to a Hindu audience (Vishwanathan, 1998) brought out in print the following year, he reiterated the same resolve, exhorting Hindus to re-invent their religion in accordance with modern republican notions. As for his own role in this deserved transformation, he volunteered all possible assistance to them toward the achievement of the goal.

Much has been discussed about certain crucial, but curiously ambiguous, aspects of Ambedkar's conversion, and the discussion on these continues till today.

(1) Why did he wait for two decades to execute his conversion decision?

(2) Why was the decision executed even after the Constituent Assembly, of which he was a very, very influential member, had drafted into the Indian Constitution, a series of measures aimed at the amelioration of the numerous kinds of disadvantages from which the "untouchables" of India customarily suffered?

[1] Quoted in Zelliot (2004).

(3) Why did he and his followers decide to convert to a newly-initiated, iconoclastic, religious system rather than opt to join one of the several established frameworks of religion which were waiting eagerly to embrace them into their respective folds?

The answers to the above questions are probably as follows:

(1) Ambedkar dealt with hurt, his hurt as a Dalit, with neither impetuosity nor petulance, but with characteristically careful deliberation.
(2) His sticking to his resolve to detach himself from his Hindu belonging, despite the inclusion in the Constitution, chiefly at his own instigation, of a range of affirmative action policies to compensate for centuries of Dalit disenfranchisement indicated a determination to entirely forsake the premises of identification as a Dalit. As Gauri Vishwanathan has explained, in opting out of the Hindu fold with his followers, Ambedkar sought to rescue Dalits from the perennial tag of downtroddenness which they were forced to wear, whether as outcasts or as the scheduled castes of Hinduism, and to confer on them a religious identity of their own.[17]
(3) Ambedkar's choice of Navayana Buddhism as the faith to which Dalits must convert was a statement on his part about the need for his people to steer clear of the orthodoxies of established religions, and in particular, the orthodoxy which was commonest to them all, that is the orthodoxy which upheld the other—worldly determination of wordly affairs. The notion of human agency was crucial to Ambedkar's theology, and along with it a belief in the ability of human beings to alter their own circumstances and that of others for the better. The image of an eternal underdog would be anathema to Ambedkar's vision of Dalit destiny (Vishwanathan, 1998).

# References

Ambedkar, B.R. 2009. "Speech at Mahad on 25 December, 1927," in *Poisoned Bread*, edited by Arjun Dangle. New Edition. Hyderabad: Orient Blackswan Private Limited, p. 259.

Ambedkar, B.R. "What Congress and Gandhi have done to the Untouchables." Appendix iv, Statement of Ambedkar on fast by Gandhi. *Dr Babasaheb Ambedkar: Writings and Speeches,* 9: 315.

Bayly, Susan. 1999. *Caste, Society and Politics in India.* Cambridge, UK: Cambridge University Press, p. 9.

Guru, Gopal. 2009. *Introduction: Theorising Humiliation,* in*Humiliation: Claims and Contexts,* edited by Gopal Guru. New Delhi: Oxford University Press, p. 18.

Premchand. 2006. *Deliverance* (Translated from the original by David Rubin), in *The Individual and Society: Essays, Stories and Poems.* Noida: Doris Kindersley India Pvt. Ltd., p. 19.

Valmiki, Om Prakash. 2006. "Joothan. A Dalit's Life," an extract from the book, trans. Arun Prabha Mukhejee, in *The Individual and Society: Essays. Stories and Poems.* Noida: Doris Kindersley India Pvt. Ltd., pp. 31–32.

Vishwanathan, Gauri. 1998. *Outside the Fold*: *Conversion, Modernity and Belief.* New Delhi: Oxford University Press.

Zelliot, Eleanor. 2001. *From Untouchable to Dalit: Essays on the Ambedkar Movement,* 3rd edition. New Delhi: Manohar Publishers and Distributors, p. v.

——— 1922. "Gandhi and Ambedkar: A Study in Leadership," in *The Untouchables in Contemporary India,* edited by J.M. Mahar. Tuscom, AZ: The University of Arizona Press, p. 85.

——— 2004. *Babasaheb Ambedkar and the Untouchable Movement.* New Delhi: Blumoon Books, p. 152.

# Knowledge and Its Dis/Contents

# 12

# Sense and Sentimentality: A Political Fable

*Sunalini Kumar*

## I

A cartoon depicting B.R. Ambedkar and Jawaharlal Nehru first published in 1949 and reproduced recently in a political science textbook published by the National Council for Education Research and Training (NCERT) became the subject of a furious political controversy in 2012. The cartoon was held by a number of individuals, civil society groups, and political leaders to be humiliating to Ambedkar and to Dalits, in general; eventually, the 'Ambedkar cartoon controversy' reached the debating chambers of the Indian Parliament, with some opposition leaders demanding an immediate withdrawal of the textbook with the offending cartoon.

In some ways, this was an unusual set of events—for, first, the Indian Parliament is not in the habit routinely of debating pedagogical matters, especially relating to specific content in school textbooks. Second, the then Human Resources Development minister Kapil Sibal took an uncommonly responsive stance to the Opposition's demand for a review of the textbook as a whole, eventually ordering such an exercise. I say uncommon because the cartoon was offending not to Nehru but to Ambedkar, a national leader who has never been well accommodated in the Congress pantheon, while of course Nehru is the fount of the nation in the mainstream historiography that the Congress party is steeped in. Indeed, the timing of the HRD ministry's intervention in the cartoon controversy, wedged between elections in Uttar Pradesh (the only state with a Dalit chief minister, and one which the ruling Congress party was seeking to gain a foothold in), and the ongoing struggle between University teachers and the Ministry over structural reforms within Indian universities was, to say the very least, interesting. Since the advisors to the textbook committee were in fact not school but University professors, by ordering a review of the textbooks, and thereby overriding the authorial autonomy of the textbook advisors, the Ministry was possibly hoping to kill two birds with one stone, disciplining university teachers and appealing to the expressly vocalized dissent of Dalits.

There is much else that can be said about the Ambedkar cartoon controversy; however, this paper takes as its provocation not the specific contours of this political event, rich as they may be, but the politics of hurt sentiment in general. There is much that bears closer examination as far as the politics of hurt sentiment as a political *thing,* as a material creature in contemporary politics is concerned. For one, as a form of politics, 'hurt sentiment' is deeply irruptive, possessing a charge that allows it to rupture and reshape the boundaries of political debate as they are drawn at that historical moment. Indeed, it appears remarkable that something as intimate, vaporous and delicate-sounding as sentiment—hurt as it may be—has come to acquire such political weight and salience in a contemporary political sphere that has been crafted around rather muscular, masculine norms—whether liberal or illiberal in their soul. What accounts for its dramatic power and particularly its capacity to strain at the seams of the liberal social contract? These are intractable questions, made more intractable by the variety and contingency of political situations that encompass the politics of hurt sentiments. To the consternation of those interested in a reasonable, rational, or at the very least legible or coherent politics, the politics of hurt sentiment appears to lend itself to political causes and objectives that belong nowhere under the same roof.

As a result perhaps of these qualities, as has occurred in innumerable instances, in the Ambedkar cartoon controversy too, a dynamic emerges wherein the hurt sentiments of the particular (community) are set up against civil liberties including the right to free speech of the general (public). Those inhabiting a liberal public sphere and its concomitant imaginative horizon have of course defended the latter, often eloquently and convincingly. However, this seldom has the intended effect, since the particularity of the sentiment that is hurt seems to only be further insulted by a generalized defense of free speech—this then becomes even more so about what Charles Taylor and Amy Gutmann have termed, a demand for recognition as much as for redressal (Taylor and Gutmann, 1992). Others have responded to this dynamic by invoking the prisms of authenticity and agency, in other words, by distinguishing a 'genuinely' hurt sentiment from one that is simply 'opportunism' or 'cynical politics'. Doing so would require isolating the 'original' hurt subject from the agencies that speak in its name – civil society bodies, special interest groups or community representatives. This distinction has been productive in identifying power structures within communities and dismantling authoritative voices that muffle alternate expressions of community and/or individual identity. However, there are times when such an exercise may fail to recognize the fluid and performative nature of identity formation in politics, insisting uni-tonally on the prior existence of the authentic agent to engender an authentic politics, and refusing to concede the possibility of meaningfully speaking for another, politically.

Perhaps it would help to take the historical rootedness of this form of politics more seriously, to trace its modern origins. A clue as to where to begin such an exercise is provided by a final peculiarity of this mode of politics that I mention here—that sentiment only appears to become public when it is always already 'hurt' thus it appears as a political reality simultaneous to its being wounded; and never previous to it. Surely, hurt is not the *sine qua non* of sentiment, surely there are non hurt sentiments. To enter these difficulties, I seek to first inquire what exactly constitutes 'sentiment' in political life; from there we may inquire into how it comes to appear in public-political life as a 'hurt sentiment'. I argue in the following pages that the politics of hurt sentiment needs to be placed firmly within the history of liberalism, that in particular it may be understood in the context of the disappearance of the language of sentiment from liberalism and the modern liberal state and public sphere. The politics of hurt sentiment is a politics about propinquity. Stated more clearly, it is a form of political thought and action that operates on the axes of distance and proximity, visibilizing, vocalizing, and interrogating the distance of the liberal state and public sphere. That distance most often manifests as liberal neutrality; however, as becomes startlingly obvious in the polemicized debate that emerges around 'defending' liberal values against particular hurt sentiments, it is not neutrality at all but in fact a particular placement of (political) objects in space and time; one may even say an arrangement of intimacies that are sanctioned by the overarching idea of neutrality.

To say this is of course to simply restate or extend the standard Marxist argument about the non-neutrality of the bourgeois state in terms of class. I will argue that in the arena of culture and identity as well, the liberal understanding of neutrality is really a (still-shaky) triumph of particular political behaviors that have over a period of time been consecrated as neutrality or impartiality. That impartiality however, overlays a much more concrete arrangement of political subjects and objects that are sanctioned within liberal societies as legitimate politics. It is beyond the scope of this chapter to investigate the full history of this 'arrangement of intimacies' as we have termed it, but we may productively explore the career of the idea and language of sentiment within this production of neutrality. Stated directly, my argument is as follows. The liberal state accommodated the idea of sentiment and nourished the sentimental mode of address and redress in public-political life far more copiously at a critical epoch in the modern period, allowing it to arrive at a specific social contract that accommodated some identities and grievances, but not others. The use of the language of sentiment however, opened up radical possibilities for reinventing the liberal public sphere and even more strikingly, the liberal legal-juridical framework in a way that is unimaginable today. Further, the *disappearance* of the sentimental mode of address in public-political life may have led to the gradual *appearance* of the politics of hurt sentiment in the same. Of course, an appeal to sentiment is not the same thing as an appeal to hurt sentiment in terms of historical trajectories; but I will return to that distinction at the end of the paper.

# II

Let us begin stating here that sense and sentimentality have an old and forgotten association. That association is most urgently demonstrated in the context of Anglo-American liberal humanitarian interventionism—I refer specifically to writing on slavery in the slave-holding and trading economies of Britain and the United States, and to an extent, in other European imperial powers. Through the 18th and 19th centuries, appeals to sentiment were commonplace in the arsenal of rights campaigners—most prominently with the Quakers and the Abolitionists. It is significant, however, that such appeals needed to be accommodated within an emerging liberal humanist discourse that affected the court and the Parliament alike. Free of the excessively self-conscious secularism that was a hallmark of latter-day jurisprudence, campaigners alternated between Christian and secular arguments, between cool appraisal and fervent appeal, between Reason and Sentiment. As early as the 17th century in fact, as Ramesh Mallipeddi has shown in his recent study of the novel *Oroonoko* by Aphra Behn, there was a complex political, esthetic and moral interplay at work in the late 17th century that effectively used sentiment and spectacle to humanize the slave body and bring it into the ambit of human rights (Mallipeddi, 2012). *Oroonoko*—a novel that enjoyed great repute on publication and continued to be reprinted and performed on stage through the following century—was the story of an African prince sold into slavery. Mallipeddi reminds us of the specific, embodied nature of the sympathy Behn generated toward the eponymous hero, Oroonoko. It was toward the individual Oroonoko—handsome, aristocratic, and tortured—and not a generalized sympathy toward *all* slaves. However, it was precisely the narrative device of the embodied white (aristocratic) female gazing upon the embodied black (aristocratic) male that generated a 'militant sympathy' in readers quite unlike the more impersonal humanitarian campaigns of the following century. No wonder, Mallipeddi writes, Behn's novel was ensured a place in subsequent anti-slavery and humanitarian campaigns.

Mallipeddi writes

> Behn's sentimentalization of slavery is contemporaneous with and yet fundamentally distinct from what David Brion Davis has described as the "Christianization of Negro slavery" in the latter half of the seventeenth century. At that time, Protestant and Quaker authors attempted to make the economic exploitation of African slaves a "moral problem" for English culture…. (Mallipeddi, 2012)

Behn's was a sympathy full of contradictions, even flaws if viewed through contemporary eyes—not only was Oroonoko an extraordinary subject in being of royal lineage among his own people as mentioned, but Behn humanized his black body only by subliminally sexualizing it and placing it among the shining objects that may be obtained for a price from the Caribbean island in which the novel is set. Mallipeddi, thus, suggests that the intensity of sympathy that could be generated for a slave must be set off against the enormous commodity fetishism afforded by European colonization of the 'wild' Caribbean, where all objects—human, beastly, and artificial—could be bought and sold. The degradation of one such beautiful natural object, inhabitant of a prelapsarian Eden, thus becomes for the consumers of Behn's novel, an occasion for empathic horror.[1]

Returning to the question of sentiment, and further of spectacle, a footnote in Mallipeddi's essay provides a clue to the mechanisms by which sympathy was produced in the English aristocratic or bourgeois public of the 17th and 18th centuries. Referring to Bridget Orr's *Empire on the English Stage 1660–1714* (Orr, 2001), Mallipeddi highlights the importance of the device of movable scenery in creating a "pleasurable assimilation of exoticism":

> Scenic background in theater and descriptive detail in narrative appear to function analogously during this period, since the scene performed the function of description in prose fiction insofar as it provided a background to the action … the use of the movable scenery offered a visual translation of the topography … the accuracy of the topographical scenes, their perspectival organization, and their esthetic enticement by the frieze, which framed the interior images like paintings, all encouraged the spectator in a pleasurable assimilation of the exoticism represented. (Mallipeddi, 2012; footnote 16).

It is this "pleasurable assimilation of the exoticism represented" that characterizes Behn's novel too, which begins with a description of the fantastic landscape of the Caribbean island in which Oroonoko's capture and torture would take place. At all times, the reader is lulled into a sensual excess, one which goes a long way in producing the shock of sympathy for the principal character—otherwise black-skinned and

---

[1] It is noteworthy that Oroonoko's wife Imoinda remains a slave-commodity for the plantation owners and even for Behn. When she is removed from the scene of Oroonoko's torture and execution, it is not so much with regard to her own emotions as with the necessity of preserving her physically and mentally for further work. A female slave was too precious to be lost to grief, even at her own husband's inhuman death.

unfamiliar. The footnote on the theatrical devices of the Restoration drama and its relation to the novel also, however, underscores the importance of perspective, and this is where we return to sentiment as a relational category in modern Anglo-American liberal humanitarianism.

# III

Contrary to the word's connotations in the contemporary world (where it is seen as having an affinity to, and even synonymous with the more personal and privatized universe of *emotions*), sentiment in the 17th and 18th centuries was a mode of feeling which was believed specifically to be an attribute of civilized folk; and civility by definition was a *relational* quality. In saying this, I bring attention to the two-pronged target of the discourse of civilization. While this discourse undeniably differentiated the white man from the black, brown, red, and yellow, it also lent itself to being used by anti-slavery campaigners to differentiate between one white man and the other in the manner of how they treated the Other—the poor man or the black slave. The idea of *sentiment* was critical to this process—it was precisely its cultivated and not primordial nature that made it such a fiery ally of the discourse of humanism and civilization. Sentiment could be married to the finer senses and values in a manner that shamed fellow citizens and undercut the thorny legal defenses of slavery launched by slave-owners and conservatives (Marx, 1843).[2] Sentiment indeed *structured* the liberal social contract to a degree that still remains relevant for human rights campaigners, but routed through a more generalized moral discourse. Perhaps the slave narrative was central to the habilitation of sentiment within the modern liberal imagination. An example is Ottobah Cugoano's "Thoughts and Sentiments on the Evil and Wicked Traffic of the Slavery and Commerce of the Human Species, Humbly Submitted to the Inhabitants of Great-Britain" (1999) which enjoyed considerable

---

[2] "Shame", as Marx famously noted, "is a revolution of a kind in itself". (Letter from Marx to Arnold Ruge in Dresden; first Published: Deutsch-Französische Jahrbücher, 1844; pp. unknown.)

success upon publication.[3] I do not wish to suggest that the use of the sentiments was timeless. The particular association of sentiment with civility, anti-slavery campaigns, Christian goodwill, liberalism, and natural justice was deeply contingent upon the emerging conditions of the 18th century Europe and the New World. However, the argument here is that for a significant period in Anglo-American political thought, the trope of sentiment was a powerful call to humanitarian intervention, even to reason itself. It was deployed copiously in the institutions of the liberal state to speak of the Other in a deeply interpersonally structured public sphere; in a sense it was the invocation of perspective vis-à-vis others. Other developments helped too, certainly. Mallipeddi conjectures that

> … with the rise of the intimate public sphere, the growth of print culture, and perhaps more crucially, the gradual feminization of ideology in the following (eighteenth) century, individual acts of sympathy began to enter, via writing, the political realm. And the concerns raised by Behn's novella about the political efficacy of sympathy—its capacity for engaging with individual misery as opposed to generic suffering—resurface with increasing frequency throughout the eighteenth century, in contexts as diverse as Mr Spectator's tearful reaction to Yarico's enslavement in Richard Steele's version of the Yarico–Inkle story in *Spectator 11* (1713), and Yorick's earnest but unsuccessful attempt to imagine the distress of the incarcerated slave body in Laurence Sterne's *A Sentimental Journey* (1768). (Mallipeddi, 2012)

The latter novel is of course arguably the foundational text within its genre of the sentimental novel. Daniel Gross in a recent essay on modern developments in the humanities argues that the invocation of sympathy in Sterne's novel depends on distancing techniques familiar to a landscape artist; in other words, it is a particular use of perspective that produces the sympathetic sentiment—not only with regard to the "incarcerated slave body" but also toward "poor, patient, honest, quiet" peasants (Gross, 2012). Commenting on a canonical passage in which

---

[3] Further, as Anthony Bogues has noted in his *Black Heretics*, in adopting the language of the masters against the practices of the masters, the slave always risked a profound disconnect and alienation from his own experiences. In Bogues' language, he found that once he had adopted the "discursive boxes" of Western political thought, he may find with W.E.B. DuBois that, "In the folds of this European civilization I was born and shall die, imprisoned, conditioned, depressed, exalted and inspired. Integrally a part of, and yet, of much more significance, one of its rejected parts" (DuBois, quoted in Bogues: 14).

the narrator Yorick chances upon an impoverished peasant family, Gross argues that it is not accidental that Yorick remains far away from the scene in a situation of spectatorship, a condition that is essential to the production of pity toward the "poor, patient, quiet, honest people." The fact that this is not the self-perception of the peasants themselves, but of the narrator seems to be well appreciated by Sterne, as Gross elaborates below.[4]

> Nowhere in this scene do we find suggestive documentation of face-to-face encounters; in fact, the pathos of this scene thrives on a variety of distancing mechanisms familiar to the landscape artist and the critical theorist, respectively... Immediately following upon a "feast of love" at the table of a large and respectful French peasant family (S, p. 119), this scene of partial spectatorship restages the classically tragic sequence that moves from horror to pity as a critical opportunity (as we will see below), not as a virtual experience. Yorick's pitiful perspective can only be understood against a romanticized landscape that includes—along with sweet dwellings—"poor, patient, quiet, honest people" who would no doubt have a very different perspective on the situation, if asked. And I imagine most of this situational complexity, including its class element, is not lost on the ingenious author, who earlier outlines the terms of a "sentimental commerce" in which "sentiment is produced not by natural immediacy but by the imbalance of social "exchange (S, p. 9). (Gross, 2010: 56 [emphasis mine])

It is interesting that while Mallipeddi believes Sterne's novel followed in the footsteps of Behn's in the previous century in mobilizing sympathy for individual misery versus generic suffering, Gross believes that it is precisely the facelessness of the peasant family that generates the sympathetic sentiment in the (bourgeois) traveler Yorick. Both emphasize the use of perspective, however. We may turn to an unlikely source for illumination. Adam Smith (1976), who Gross sarcastically refers to as the "patron saint of universal emotion" in the same essay, revised his work *Theory of Moral Sentiments* (hereafter, *TMS*) toward the end of his life. Not surprisingly, a bulk of this work is dedicated to establishing the essential selfishness of human beings, thereby confirming Gross's judgment of him. In all his works, Smith paints a picture of a post-feudal, mercantilist-capitalist universe in which disorder continually threatens the relation between

---

[4] It would be relevant to mention here that Lawrence Sterne was socially acquainted with Ignatius Sancho—the author of one of the best-known slave narratives.

classes, fabulous fortunes are to be made and lost, and competition is becoming a 'natural' law. However, it would be difficult to ignore the almost obsessive concern displayed by the patron saint of universal emotion (and at least one of the saints of what C.B. Macpherson has termed "possessive individualism") regarding overall social balance, harmony, and indeed, 'propriety'. While the warp of Smith's thesis is the universalizing language that became the hallmark of liberalism in latter ages, the intricately woven weft is a bourgeois patriarch's anxiety regarding the effects that individual actions may have on others. Reading Smith now in the 21st century, one cannot help notice that his world was structured deeply by notions of good behavior, manners, and form; indeed, by Christianity. Let us begin with the more familiar ideas of Smith; in the following passage he argues that a person's reaction to external stimuli is conditioned by their individual tastes, habits, and "acuteness of the faculty of the mind":

> The beauty of a plain, the greatness of a mountain, the ornaments of a building, the expression of a picture, the composition of a discourse, the conduct of a third person, the proportions of different quantities and numbers, the various appearances which the great machine of the universe is perpetually exhibiting, with the secret wheels and springs which produce them; all the general subjects of science and taste, are what we and our companion regard as having no peculiar relation to either of us. We both look at them from the same point of view, and we have no occasion for sympathy, or for that imaginary change of situations from which it arises, in order to produce, with regard to these, the most perfect harmony of sentiments and affections. If, notwithstanding, we are often differently affected, it arises either from the different degrees of attention, which our different habits of life allow us to give easily to the several parts of those complex objects, or from the different degrees of natural acuteness in the faculty of the mind to which they are addressed. (*TMS*, pages 14–15)

Unsurprisingly, Smith believes that individuals have no sympathy for others if they cannot relate to their suffering. This is in marked contrast to the sentimental or spectacular-sympathetic modes adopted by Behn or Sterne. However, for Smith, the matter doesn't end there—the sentiments we feel are and must be constantly subjected to judgment by others.

> The sentiment or affection of the heart from which any action proceeds, and upon which its whole virtue or vice must ultimately depend, may be

considered under two different aspects, or in two different relations; first, in relation to the cause which excites it, or the motive which gives occasion to it; and secondly, in relation to the end which it proposes, or the effect which it tends to produce. (*TMS*, page 13)

Thus, fascinatingly, a sentiment is justified not only in terms of the original cause which excites it, but contrary to the versions of Benthamite liberalism that became associated with liberalism irredeemably later on, also in terms of the effect which it tends to produce. Smith's extraordinary discussion in the following pages of *TMS* hopes to "produce among mankind that harmony of sentiments and passions in which consists their whole grace and propriety." Such a balance is not 'natural' but cultivated:

> ... that there may be some correspondence of sentiments between the spectator and the person principally concerned, the spectator must, first of all, endeavour, as much as he can, to put himself in the situation of the other, and to bring home to himself every little circumstance of distress which can possibly occur to the sufferer. He must adopt the whole case of his companion with all its minutest incidents; and strive to render as perfect as possible, that imaginary change of situation upon which his sympathy is founded... (*TMS*, pages 16–17)

Smith also advises constant striving since one's natural selfishness threatens to undo one's capacity for sympathy:

> After all this, however, the emotions of the spectator will still be very apt to fall short of the violence of what is felt by the sufferer. Mankind, though naturally sympathetic, never conceive, for what has befallen another, that degree of passion which naturally animates the person principally concerned.... The person principally concerned is sensible of this, and at the same time passionately desires a more complete sympathy. He longs for that relief which nothing can afford him but the entire concord of the affections of the spectators with his own. To see the emotions of their hearts, in every respect, beat time to his own, in the violent and disagreeable passions, constitutes his sole consolation. But he can only hope to obtain this by lowering his passion to that pitch, in which the spectators are capable of going along with him. He must flatten, if I may be allowed to say so, the sharpness of its natural tone, "in order to reduce it to harmony and concord with the emotions of those who are about him." What they feel, will, indeed, always be, in some respects, different from what he feels, and compassion can never be exactly the same with original sorrow; because the secret consciousness that the change of situations, from which the

sympathetic sentiment arises, is but imaginary, not only lowers it in degree, but, in some measure, varies it in kind, and gives it a quite different modification. These two sentiments, however, may, it is evident, have such a correspondence with one another, as is sufficient for the harmony of society. "Though they will never be unisons, they may be concords, and this is all that is wanted or required." (*TMS*, pages 16–17 [emphasis mine])

It may appear strange to the contemporary eye that sentiment and affections must thus be balanced interpersonally through constant endeavor, almost like the Smithian invisible hand of the market that balances micro and macroeconomic forces. However, this seemingly technical description of social commerce must not mislead us—it also seems to have been powerful enough to segue into an argument against slavery in the same text. Of course, Smith is no anti-racist—the distinction between the "barbarous" and "civilized" nations is clear in his mind. However, unlike the popular notion of the barbarous nations as emotional and the civilized nations as rational, for Smith it is exactly the opposite—to be passionate and to have an excess of sentiment is a sign of civilization. Thus, he holds the French and Italians, with their excitable and emotional behavior, to be more "polished" than the English, who are educated with a "duller sensibility" (*TMS*, page 187).[5] Again, and this is where his argument becomes an anti-slavery position, the difference between the civilized and barbarous nations is due to differing levels of material security. In his words:

> Among civilized nations, the virtues which are founded upon humanity, are more cultivated than those which are founded upon self-denial and the command of the passions. Among rude and barbarous nations, it is quite otherwise, the virtues of self-denial are more cultivated than those of humanity. The general security and happiness which prevail in ages of civility and politeness, afford little exercise to the contempt of danger, to patience in enduring labour, hunger, and pain. Poverty may easily be avoided, and the contempt of it therefore almost ceases to be a virtue. The abstinence from pleasure becomes less necessary, and the mind is more at liberty to unbend itself, and to indulge its natural inclinations in all those particular respects. Among savages and barbarians it is quite otherwise. Every savage undergoes a sort of Spartan discipline, and by the necessity of his situation is inured to every sort of hardship.

[5] Of course, this was also a not-very-subtle bromide by the passionate Scotsman Smith against the reserved and imperious English!

Smith then uses the fine contrasts between civilized and barbarous nations to argue for the liberation of suffering, stoic slave from the "wretched" slave owner.

> There is not a negro from the coast of Africa who does not, in this respect, possess a degree of magnanimity which the soul of his sordid master is too often scarce capable of conceiving. Fortune never exerted more cruelly her empire over mankind, than when she subjected those nations of heroes to the refuse of the jails of Europe, to wretches who possess the virtues neither of the countries which they come from, nor of those which they go to, and whose levity, brutality, and baseness, so justly expose them to the contempt of the vanquished. (*TMS*, page 186)

In a sense, Smith produces the most radical sympathy for the slave by producing a sociological and not naturalistic theory of their stoicism, even if he succumbs to the fatal temptation to make Africans exotic by rendering them as "nations of heroes"—(here the heroism qua Behn, is extended to the entire group, and not merely to the individual). Here too, Smith mobilizes, to use Gross's description of Stern's novel, sympathy by drawing attention to the "imbalance of social exchange" between the civilized and barbarous nations and people. Perhaps is impossible to understand these associations except through Smith's Christian conscience. In the following passage, he describes the effort required to be a good Christian. The effort, it is clear, consists—yet again—of making an imaginative journey from one's own situation to another's. In other words, to develop sympathy which "carries us beyond our own person."

> As we have no immediate experience of what other men feel, we can form no idea of the manner in which they are affected, but by conceiving what we ourselves should feel in the like situation. Though our brother is upon the rack, as long as we ourselves are at our ease, our senses will never inform us of what he suffers. They never did, and never can, carry us beyond our own person, and it is by the imagination only that we can form any conception of what are his sensations. Neither can that faculty help us to this any other way, than by representing to us what would be our own, if we were in his case. It is the impressions of our own senses only, not those of his, which our imaginations copy. By the imagination we place ourselves in his situation, we conceive ourselves enduring all the same torments, we enter as it were into his body, and become in some measure the same person with him, and thence form some idea of his sensations, and even feel something which, though weaker in degree, is not altogether unlike them. His agonies, when

they are thus brought home to ourselves, when we have thus adopted and made them our own, begin at last to affect us, and we then tremble and shudder at the thought of what he feels. (*TMS*, pages 2–3)

A little later in the text, Smith argues

And hence it is, that to feel much for others and little for ourselves, that to restrain our selfish, and to indulge our benevolent affections, constitutes the perfection of human nature … as to love our neighbour as we love ourselves is the great law of Christianity.… (*TMS*, page 19)

# IV

In time, sentiment all but vanished from the language of the liberal state, to be replaced by a decidedly unsentimental language of individual rights, needs and entitlements—a set of welfare concerns that Hannah Arendt describes as anti-politics in *The Human Condition* (Arendt, 1998). Speaking of the rights discourse in particular, Lynn Hunt argues in her magisterial *Inventing Human Rights* that the powerful language of natural rights emerged in the 18th century only to be eclipsed in the 19th century and re-emerge in the more formal legalism of the Universal Declaration of Human Rights in the mid-20th century (Hunt, 2007). It is beyond the scope of this paper to properly investigate this complex history; however, one may conjecture that it is related to a shift in the understanding of liberalism as a whole philosophy of life, an entire way of being, a moral order, and liberalism as a system of individual rights and utilities to be enforced by a welfare state.

It is possible that the rise of what Michel Foucault (1990) has termed biopower—the management of the entire biological life of human beings by an impersonal authority—has evacuated the social contract of the violent charge of diversity and alterity. Rather, since diversity is nowhere close to disappearing, the historical development of this biopower-as-liberalism may have rendered mute the language required to speak of that diversity and indeed of the capacity to speak of the Other. The argument here is not that sentiment as an eternal human attribute somehow balanced or softened liberalism, but precisely that it is a historically constructed category that was central to the development of natural rights and liberalism. We may term this amalgamation of opposites productive insofar as it laid the foundation for appeals to human rights to be made *within* the emerging unsentimental language of liberalism, to meld sentimental and rational appeals in the growing outlawing of both private torture and public punishment for instance. Has the disappearance of the language of sentiment as the governor of interpersonal exchange, as simultaneously social harmony, Christian goodwill and natural justice re-located the moral force of sentiment in a very different politics—a politics of recognition as it is sometimes called, or we may call it a politics against distance? Indeed, one could go as far as to ask where would liberalism and, in particular, the rights that underpin liberalism's social contract and that appear to be endangered today with the politics of hurt sentiment be without the idea of sentiment itself?

We may return to Gross' essay briefly for clues. Commenting on one of Charles Darwin's lesser-known works *The Expression of the Emotions in Man and Animals,* Gross argues that contrary to the manner in which Darwin has been interpreted by the 20th century scholars like Paul Eckman who are invested in discovering a "science of emotion" which claims to follow Darwin "and which has recently infiltrated the humanities like a Trojan horse...," Darwin's own understanding of emotion in this work is decidedly rhetorical, skeptical, and humanistic (Gross, 2010: 36). Gross' philosophical skepticism regarding universal emotion has a striking relevance to our own discussion on sentiment as perspective. In a sense, sentiment can be connected to humanism, with all its possibilities for politics, in a manner that a universalized understanding of humans as 'emotional' creatures cannot. Here, it would be important to note that while the liberal state and its rights-making apparatus no longer accommodate the language of sentiment, the idea of harm or injury is highly familiar to juridical and popular discourse as far as historical or personal injustice is concerned. For example, Saba Mahmood writes in the context of the Danish cartoon controversy of 2009 that in fact the notion of injury permeates legal and popular discourse in the West, a fact that makes the hopelessly polarized debate over the cartoon all the more surprising. About this debate, Mahmood states

> Little attention has been paid to how one might reflect on the kind of offence the cartoons caused and what ethical, communicative, and political practices are necessary to make this kind of injury intelligible. The lacuna

is all the more puzzling given how complex notions of psychic, bodily, and historical injury permeate legal and popular discourse in Western liberal societies; consider, for example, the transformations that concepts of property, personal injury, and reparations (to settle collective historical harm) have undergone in the last century alone. (Mahmood, 2009: 842)

Mahmood's reflections on 20th century Western societies are striking as she is in fact pointing to the extent to which the development of group rights within liberalism depend on mobilizing the idea of (collective) injury—a connection that the political scientist Will Kymlicka has used fruitfully in his influential theory of multiculturalism (Kymlicka, 1998). Of course, Mahmood's invocation of the idea of harm rather than hurt also has the effect of displacing the rather peevish overtones of the latter, restoring us collectively to the discussion of something urgent and quite specific, that is, injury.

As far as *hurt* sentiment as a trope is concerned, it appears to have remained in contemporary politics as a disembodied echo of the previously robust sentimental discourse as a whole. On the one hand, the reclacitrance of the sentimental discourse allows the eruption of a politics of recognition and specific injury against liberal 'neutrality', thereby forcing a reimagination of the public–political. On the other hand, the disjunct between the politics of recognition and the seemingly bloodless thythms of biopolitics also allows the state to *selectively* represent uncomfortable demands for redressal of hurt sentiment as farce and excess. In this, the role of courts is critical, especially with reference to postcolonial societies where the law can be an overwhelming and monolithic site of appeal and redressal. Lawrence Liang argues in the Indian context for example that the courts are not merely adjudicators but may be credited with introducing the idea of hurt sentiment in public life. Liang believes this may be a remnant of the colonial prejudice about "emotionally excitable subjects" who needed to be protected from themselves. He writes:

Section 153A and Section 295A of the Indian Penal Code (IPC), which deal with hate speech in India ("promotion of hatred, enmity," "outraging religious feelings," "insulting a religion," etc.) are not provisions that merely describe an objective, affective state called hatred, but through such descriptions also constitute a legally and socially recognisable category called hate. When these laws were introduced in the colonial period, an underlying assumption was that there was a need for a rational and neutral arbiter (the colonial State) to govern the relationship between "emotionally excitable subjects" prone to emotional injury and physical violence. But this was a self-fulfilling prophecy because once you have a law that allows for the making of legal claims on the basis of charged emotional states, you begin to see the emergence of cases that steadily cultivate a legal vocabulary of hurt sentiments. (Liang, 2012)

While Liang's tone is decidedly cautionary, other scholars have pointed to the affective nature of law itself, to the similarity between law and literature, and to the deep dependence of legal writing on literary narrative-forms and tropes (Reichman, 2011).[6] Taken together, these arguments would in a tangential way amount to rehabilitating sentiment somewhere at the centre of modern juridical and political imaginations. At the very least, they would construct a channel between the avowedly bloodless, impersonal nature of law and the effusive excesses of sentiment. We may appeal for the politics of hurt sentiment to be met with a politics of sentiment so that it may dent and counter, sans the absurd threats of silence or violence, the overwhelming authority of law which arrogates the power of adjudicating all interpersonality from its Kafkaesque inclines.

# References

Arendt, Hannah. 1998. *The Human Condition*. Chicago: University of Chicago Press.
Benjamin, Walter. 1974. *Theses on the Philosophy of History*. Frankfurt: Um Main Verlag Suhrkamp.
Bogues, Anthony. 2003. *Black Heretics Black Prophets*. New York: Routledge.
Cuguano, Ottobah. 1999. *Thoughts and Sentiments on the Evil and Wicked Traffic of the Slavery and Commerce of the Human Species, Humbly Submitted to the Inhabitants of Great-Britain*. New York: Penguin.
Foucault, Michel. 1990. *The History of Sexuality: Volume I*. New York: Vintage.
Gross, Daniel. 2010. "Defending the Humanities," in *Critical Inquiry 37* (Autumn), pp. 34–59.
Hunt, Lynn. 2007. *Inventing Human Rights*. New York: WW Norton and Co.
Kymlicka, Will. 1998. *Multicultural Citizenship*. Oxford: Clarendon Press.
Liang, Lawrence. 2012. "Love Language or Hate Speech," in *Tehelka*.
Macpherson, C.B. 1962. *The Political Theory of Possessive Individualism*. Oxford: Clarendon.

---

[6] See for instance the work of Ravit Reichman on the manner in which modernist literature helped to reshape law in the interwar period, and eventually to evolve a way in which the unfathomable loss of war could be accounted for in juridical discourse through concepts like Crimes against Humanity.

Mahmood, Saba. 2009. "Religious Reason and Secular Affect: An Incommensurable Divide?" *Critical Inquiry*, 35(Summer 2009): 836–862.

Mallipeddi, Ramesh. 2012. "Spectacle, Spectatorship, and Sympathy in Aphra Behn's Oroonoko." *Eighteenth-Century Studies*, 45(4): 475–496.

Orr, Bridget. 2001. *Empire on the English Stage, 1660–1714.* Cambridge: Cambridge University Press.

Reichman, Ravit. 2009. *The Affective Life of Law: Legal Modernism and the Literary Imagination.* Stanford: Stanford University Press.

Smith, Adam. 1976. *The Theory of Moral Sentiments.* Oxford: Oxford University Press.

Taylor, Charles and Amy Gutmann. 1992. *Multiculturalism and the Politics of Recognition: As Essay.* Princeton: Princeton University Press.

# 13

# The Return of Daya

*Prasanta Chakravarty*

A close friend of mine—a fine political philosopher with nuanced artistic sensibilities—once suggested that he is inherently suspicious of blithe gaiety in relationships, friendships, and in public exchanges. Gaiety smacks of happiness; indeed it is happiness: a deficient and shrill routine. It shuts off intellectual pessimism, the very basis of criticality. One must take time, let matters marinate ("jaarano" he proposed in Bangla) and not be prematurely upbeat and exuberant while forging bonds and taking actions. The deficient modes of resting and concealment are important preconditions in order to take on varieties of political manipulation, social one-upmanship, and literary cleverness that beset our time.

What had actually made my friend restive, I suspect, was a certain accommodative circumspection and glare that characterize expressions of literary *talent* and political *acumen*, an attribute otherwise known as *correctness.* That insouciance might lead to quick opinion mongering and uncritical conclusions, operating merely within the ontic upper crust, is the needling point. It is with a similar enthusiasm for a supposed 'pickling effect', to keep conflicts 'low key' and place them as more serious *concerns*, that we notice a proliferation of the subjective, claims for a certain authenticity that gets best reflected in memoirs and autobiographies—freshly tailored, translated, and often revived in recent times. That such retrievals of community memory and/or fashioning of interiority via the autobiographical are being accepted and advocated by social scientists (a mode usually fancied by those in the humanities) is not merely a declaration against 'doing' political economy or taking on the empirical fundamentals of analytical thought, but a more interesting drive to locate the authentic through a process of methodological revelation. Confessionary drama, reality shows, and sundry blog-diaries affirm a remarkable rise in collective narcissism where questions of authenticity are unmistakably amalgamated with a certain performance—to act, sell, often to produce and exhibit *exemplary cultural lives*. And exemplary friendships and bonds around such lives. In such a milieu what price concealment and marinating?

# Not Trauma No Nostalgia

In Bangla literature, the greatest success story in recent times has been a post-partition memoir: *Dayamayeer Katha* (*Dayamayee's Tale*), Sunanda Sikdar's maiden work. Upon its arrival in January 2008, it received both critical and popular acclaim and in no time traversed the distance from being a cult hit to becoming an instant classic. In Bangla, partition and/or resettlement narratives are not a new phenomenon. One immediately recalls Tapan Roychoudhury's *Romathan Othoba Bhimrotipraptor Paracharitcharcha* (and the lesser work, *Bangalnama*), Mihir Sengupta's *Bishadbrikkho*, and *Ujaani Khaaler Sonta*, Manas Ray's *Kata Deshe Ghorer Khoj*, and Indubaran Ganguly's *Colonysmriti*. And now, of course, there is a spate of fresh testimonies: Adhir Biswas' *Deshbhager Kawtha*, Nilima Datta's *Ujaan Srote*, or Mrinal Chakraborty's *Amar Ei Aparahnarekha*, for instance. Some incisive novels and short stories have also accumulated over the years. So, what is it about Sikdar's book that catapults it both to the bestseller list even as it commands reviews and commentaries in snooty little magazines? There are several reasons possible: a crystal clear prose, structuring of the narrative in little self-sufficient snippets that relate to a larger inconclusive journey (about which she has written in recent newspaper articles), effective managing and distancing of the space-time continuum and the sheer polyphony of colorful characters that people her firmament.

But the book is not only about effective circulations of speech-acts. There are many proceedings that make the work special, and which I would venture, make it at once historically ensconced while transporting it beyond the narrative of the after-effects of mass exodus. The two axes around which the whole idea of grievance and memorialization of Partition and multiple and future possibilities of the very condition of being perpetual refugees are usually established are: trauma and nostalgia. This book manages to shake off the immense traction of these two narrative motifs which used to produce a different kind of political investment in the context of that momentous event and its aftermaths.

Somdatta Mandal tells us that Nemai Ghosh's *Chinnamul* (1951), Ritwik Ghatak's *Meghe Dhaka Tara* (1960), *Komal Gandhar* (1961), and *Subarnarekha* (1962), Buddhadeb Dasgupta's *Tahader Katha* (1992), Masiuddin Shaker and Sheikh Niamat Ali's *Surya Dighal Bari* (1979), Tanvir Mokammel's *Chitra Nadir Pare* (1999), and Supriyo Sen's *Way Back Home: A Documentary* (2002) are crucial Indian and Bangladeshi cinematic memorializations of the 1947 Partition of Bengal, particularly relevant in light of the relative scarcity of Bengali prose on the subject. Mandal explains how Partition is represented in Bengali literature and film as a metaphysical wound afflicting the mind, not the body, and characterized as nostalgia, not madness. Sometimes, creative writing took an opposite, ameliorating turn, as in Salil Sen's play *Natun Ihudi* and Tulsidas Lahiri's *Banglar Mati*. Both the plays depicted the middle class desire to valorize some kind of cultural unity and propagate the rhetoric of religious harmony. Poetry, a more imaginative and sensual genre, in creating an affective distancing, has been more complicated in depicting the overwhelming theme of radical fracturing.

That nature of investment we rarely see in Bangla prose, which invariably returns to motifs of trauma and nostalgia. Naturally, a visceral sense of hurt gets subtracted to either ameliorating, nihilistic, or legal-behavioral modes of seeking a closure that are non-poetical, non-political. The idea of justice in such imaginations is either *retributive* (based on a sense of radical antagonism or opting out altogether from the historical happenings by highlighting meaninglessness of our existence) or *restorative* (seeking reconciliation, forgetting, and moving on in order to begin afresh, giving a premature closure in the process). Can we avoid in imaginative literature retributive and restorative ways of seeking justice, especially while dealing in such cases of immense personal and collective injury? A larger point is at stake here: can we recalibrate our settled idea of justice and art afresh? Is it possible to remind ourselves of the significant role that esthetics plays in themes that otherwise seem to be merely juridical-political?

# Two Paradigms and the Equity of Philia

It is a different kind of tryst with her times for Sikdar: First, a very subtle politicization of the genre of the memoir without it getting busy, exemplary, or politically correct, and second, more importantly, a categorical rejection of a life-world that thrives on a philosophy of marinating and inwardness. There is cruelty, retribution, pain but no refractory, indifferent grief (*bishaad*). *Dayamoyee's Tale*, at the bedrock level, celebrates unobtrusive sharing and equity and revels in exchanges of unnecessary and limitless love. It does not forget, but calibrates and fine-tunes memory to such an extent that there is scant scope for wide-eyed exuberance around 'affective' this and 'subjective' that. It does not care to give us a *representative* narrative of trauma and tribulation; it gives us an everyday, situated account of one person's impressions over her surroundings, without an iota of sentimentalizing. The overarching rubric of *daya* (she uses *meherbani* too) Sikdar wields like a master craftsperson in order to achieve such an effect. This particular mode of interaction (individually and collectively) surely comes from a cultural sense of cooperative mutuality, a natural form of straightforward camaraderie that springs forth and develops from actual liking of other human beings and creatures. The important idea is to *really know* another person, investing in every single social relationship or a situation with passion and investment. In ancient Greece this is what would be called *philia* (though its origin is brotherly love): when one talks about the character or disposition that falls between obsequiousness or flattery on the one hand and surliness or quarrelsomeness on the other. This form of mutuality may also lead to a self-sufficient mode of fulfilled life and act as a strong buffer against the excesses of rampant individualism/communicative interaction and a resilient provocation to the obverse ethical modes of non-engagement and surpassing detachment from our everyday political predicament.

In his writings on Gandhi, Ajay Skaria has cautioned us against translating *daya* as compassion. Daya is rather coterminous with a pervasive love, opposed to *tiraskar* (hateful chiding). Skaria says: "… *daya* and *prem* point to the practice of *ahimsa* as the infinite giving of oneself and such infinite giving can be conceptualized, paradoxically, only as the very practice of finitude." There is nothing metaphysical about *daya*, though God may be the primary practitioner of *daya*. God's infinitude involves rather a radical finitude in human interactions, so that practicing and acceptance of *daya* provide a peculiar and exemplary freedom from settled dogmas leading us to an open-ended sense of humility. But is the cultivation of such humility and giving-of-oneself sufficient to capture the contested terrain of everyday practice and historical contests? How can personal realization of relationality lead to a configuration of the public-political?

Ranajit Guha, on the other hand, argues for a different trajectory of *daya*, in the context of Ram Mohan Roy and the modern Indian experience. Apart from reason and *shastric* thinking, Ram Mohan, Guha dwells, is particularly enamoured by the fostering and promotion of worldly, practical knowledge. And here Ram Mohan marries ideals of courage, asceticism, judgment, and perseverance to what will eventually come to be celebrated as the very foundation and index of our contemporary existence: communicability. From Vico through Shaftesbury, from Hutcheson through Hume to Immanuel Kant—a demand for universal assent for mutual communicability is in a way the story of modernity. And at least one cornerstone to such an ideal of communicability is the cultivation of empathy (*sahanubhuti* or *samavedana*) among modern agents. For Guha, it is this liberal idea of *daya* that could have taken the nation in an ethical direction. But that was not to be. Instead we took a provincial and narrow religious and political turn leading infamously to Bankimchandra's commemoration of a counter ideal—that of muscle-power (*baahubal*). One can see Guha's ideals of *daya* are almost a reversal of Skaria's. A notion of *daya* that relies on collective/associative (*saha*) + empathetic feeling (*anubhuti*) and equal/associative (*sama*) + anguish (*vedana*) are likely to be suspicious of the limits of finitude and unlikely to conceive interactions based on non-judgemental passion and love in both personal and public life. What kind of interiority does such a notion of *daya* suggest? And what may be the implications if we attempt to chart Indian modernity by dovetailing it with such an ideal of empathy?

# Conflicts, Tussles, Fabrications, Death

The tale (*katha* is both a non-fictional *akhyan* and a personal narrative) begins in retrospect when little Daya had not transformed herself into Sunanda (Kankan), her Hindustani identity. It is 1971 and their *kamla* (manual worker), a Mussalman copyholder whom she considered to be her brother, sells his last belonging and his cow and comes to visit her in India. This initiates a reluctant recollection of 9 years—1951–1960, which forms the basis for the narrative time. The locale simultaneously shifts to Dighpait village in Bangladesh, where she had spent those years with her foster mother when her parents had left for India. It is here that her tale unfolds.

Dayamayee tells us right at the outset how religion and caste structures were entrenched in her village, and yet it is through her account that we appreciate the shades of some changing equations. Her said brother, Majom, was looked upon with suspicion by her Hindu brethren and yet Daya learns the diurnal intricacies of everyday Islam from him and other acquaintances. Her foster mother, a benevolent but hardened widow, is quite categorical in her warnings when Daya goes to play with Muslim neighbors: "Have paan, have jaggery but be careful not to touch water. That's when you lose *jaat*." But little Daya did flout her mother's strictures. And did it often.

The two communities have a distinctive relationship with land. While Hindus refrain from getting into the fields owing to their social position and stature, the sheikhs (Muslim landowners) till the land themselves and seldom look for a helping hand: "Sadi Sarkar is so well to do. Even his children are matriculate. But gathering his *tafan* and girdle, one sees him pushing the yoke every morning," says a scion of the reigning Hindu zamindar family.

In a community marriage, the village Brahmins and Kayasthas are made to sit in the inner courtyard, the *kaivartas* and *jolas* in the central-courtyard and Mussalmans in the outer-yard. Since the zamindars and the groom's family were being served in the inner courtyard, there was no dearth of mutton, curd, and other sweets. In the central-courtyard, sweets were served, but not curd. The outer yard was supplied with just meat and fish. The *maulavi* saheb, having got a whiff of the distinctions, was greatly offended and was about to quit the scene. The organizers then cajoled and jockeyed, appealing to the precarious financial status of the bride's father and the necessity for the marriage to take place that very night. The *maulavi*, putting fraternal concerns centre stage, agrees to overlook caste and class, but only for the time being. Such a transference is possible not due to goodwill and empathy, but owing to a much larger sense of ethical responsibility that could be politicised at will.

In Dighpait *ripuchis* (refugees) from India are a lurking subterranean presence. Says little Daya: "I guessed what *ripuchi* might mean. *Ripu* means one's enemy. Reading of Ramayana made me aware that Ram and Ravan are each other's *ripu*. I understood that Samsher-chacha and his family were my Ma's *ripus*." And then she goes on to argue with her foster mother—how *ripuchis* are not a girdle-waving breed but have something akin to Mussalmans, which made her mother see red. It is through these direct and pesky rearguard arguments that Daya often, very subtly, ushers a change in her foster mother so that when a poor, frustrated fresh arrival from India ventures on to steal some fish from an enclosed pond, and is caught and derided, she retorts by appealing to a deeply responsible sense of *daya*, duly politicised: "In God's kingdom, fruits lying beneath the trees, fishes in the local ponds, are everyone's right. That is what we have known." There is a remarkable entanglement of the language of common rights with that of nature's bounty, local political tussles with much larger concerns. And Daya realizes soon enough that if any *ripuchi-chacha* brings money, can read and write, talk his way through, he can ensure his rights to the jungle and deal in timbers. Some refugees are more equal than others. The idea of *daya* is materialized.

There is entrenched impatience against the pervasive caste hierarchies from inside, throughout the narrative without ever-inculcating pre-emptive secular dismissals: "Ours is the religion of *paraan* (spirit/soul) saving, not dabbling in luxurious ideals and castes," a central realization that Majom weaves into Daya at a tender age, which gets diffused into everyone with whom she comes into contact, including her readers. The local zamindars, Bhuiyas, the surrogate hands of governing, come across not just as callous and unjust, but as detached and completely unaware of the basic relational aspects of living. A strange breed, they are caught between ancient norms and forces of modernization. They try to reverse the processes of *daya* time and again, but are unable to meet its complexity with any long standing counter-move.

And then there is the telling puzzlement about Motilal's son Jawahar about whom Daya learns from a refugee relative who was, at that point, trying to settle in Dandakaranya. Jawahar has given them everything—land, though slightly hard and seed grain to sow, initiatives to start lives afresh. Even people in Dighpait kept singing paeans on Motilal's son when they hear this bit of news.

But little Daya experiences strange goose bumps—Dandakaranya of the Ramayana? Something ominous about it, isn't it? Something not right. Can *meherbani* reach there, touch those seeds? And all these at the backdrop when her foster mother is worried sick about Jawaharlal's changing relationship with Ayub Khan.

The immanent and the hidden sometimes conjoin and foment terrible tragedies, not just in distant Dandakaranya, but in the vicinity of the remembered village. An untimely death befalls the beautiful Sudhir-da, who used to be an extremely gentle presence in the neighbourhood. He would often colour his dhoti in pink or in a yellowish tinge, sometimes would don a sari as a dhoti, loved to do his rather longish hairs, spend his spare time in the inner courtyards, helping the womenfolk in making wicks, processing pulses, and grating coconuts. But being gullible and malleable, he was used at one point by some influential members of the community to scare a family through his antics. The same people stabbed Sudhir-da to a brutal death once the whole affair came to light. A shocked village is silenced. Moral indignation coupled with retribution indeed hides fatal potentialities—and neither contractual empathy nor any language of infinite responsibility provides us with any clear answer about thinking radically on relations within the community during such times of crisis. Sikdar's narrative powerfully pitches *daya* at a level where it steadfastly shuns all overstatements about the confessional, but also carefully distances itself from a plea to the modern ideals of sincere social exchange. People could be deeply attached and be cruel at the same juncture. Violence is constitutive of *daya*, not its obverse, as Gandhi would have us believe.

# Those Who Can Be Curious

In *Love's Work*, Gillian Rose recounts with elation her qualification in unhappy love affairs. She reflects on someone who loves and desires you, and glories in his love and desire and you glory in his ever strange being, which comes up against you, and disappears again and again, surprising you with difficulties and bounty. To lose this is the greatest loss, a loss for which there is no consolation. She has this to say: "There is no democracy in any love relation: only mercy. To be at someone's mercy is dialectical damage: they may be merciful and they may be merciless. Yet each party, woman, man, the child in each, is absolute power as well as absolute vulnerability." This unchristian sense of mercy comes close to Daya's tale. She would record the joyous and the joyless with an equal degree of curiosity (not equanimity). Things, events, and relations would surprise her and this element of amazement is key to the kind of readership that the work enjoys. Despite the varied degree of inward pulls which could only be upended by dabbling in daily tribulations, this is an absolute and untainted celebration of our kaleidoscopic existence, looking strangely and askance at the profound 'pickling effect' that our best minds on the subjective have been demanding from us.

This tangible, accessible mode of love is best exemplified by Bhuli-pishima, Daya's aunt and a widow at 10. Despite her scant formal education, she was blessed with an intuitive interior space (*mukto antahkaran*—a phrase quite distant from Cartesian cogito or Locke's idea of personhood). Her life's story was to travel in trains, living from ashram to ashram. Sometimes traveling ticketless, she would be forced to alight at some unknown railway platform, where she would stay for months, take bath under roadside taps, create new relations and do sundry work. And then may be board another train one day and the ticket-babu this time may have been *dayabaan*, allowing passage to her next destination. She had discovered great joy in nourishing curiosity for things and relations in the process. Bhuli-pishima, as she recounts her endless experiences across the country, confides: "Daya, human beings are incredibly bountiful and giving; they give sleepers and shawls to complete strangers!" She would survive on a pension earmarked for widows, but would often distribute that little money to friends and loved ones. Riots she witnessed and yet considered those as an aberration in human experience, not the norm. But her abundant nature was not a fruition of any inward pacifism or liberal pluralism; it was an active mechanism that stemmed from a thought-out belief in struggling with everyday conflicts, difficulties and humiliations. This is how an acute sense of *philia* might work in our everyday transactions.

There is an equally compelling snippet about Modi–*bhabhi*, who turns completely unhinged as her fiancé Suresh is forced to depart for India. It is Daya who develops a special friendship with Modi and convinces her to continue stitching intricate cotton quilts for Suresh. Daya promises to deliver the quilts to Suresh once she crosses the border and reaches Hindustan. The important thing is to realize that the workings of *daya* in such situations are inextricably bound to a life-world suffused with curiosity: which in this case gives rise to habitual engaging with someone whom the community considers mad and which in turn is layered by her anticipation and inquisitiveness to see a finished hand-woven artefact.

Nature works in tandem with sentient beings throughout the narrative, which brings Sikdar close to the memoirs of Monindra Gupta or Mihir Sengupta, for she often recalls her lost world through the undergrowth and foliage. But then again, natural bodies are actively left unromanticised. Majom prays to Allah and Daya listens with rapt attention: "Keep everyone contented—humans, animals, trees and shrubs, insects of all kinds." A whole section is reserved for relating the bovine world to the readers. When one of their favourite cows Buri breathes her last, to Daya's enquiry whether she was Mussalman, her foster mother replies that since animals are unlikely to have caste slots, Buri could be buried without complications.

Much of the charm in Daya's tale lies in putting your feet up and partaking in the interstices of the everyday, the poetics of history as it were. That young Daya is unable to read books beyond the two epics, since she is unable to decipher *juktakhhars* (conjuncts) and yet she waits with baited breath for someone to get the *Ittefaaq* newspaper from Dhaka-Maimansingha, is an outward manifestation of an angst in which the reader participates with a deep anxiousness but with little anguish. Stories (*shastar*, in the local tongue) abound anyway and Dakkhinaranjan Mitra-Majumdar, one of the best known exponents of Bengali children's tales, Daya tells us, got hold of his most famous stories from the many that circulated under the double Banyans in Dighpait. As the nephew of the local zamindar he would be a regular at those story-telling sessions before he travelled to Calcutta, compiled the tales and published them as "Grandma's Kitty" (*Thakurmar Jhuli*). When the local storytellers would complain about this development, Daya's foster mother would ask them not to be resentful of others' success but rather revel that the turnings of their everyday existence were now circulating in print. Is it a self-reflective articulation on Dayamayee's part, whose tales are now being circulated in a similar fashion through the world of print?

The very idea of curiosity and the ability to be existentially surprised and infect, colour others in that meaningless exercise is the body and soul of Daya's narrative. Do we need to be performing either the confessional or the testimonial in order to be true to our inner turnings or to capture and chronicle sociological datum? Conversely put, can we avoid performing and look for a self-reflective depth? Manas Ray has written against the ethnography of the partition narrative, an approach that seizes the representative writings and thrives on presenting the spectacular to the purported reader and thus claims a certain authenticity over the events and lives caught up in the turmoil. This Michel De Certeau has called fake heterology. *Dayamayee's Tale* is hardly interested in the spectacular.

In fact, the narrative traverses well beyond the actual events and creates a deliberate distancing from the empathetic framework of *samavedana* which Ranajit Guha recommends. But the cultivation of humility and acceptance of the finitude of one's existence is never inward looking. Nor surpassing. And never romantically idealistic. It is not the ethical position of *agape* or *karuna* that Sikdar's idea of *daya* performs. It comes closer to that other idea of robust sharing and camaraderie: *philia* and the politics that this latter mode might spread and infuse in the wake of grievous, relentless and banal infliction of injury and incapacity, which is our daily existence. The workings of *daya* can be felt and touched, mired as it is in the world of negotiations and strategies. But the basis of such negotiations is the ability to be surprised endlessly and scatter that ability through wanton deeds of love.

# Bibliography

Aristotle, 1999. *Nicomachean Ethics.* Trans. Terence Irwin (2nd edition). Hackett.

Bagchi, Jasodhara, Subhoranjan Dasgupta, and Subhasree Ghosh. 2009. *The Trauma and the Triumph: Gender and Partition in Eastern India*, Vol. 2. Kolkata: Stree.

Chakrabarty, Bandana. 2007. "Partition: Between Memory and Representation," in *Reading Partition/Living Partition*, edited by Jasbir Jain. Jaipur: Rawat Publications, pp. 173–184.

Chakravarty, Tapati. 2002. "The Paradox of a Fleeting Presence: Partition and Bengali Literature," in *Pangs of Partition, Vol. 2: The Human Dimension*, edited by S. Settar and Indira Baptista Gupta. New Delhi: Manohar, pp. 261–282.

Guha, Ranajit. 2010. *Daya: Ram Mohan Roy O Amader Adhunikota* (*Ram Mohan Roy and Our Modernity*). Kolkata: Talpata.

Mandal, Somdatta. 2008. "Constructing Post Partition Bengali Cultural Identity through Films," in *Partitioned Lives, Narratives of Home, Displacement and Resettlement*, edited by Anjali Gera Roy and Nandi Bhatia. New Delhi: Dorling Kindersley India.

Ray, Manas. 2010. "Aapon Katha: Mithya Shotyor Prattahik Kabyo," (Story of the Self: Everyday Poetry of Falsehood and Truth), *Nibondho Boichitrer Teen Dawshok*. Kolkata: Chawrjapawd.

Rose, Gillian. 1997. *Love's Work*. London: Vintage.

Samaddar, Ranabir (Ed.). 1997. *Reflections on Partition in the East*. New Delhi: Vikas Publications.

Sikdar, Sunanda. 2010. *Dayamayeer Katha* (*Dayamayee's Tale*). Kolkata: Gangchil.

Skaria, Ajay. 2010. "No Politics without Religion: Of Secularism and Gandhi," in *Political Hinduism: The Religious Imagination in Public Spheres*, edited by Vinay Lal. New Delhi: Oxford University Press.

Sontag, Susan. 2004. *Regarding the Pain of Others*. New York: Picador.

# 14

# Of JAB and Hurt: Exploring Spaces of Resistance within the University

*Vinita Chandra, Rina Ramdev, and Giti Chandra*

This chapter is an attempt to capture the energy of an intervention, a moment of activism in the University that revolved around the idea of 'hurt'. This was a context that was being urgently debated in the years 2010–2012 during which time Delhi University was bringing in a slew of changes beginning with the Semesterized model to replace its existing Annual mode of examination at the undergraduate level despite large-scale opposition to it. When teachers individually and along with their union, the DUTA (Delhi University Teachers' Association), began a series of protests, opposing the 'reforms' which were undemocratically being ushered in, the University retaliated by issuing public statements on how teachers were 'hurting' not just the ethos and spirit of the University but that of the teaching profession as well.

In the face of the concerted attack on academics in the recent past, in the name of necessary reforms in which anyone who voiced opposition was labeled as a 'nay sayer', and the increasing repressive methods of the authorities to silence challenges to their so-called reforms, it has been almost impossible to separate our role as knowledge professionals inside the classroom from the activism that has become part of our daily routine outside the classroom.

There is a strong body of discourse and praxis that inextricably links academics and politics—what we teach and what we do not, or are not allowed to, teach, how we teach, how we evaluate, how often we evaluate, whether we want students to have a deeper understanding of concepts and issues or whether we want them to simply regurgitate information twice a year, and whether our object is to train young people to be marketable or whether we train them simply to have a higher education, are all political decisions. Until recently these decisions were taken through lengthy debates, discussions, consultations, circulating drafts of ordinances, taking feedback, and then implementation through due legal procedure. Whether or not one agreed with the new internal assessment scheme, the restructured BA Honors and BA Program courses, the fact is they were introduced over a period of time with due process and, therefore, did not invite protest or agitation. But the new regime of the last few years made rational procedure seem a thing of the past, now long gone.

While we were drafting and organizing this presentation, we had to try and find a theoretical framework that would suitably peg the movement and its struggles and also challenge here the University administration's charge of 'hurt' against the protesting teachers. In this we would like to draw up a short history of the events that led to the 'passing' of Semester by statutory bodies at the University and the coercive tactics that were at play therein.

# Labor and Learning

Within the growing culture of surveillance, intimidation, and repressive legislation that the University administration now operates through, there lies an attempt at delegitimizing and subduing acts of protest by teachers in different ways. On the one hand, the University invokes the idealization that teaching as a profession has always been mired in, within which the protesting teacher is shown up as harming and hurting not just students and the functioning of the University at large but crucially also the exalted casting of the teacher herself that exists in the public imaginary. This exaltation comes from the widely circulated image of the teacher as the lofty harnesser and wielder of ideas within an abstracted realm unmediated by history and economy, and materialist contexts. This circumscribes intellectual output by sublimating it within the ideational domain of logos, as opposed to the instrumentalist conception and political model of the worker's labor. Within these modalities, there is an insidious removal of the teacher from the discourse of labor and rights. Even as it does this, the administration on the other hand also evokes quantifiable categories to ensure that stipulated hours are clocked within the classroom 'teaching', while disaggregating it from research and study that remain uncalibrated. This quasi-Weberian model of rationalization rests on a bureaucratic understanding of technically ordered efficiency that insists on a quantification of work to arrive at figures of optimal output, even as the exalted teacher figure is placed above the calculable logic of productivity and its control. The University administration, thus, uses a selective evocation and understanding of teachers' work, invested as it is in strategic delimitation without any attempt at a delineation of its complexities.

The teacher organizing resistance and inhabiting sites of struggle is seen as 'hurting' the ethicality of the larger service ideal imposed upon the teaching community. In this, the protesting teacher is sought to be located within the unethical realm of politicking and not politics, with no apparent political goal outside of a destructive project. The University's moral outrage attempts at mobilizing public opinion against teachers by claiming that the apolitical, sanitized, and exalted nature of the social service rendered by teachers hangs precariously by their exertion of a certain kind of political agency. This negativizing of teachers' resistance not just countermands their right to protest within the ethics of political action but also precludes the possibility of any kind of critique of academic practices that the protesting teacher demands.

In 2008, the Delhi University announced its plan to introduce the Semester model in undergraduate teaching and soon after in a superficially consultative attempt sought the views of teachers through staff associations of colleges. By mid-2009, there was an overwhelming rejection of the impending Semester implementation by academics across the political spectrum. This resulted in a bitter battle of attrition between the University administration and teachers. DUTA, the trade union body's combative stand against the mode of implementation of the Semester system was suppressed by a PIL in the court soon after. In January of 2011, a small group of English teachers across University campuses came together to re-engage with the debate in a loose confederation that was to be later called JAB or Joint Action Body. Because of its protean nature, JAB acquired a wide base with a large representation of teachers across disciplines, solidarizing them as they challenged the pedagogical rationale behind semesterization.

JAB mobilized the anti-semester struggle through a renewed call for General Body Meetings across departments and also through its call for more pedagogic engagement at the level of COCs (Committees of Courses) outside of coercive administrative diktats. Along with this, it organized a Press Conference, a candlelight *Jashn-e-Azadi* and open-air teaching. It was this teaching, outside the classroom space, that became a rallying point for the administration to 'expose' the teacher as recalcitrant and unruly. The University administration constructed a narrative of 'hurt' to highlight this performative moment of protest as wrong and violative of the ethical responsibility of the teacher, while at the same time reporting it to the court as a defiance of its injunction. What is interesting here is that even as there was no disruption of teaching, it was the moment of protest that was sought to be subdued, within which teaching itself was deemed disruptive and hurtful. Resistance came not from a withdrawal from work but from a resistance embedded and drawn from within work. What the University has an issue with is not whether teaching is undertaken within quantifiable models of efficiency and productivity but the resistance gestured at making work and the act of teaching itself events of offence and hurt. The ironic model of protest comes from work and it becomes both a mode and pretext for resistance. Even as teachers are seen as not striking work in this, the larger semantics of strike and disruption are used to prove how 'teaching' itself becomes a mode of protest. Within this logically fallacious, self-refuting problematique, it is the act and moment of protest that becomes an issue for the University.

The teachers' position and protest are in fact rooted in a progressive understanding of ethics as it aggressively attacks the University's neoliberal agenda through academic reforms like Semesterization. Such ethics engage with higher education policies and the social service sector in an attempt to resist top-down neoliberal reforms. In this if at all the hurt is real, it is a conscious act of hurt aimed by the teachers not at society and social progress but at the interests of the ruling political establishment.

Judith Butler identifies injurability and violent aggression as the two limits of political life. If we think of these as bracketing off conditions of protest, it is difficult to know where to place the academic as a protestor. As Arundhati Roy pointed out to us in her speech at the JAB organized, *Jashn-e-Azadi*, the guns of the state are not trained at us. We are in no danger of physical harm. We are not, in her experience, the man in the hollow tree trunk who hid, and was immobilized and silenced, while armed men patrolled the fields searching for people like him to kill. The image came to her unbidden, she said, while listening to the songs and poetry with which we ironized our silencing.

We could have argued that the silenced, immobilized man, cabined, cribbed, confined within the dead hollow of what used to be a living tree may well have been an apt image for an academic community ordered by the Delhi High Court not to even "harbour notions of peaceful protest in their minds." We could have argued that symbolic guns were, indeed, aimed at us by the state, that the injury and hurt and perhaps death, that we were in danger of, were to an entire system of education, that the damage to young minds and their education and their future was as ugly and as imminent as the wounding of the body. We could have. But we did not.

The hurt, we had borne witness to, was not in the teacher's apparently un-ethical deterritorialization of work—outside of the institutionally consecrated space of social service—but in the massive assaults launched by the university on the rights and interests of a community bound by a pledge to intellectual freedom. In hurting the imaginative sentimentalism surrounding the figure of the teacher as distinct from exploitable-and-violable labor, JAB was trying to obvert popular memory in order to reclaim the space of reason and debate. We were performing and renegotiating acts of memory to make visible the evidence of violence, not as leaving behind the trace of a wound or the mark of mourning but as necessitating a new politics of hurt. Our movement, hence, was about organizing a collective conscience not around the claims of violence, but beyond their apparent convergence in a moment of becoming political in the field of the ethical.

# Between the Wound and the Voice

Here we could attempt an explanation with a simple question:

What is the opposite of "Remember?"

To forget: the word "forget" comes from the idea—to forego. To loose rather than to bind. To allow to go, rather than to fix in place. This is one notion of memory and narrative: to fix, to coalesce, to bind events into a series of cause and effects, or, at the very least, into a linear chain of incidents over time.

But suppose we were to suggest that the opposite of Remember is to Dismember. What then?

What if we were to take the body to which violence has been done, which has been literally, physically, maimed, crippled, broken, ripped apart; and to place it at the centre of any causal, linear narrative? Ever since Elaine Scarry's 1986 book, *The Body in Pain*, and Cathy Caruth's *Trauma: Exploration in Memory* (1995), the formulation, "Silence marks the site of trauma" has become the foundation of much of our understanding of how narratives are constructed or destroyed in the absence or presence of the violenced body. The presence or even the image of the violenced body has the power of silencing everything around it, rendering it insignificant, trivial, unimportant. This is what makes the rhetoric of violence so powerful. Once inserted into the narrative, it bends everything around it, refocusing the events, incidents, images and silences of the narrative to reflect on and upon itself. In return, it grants to the narrative a primacy and an urgency that it could not otherwise possibly acquire through mere material significance or rational argument.

This is why the imagery and rhetoric of violence is so critical to so much protest: the violenced body issues an imperative in its performativity—we ignore it at our peril. Through it, performance and protest are intimately fused and at once acquire an almost primal immediacy. It is, in other words, the most powerful tool any protest can hope to have. Why, then, one may well ask, did we not make use of it?

So in this last section of this paper, we would like to focus on the things we did not do, and why; and also, the various ways in which we managed to piece together a politics of inarticulacy that allowed us to renegotiate the boundaries of violence that were drawn for us by the university. We are academics. We believed ourselves to be rational people who live and evolve through discussion, argument, persuasion and the presentation of evidence. The General Body Meeting of the Department of English was a thundering evocation of the intelligence, humor, learning and wit, with which we can do this. But that milestone meeting was not a protest. And protest is, after all, aligned with performance. We did not really need a decade and more of Affect Theory to know that we must also perform our anger and hurt, even while we detail our rational arguments.

The political uses of performativity were, indeed, exploited by JAB when we staged the white, silent *dharna,* or the teaching outdoors or the *Jashn e Aazadi* and the candlelight vigil. And useful as these events were, in clarifying our positions to ourselves and publicizing our hurt and defying our constraints, they were not really effective in capturing the imagination of a nation whose future was at stake, far more than our jobs were. And without the rhetoric of hurt, we made ourselves once again vulnerable to what Butler calls the "allocation of stigma" (Butler, xvii): the ease with which teachers can be stigmatized as lazy shirkers, desirous only of doing less work, of having concerns that are, after all, bourgeois, and not as attention-worthy as, say, the man in the hollow tree.

The allocation of stigma effects a silence that is all the more powerful in that every protest damns the speaker further and confirms her complicity more conclusively with every word. Each rational argument becomes tainted with the stigma of workers who refuse to do their job. Speech takes the place of labor; memos and pamphlets, information, and fact sheets are seen as substitutes for the work we are supposed to be doing. The allocation of stigma renders things unsayable by stigmatizing the speaker, thereby robbing the speech—act of its political power and the words of their rationality.

How then, is it possible to effect a space between 'injurability' and 'violent aggression' that encloses both rational discourse and the performance of affects within which to locate the academic protest? Here, we would like to discuss two incidents.

When the Head of the Department of English called a Committee of Courses meeting at the Arts Faculty, a large group of English Teachers decided to sit silently outside the room. We did not see this as an act of protest, but rather as an immediate reminder to everyone at the meeting that they had an obligation to stand by the resounding resolution of the General Body Meeting of the departments of English held earlier which overwhelmingly rejected the proposed Semester System. Rina was a part of the Committee of Courses and was inside in the meeting and outside only Vinita and Giti managed to make it to the actual room before the doors of the Arts Faculty were barred and the rest were not allowed to enter. Before the meeting began, three guards had been posted in the corridor, blocking our way (Photograph 14.1).

At first, they adopted the aggressive posture of guards, keeping their backs turned to us, legs apart, arms crossed, backs ramrod straight. Clearly, this positioned us as potentially violent people. After a while we asked them to get themselves chairs since we were not going to 'do' anything and the meeting could take hours. Once sitting, they ordered tea and had the courtesy to offer their cups to us first. By the time they were enquiring solicitously if there was enough sugar for us, that boundary between violent protestor and guard had long since vanished and we joined their line and stood alongside (Photograph 14.2).

**Photograph 14.1**

*Guards at the Arts Faculty*

Source: Authors.

Meanwhile, Rina's steady stream of messages from the meeting detailing the proceedings became the groundswell of an increasingly hostile and openly aggressive position adopted by the authorities.

It must be said that much of this permeating of the artificial lines that cast non-oppositional parties as violent protestor and aggressive guard was deliberate on our part. A small subversion, yes, but important to our sense of a non-violent, rational and democratic process of negotiation and debate.

The second instance saw far more unpleasant aggression. In April 2011, many of us decided to attend a meeting called by the Head of Department for English Faculty on the restructuring of courses. We went with sheets of information, data, ordinances, legal procedures and so on to present to the meeting. When we declined to leave, the Dean called in bouncers and asked them to throw us out.

Several men, some in uniform, were commanded to remove us physically. And yet interestingly, they refused. And this time the body

**Photograph 14.2**

*Guards and the Guarded*

*Source:* Authors.

language was: arms crossed, hand holding hand either in front or behind the back. Refusal to act.

So imagine a scenario in which the Dean, senior functionary of the university, is standing in the middle of a large room shouting at the bouncers to get rid of us. *Nikaal do in logon ko! Pakad kar bahar kar do!* And the bouncers standing rock still, not moving. And a large group of academics, armed only with sheets of data, sitting silently. Only one of the bouncers was goaded enough to actually touch another colleague on his shoulder but backed off immediately. Eventually, the Dean asked them to leave and we were allowed to speak.

It is possible that the bouncers were better aware of the consequences of physically touching any one of us than the Dean seemed to be, although they must also have known that any consequences would be visited upon the Dean rather than on them. Whatever the case, we like to think that their refusal to touch us was their silent revolution. Resisting this aggressive demand upon them to transform themselves from informal campus security to violent and abusive vigilantes over peaceful and rational discussants at a meeting of our peers, the bouncers denied the Dean the power to construct us as violent protestors in need of eviction.

These were small acts of subversion, but critical to our sense of who we are as a community and what our struggle means in academic discourse, as protest and as performance. This was something that the rhetorical equivalent of the man in the hollow tree would have denied us. And yet, it is through these appropriative acts of what we called a political performance of inarticulacy that we made apparent the dual forces of hurt that were rallied around in the university. First, the strategic silence through which we registered our 'wounded voice' did in fact mime the forceful repression of dissent that the university administration systematically subjected its workforce to. The 'hurt'-tactics deployed by the university in bulldozing its reforms through statutory bodies and processes ironically became part of our vocabulary of protest, by heightening the injustices of silence when reproduced within a space consecrated to debate. The absence of a 'violent voice' only served to accentuate the routine violence that absented it. Second, the measures resorted to by the university authorities in attempting to curb our wounding voice(lessness) through a regular militarization of a teachers' movement proved yet another point. It effectively turned around the charges of 'hurt' levelled by the administration against the teacher–protestor vis-a-vis the a-political project of social welfare. Our protest made apparent that a policy of the most palpable belligerence had become the default condition of experiencing the institution. The 'hurt', it made amply clear, was not in what we 'did' but in what the university apprehended of a community bound—as we say—by a pledge to reason. In other words, the 'state of hurt' became the 'state of the university', in a compulsive–preventive censorship of a resistant muteness.

# References

Butler, Judith. 2006. *Precarious Life: The Powers of Mourning and Violence.* London: Verso.

Caruth, Cathy. 1995. *Trauma: Explorations in Memory.* Baltimore: Johns Hopkins University Press.

Scarry, Elaine. 1985. *The Body in Pain: The Making and Unmaking of the World.* New York: Oxford University Press.

# The Dirty Picture

# 15

## Sexuality, Mediation, Commodification: The Business of Representation

*Karen Gabriel*

### I

The year 2012 dealt the popular Indian rapper Yo Yo Honey Singh a well-earned parting blow, the consequences of which continued to reverberate through 2013 as well. Instead of basking in the adulation of fans on New Year's Eve at Bristol Hotel, he found himself at a loose end, the subject of a censorious e-campaign and stuck with an FIR alleging obscenity and incitement to crimes against women. He was christened the "King of Rape Rap," a well-deserved epithet as this sterling instance of his creativity demonstrates.[1]

Following the uproar over Singh's songs that came under close scrutiny and condemnation after the December 16 gang rape, his

---

[1] The following lyrics are from one of the offending songs, reportedly by Singh, evocatively titled, "Ch**t Honey Singh."

Come let me f*ck you/I'll cleanse you of your desire to be f*cked/After f*cking you, I'll slipper you/I'll make you suck my c**k while I piss in your mouth [Author's translation]

For the rest of the lyrics, see http://www.elyrics.net/read/h/honey-singh-lyrics/choot-honey-singh-lyrics.html.

*Author's note*: Asterisks inserted by publisher. The editors and author, however, believe that every expression, however 'inappropriate' or 'offensive', has the right to be subsequently represented in full—not as endorsement of the views therein, but as a means to provoke critical debate/discussion.

lawyer issued a denial on his behalf.[2] Despite the denial and Singh's nervous protestations, few people protested against the gag—the show was cancelled, his videos and songs were edited and sites carrying his adult lyrics were temporarily inaccessible. In fact, there appeared to be a general consensus that Honey Singh got what he deserved, possibly because the incident happened soon after what is now known as "the Delhi rape."

It is still not clear why the rape capital of India, Delhi, reacted to the rape of Jyoti Singh Pandey[3] as it did. The horrific and tragic sexual assaults that have preceded and followed the Delhi gang rape have been ignored.[4] For instance, the abduction, three-day confinement, gang rape, and genital mutilation of a five-year-old girl in East Delhi just five months later on April 15, 2013,[5] elicited a comparatively tepid response, as did the attack, rape, and slit throat of a six-year old in a south Delhi public toilet on April 26, 2013. But the December 16 tragedy inflamed Delhi. Amid strident calls for chemical or physical castration, torture, and death (whether by legal means or by lynching) for the rapists, by men and women of all political dispensations and ages, the electronic

---

[2] The denial notice issued by lawyer Pragyan Pradip Sharma, on behalf of Singh states, "Honey Singh wishes to clarify through this notice that he has no connection whatsoever with the said songs. My client has already written to various digital platforms to immediately take down the video/songs and is also considering appropriate legal action for defamation, loss of reputation and violation of privacy."

[3] For some reason, the epithet Nirbhaya continues to be used, especially since her father Badri Singh, disclosed his dead daughter's identity on January 5, 2013 to remove the stigma of rape: "We want the world to know her real name.... My daughter didn't do anything wrong, she died while protecting herself.... I am proud of her. Revealing her name will give courage to other women who have survived these attacks. They will find strength from my daughter." While Indian law prohibits naming a rape victim unless she authorizes it, if she is dead, she may be named if her family agrees to it. See http://www.mirror.co.uk/news/world-news/india-gang-rape-victims-father-1521289. Various responses and analyses of the Delhi rape may be found at www.sanhati.com and elsewhere.

[4] "Delhi has witnessed 806 rape cases this year until June 20, a sharp increase from 330 for the same period last year. Delhi Police statistics show that the east district is the worst offender with 122 cases, followed by the southeast district which has witnessed 106 cases and southwest that has seen 102 cases. The three districts had reported 45, 56, and 42 cases, respectively, last year...." The jump in the number of molestation cases is even steeper, with 1,780 cases reported in the Capital in the first six months this year against 270 for the same period last year.

At 230, upmarket south Delhi has reported the highest figure, followed by west with 209 and east with 200. The three districts had witnessed 20, 25, and 35 cases, respectively, last year. http://www.hindustantimes.com/India-news/NewDelhi/Delhi-witnessed-806-rapes-in-2013-until-June/Article1-1085015.aspx

[5] The child was rescued more than 40 hours after the incident from the building in which she used to live. The doctors said she was undernourished and weighing only 20 kg. The child was shifted from Swami Dayanand Hospital to AIIMS for treatment after public protests.

media in particular sponsored debates about aspects of rape. Many of the TV shows showcased bloodlust and misogyny in equal parts, notwithstanding the discomfort of some of the anchors, panelists, and viewers. More nuanced, politically experienced, and humane feminist voices like Flavia Agnes' were heeded to only later.[6] Despite the presence of women activists (some of whom were rather bloodthirsty), some panelists doggedly insisted that women *invite* rape. Aggravating disputes over the finer points of women's culpability in their own rapes were common. There was much speculation about the usefulness of such voices on serious panels and the impact of these speakers on public opinion, given the context. They tended to further downgrade the idea of free speech to cacophony and political one-upmanship, a tendency that prevails anyway on most 24/7 English language news channel talk shows.

Even while anxieties about such opinions were relatively delimited given the public outcry against the gang rape and the government's unnerved responsiveness, there were speculations about the need for some moderation or regulation or course correction. One of the outcomes of the need for these was the ritualistic cancellation of Honey Singh's show.[7]

The Honey Singh incident, occurring as it did in the immediate aftermath of the Delhi gang rape, raked up the old issue of the impact of representation on life once again. Does art or kitsch affect life? Does it influence the way we think, our actions, the course of history?

Far from being a settled issue, the longstanding debate about the relationship between the real and the representational worlds is as old as art itself. The debate intensified greatly first, with the advent of camera, then, with the arrival of cinema, and then again, with the development of the mass media. The technological advancement that facilitated the camera's proficiency with verisimilitude (photography) was outdone only by cinema's proficiency with movement (the moving picture). The camera, intensified the scopic regime, and seemed to capture movement faithfully, and spectacularly *bring life to life* for all to see and deliberate on both immediately (while viewing) and at leisure (while reviewing). The camera's approximation of the human eye—by matching it—and then its enhancement of the capacities of the human eye—through magnification, illusion, voyeurism, spectacle, and speed

---

[6] http://www.asianage.com/columnists/rape-death-349

[7] Shah Rukh Khan salvaged Honey Singh by including him in his September 2013 international music tour that included New Zealand and Australia, and evidently without any consequences. Protests over Honey Singh are over.

management—promised to reveal what the eye itself sometimes failed to see. More so given the work of *mise-en-scène*, which enabled subtle ideological orientations. In fact, verisimilitude and life-like movement combined quite lethally to minimize the suspension of disbelief. Political questions were asked: was the camera an instrument for the 'pure' transcription of reality or was it obliged to assert the constructed-ness of the 'real'? Was the function of cinema the re-presentation of physical reality as Jean-Luc Godard argued, or was it to construct reality and its meanings, and to reveal how these are constructed, as Sergei Eisenstein maintained? In so many ways, the colorist impulse and the 'slice of life' dictum that was central to 'function of art' debates were revisited within the renewed technological context of the moving image both within and outside of its novelistic and theatrical cousins' naturalist idiom of despair and degeneration. The voyeuristic tendency inherent in the camera, that modernist instrument par excellence, was greatly accentuated by its dramatic and technological capabilities, and heavily fueled by its intense market reliance. It was only by and by that the alignments between the cinematic mode and commodification under capital were properly apprehended as impoverishing its aesthetical modernism. The lay understanding was that films were screened to what trade analysts and distributors called, 'the masses' and the 'classes', alike. In fact, the industry's approach used to be, "the more the merrier." Tickets were priced competitively, urban cinema halls were enlarged to an average capacity of 900 seats, luxury features such as cushioned seats, air conditioning, and upgraded sound were introduced to draw crowds to the very experience of cinema-going, not just a film. The PricewaterhouseCoopers and FICCI Reports of 2007 and 2008 note that, in India alone, films draw an estimated audience of 23 million per day. This does not include the diasporic audience or those who watch films on television. The scope of the cinema as a mass medium is then substantial, and it was expected to function within state-approved parameters for the mass media.

## II

The founding idea behind the government-owned mass media was not profit; it was to educate and entertain all sections of the people, a view that governed the state's approach to and policies on cinema till the mid-1990s.[8] However, the only segment of cinema that remained genuinely driven by this motto and by a relative freedom from box-office compulsions was the National Film Development Corporation (NFDC) funded film. While the film industry openly avowed and perceived itself to be a part of the continuing nation-building project, it remained equally committed to profitmaking and structured itself and conceptualized the nation accordingly. The state understood this and took a disapproving distance from the industry and its interpretation of nation and nation-building. The NFDC films, on the other hand, tended to follow the foundational first principles set by the state for the mass media while remaining heavily invested in formal, idiomatic, and thematic experimentalism. The commitment of the likes of Bhupen Hazarika, Chetan Anand, Balraj Sahni, Bimal Roy, and K.A. Abbas of the Indian People's Theatre Association (IPTA) and Prem Chand, Kaifi Azmi, and Ismat Chughtai of Progressive Writers' Association (PWA) to these principles and their contributions to cinema helped steer the course of cinema in the 1940s and part of the 1950s. But with the post-war decline of the studio system, cinema was slowly starved of legitimate sources of cash and soon became open to all manners of financial speculators. The shadow of disrepute that had tended to follow mainstream cinema particularly after the 1940s thickened and by the middle of the 1960s cinema had become a somewhat murky business.

By the 1970s, as mainstream cinema's commercial dependence on people unconnected with filmmaking soared, the entity called 'commercial cinema' came into existence, marking by its very nomenclature an alignment with the box office or profit at the apparently acceptable cost of its artistic credentials. The field of esthetics was left to the 'art film' makers, and their niche audience, till 'middle' cinema resolved to walk both lines. Films nevertheless, through all of this, remained strongly aligned with the productive agenda of creating Andersonian imagined communities. The industry's nexus with the underworld and the underworld's nexus with politicians and the police made filmmaking risky in unprecedented ways. But it also determined it in ways that only gradually came to light. For instance, it is now better known that Amitabh Bachchan's characters in *Deewar* (Yash

---

[8] See Abhilasha Kumari's (2008) *Media: The Key Driver of Consumerism Macro-Micro Linkage and Policy Dimension—A Case Study of FM Radio* for an excellent discussion of some of these issues.

Chopra: 1975) and *Mr Natwarlal* (Rakesh Kumar: 1979), and Pankaj Kapur's character in *Maqbool* (Vishal Bharadwaj: 2004) were loosely based on early underworld investors in the industry like Haji Mastan, Karim Lala, Varadaraja Mudaliar, and Yusuf Patel. Then, in 1997, T Series owner Gulshan Kumar was murdered by Abdul Rauf Dawood Merchant, alias Rauf Raja, allegedly a hit man of the Abu Salem gang, for non-payment of extortion money. In 2001, diamond merchant–financier Bharat Shah was arrested for laundering underworld money, and a can of worms was opened. An established network of connections between the police, the underworld, the politicians and the business community was revealed.[9] Unfortunately, cinema's intimate relation with the 'real world' of commerce is seldom registered *theoretically* in mainstream film studies. Now, we increasingly see the intimate connection. Cinema is now almost exclusively controlled by big business and is a part of a huge transnational industrial complex that is only growing. It has slipped almost wholly into the private financial hands of giant transnational corporations and is undergoing massive and unprecedented structural changes. Simultaneously, significant idiomatic, thematic, and ideological changes that correspond with the impulses of their ascendant economic drivers are becoming evident.[10] Despite the current digital shift and the resulting relief from some problems and expenses associated with filmmaking and processing, the heavy reliance on technology and capital remain and, even increase.

Neither the state nor filmmakers ever made the mistake of separating cinema and the material world within which it occurred. Notwithstanding the short shrift, it gave the Patil Committee Report, the state kept a keen eye on both money matters and content from the time of cinema's inception.[11] The state viewed cinema as both a

[9] See Gabriel 2010 for a longer discussion of these events, and Barnouw, Erik and S. Krishnaswamy (1963) for a comprehensive discussion of the early industry.

[10] For a more detailed account of the political economy of contemporary cinema, see Gabriel (2013a) *Changing Frames: Globalisation and Convergence in Bombay Cinema*, in *The Globalization of the Media: Issues & Approaches*, P.K. Bandhopadhaya and Rajesh Das (eds.). London: Anthem Press, 2013, and 2013(b) http://www.frontline.in/arts-and-culture/cinema/market-and-the-medium/article5185959.ece.

[11] In an attempt to curb financial unaccountability and other undesirable changes, the Indian government appointed the S.K. Patil Film Enquiry Committee in 1949 to enquire into all aspects of the film industry. The Committee enquired into a range of issues plaguing the film industry including the decline of the studio system, the rise of private and temporary entrepreneurs, the star system and the black market. It submitted its report in 1951, but the state took a note of some of its recommendations only in the 1960s.

cash cow, and as a potentially harmful and corrupting mass medium. With regard to the objectionable and harmful content of cinema, both the imperial and the post-colonial state raised the issue of the impact of representation on life in the particularly controversial contexts of sedition, national interest, violence, and sexual explicitness.

When deliberating on the cinema's proclivity to incite, governments have frequently focused on its ability to influence public opinion.

> The Supreme Court in a judgement three years ago said that film censorship becomes necessary because a film motivates thought and action and assures a high degree of attention and retention as compared to the printed word. The combination of act and speech, sight and sound in semi-darkness of the theatre with elimination of all distracting ideas will have a strong impact on the minds of the viewers and can affect emotions. Therefore, it has as much potential for evil as it has for good and has an equal potential to instill or cultivate violent or good behavior. It cannot be equated with other modes of communication. Censorship by prior restraint is, therefore, not only desirable but also necessary.[12]

It was not just the state, but also the women's movement and various communities and social groups that found cinema's ability to influence and seduce dangerous. Demands for the state regulation of images, speech, and discourse have come from groups across the social and political spectrum. The influential nature of the medium was raised in all cases. It appeared then, and rightly so, that verisimilitude and movement were not solely responsible for cinema's credibility.

# III

The specific viewing protocols of cinema—community viewing, darkened halls, magnified sound and images—and even the esthetics of realism (as these were observed and mediated by the medium across cultures and genres) may be seen to contribute to its perceived powers of persuasion. But quite apart from these, the spectacular, larger-than-life

---

[12] Section 3.3 of the CBFC document "Film Censorship: What Everyone Should Know," http://cbfcindia.gov.in/CbfcWeb/fckeditor/editor/images/Uploadedfiles/file/Publications/Film_censorship.pdf the government has introduced a series of regulatory measures to address other media such as The Cable Television Networks (Regulation) Act, 1995 and Information Technology Act (2000).

nature of the medium's apparatus and its images themselves inspire conjectures about the persuasive impact of the moving image and its corresponding truth value. The enhancement of its approximation to 'real' life and, therefore, its truth-bearing potential, paradoxically enough, was in direct proportion to its penchant for the spectacular and the dramatic.

The consequent extravagant, and yet life-like, moving spectacle was seen as enthralling and credible on the one hand and distracting and misleading on the other. Moreover, it frequently wrapped its portrayals and understandings of the world in framing narratives that persuasively offered the viewer an ideological interpretation of life and the world. These narratives themselves were saturated with the seductions of coherence, linearity, clear causality, and resolution, all of which earnestly proposed a specific ideological approach to life, conflict, social order, and fulfillment. There were classic palliatory explanations offered to classic problems of oppression, inequality, and struggle. Of course, cinemas from different cultures complicated this debate, but cinema itself continued to remain in a position to make powerful truth claims, and sometimes did so explicitly, as in the case of the documentary mode.

Add to the above arguments factors like established and common shot-taking methods that visually create a coherent world, and we see how narrative film and its typical characteristics fueled the terms of the debate about the relation between art and life, between representation and reality, between cinema and truth, between cinema and belief, and between truth and belief. Given its routine engagement with the domains of fiction and drama, cinema, in addition to disseminating knowledge and opinions in the public domain, was also viewed as instrumental in shaping the imagination itself. Indeed it has been convincingly argued that the cinematic engagement with phenomena, be these social (gender regimes, sexual practices, and caste hierarchies) or techno-scientific (science fiction and the war film), serves to prepare the audience both imaginatively and emotionally for social, technological, and scientific transformations of the world that may otherwise appear unacceptable, incomprehensible, and alarming (cyborgs, clones, genetic engineering, robotics, zombies, etc.).[13]

---

[13] See for example Haraway in During (ed.), 1999.

The elision of vital but contentious issues—caste, race, class, alternative gender regimes, and sexual practices—or the explicit or implicit recommendation of status quo in these domains, is the effect of specific production modes, and may have the effect of delimiting the possible worlds one may imagine or restrict the imagination of these within the ideological framework recommended by the more common and popular, if orthodox, representations of the medium. Even while conceding that there is no passive Pavlovian acceptance of proffered images and realities but rather an active engagement with them (Fiske and Hartley, 2003; Michele 1986),[14] it is necessary, as we will see, to understand the logistics and terms of engagement.

First, cinema was hailed as a democratic form that catered indiscriminately to the educated and the illiterate, the rich and the poor. Early on in its urban avatar, cinema's only visible concession to class distinctions was in the arrangement and pricing of seats in the cinema hall. Though this, as we shall see, is a severely partial story that glosses the imperatives of commerce and the quantum and distribution of money involved, and decision-making centers and logistics within the industry, it is a popular one that acknowledges the reach of this mass medium.

Second, despite its information 'overload' of 24 frames a second, film has also been seen as carrying historically 'poor' material, that is, material that is not worth knowing or that can be counted as historiographically valuable (Ferro, 1988; Rosenstone, 1988).[15] The result of the combination of cinema's putative *poor information load*, its insistence in dealing with national and social issues as part of its contribution to and preoccupation with the idea of the nation and nation-building, and its alleged influence over the public domain, was considerable anxiety and vigilance in the state and within society. Very soon, it became the only art form to face compulsory and systematic pre-release censorship. That was considered to be the only way to minimize potential 'hurt sentiments' and the socio-political fallout of these. This task was eventually given to the Central Board of Film Certification (CBFC), which has to certify every film—whether Indian or foreign—that is released in India. The CBFC has come in for both criticism and praise and their task appears to be getting

---

[14] For discussions see Fiske and Hartley (2003) and Michele (1986).
[15] See Ferro (1988) and Rosenstone (1988) among others.

only more politically difficult since the national proneness to taking offense is on the rise.

# IV

Over the last 15 years or so, the discourse of hurt has appeared as a renewed one in the realm of the political, with consistency and pervasiveness that have given rise to such disparaging epithets as "the republic of hurt sentiments." The suspicion that the hurt sentiment is often a manufactured one, seeking to attain to community/group/ section dominance rather paradoxically by alleging the weakness/ vulnerability of the community in the face of a particular form of 'hurt' is not entirely without a reason. There are a host of instances to validate this opinion, which include the Ambedkar cartoon controversy, the A.K. Ramanujam case; the harassment and exile of M.F. Husain and the destruction of his art; the attack and arrest of Chandramohan Srilamantula at the Fine Arts department of the Maharaja Sayajirao University (MSU) in Vadodara, Gujarat; the 2007 ban on AXN and FTV for their risqué and adult content; the ban of Rushdie, Taslima Nasreen, *Kamasutra* (Mira Nair: 1996) and Deepa Mehta's *Fire* (1996) and *Water* (2005); the protests over Kamal Hassan's *Hey! Ram* (2000) and *Vishwaroopam* (2013); and "Operation Majnu"—the list goes on and on.[16]

All of these instances accentuate the fact that the site of the sexual, like the domain of the political, has been a key domain of censorship.[17] Like the debates about the influence of art or representation on life, the one about censorship *per se* and specifically of sexual content is twofold. First, do representations of sexuality (or any other phenomenon) influence the way we think about it; and second, if they do, should they be regulated. Though both parts of the debate remain unresolved, people have taken sides giving rise to what are rather misleadingly known

---

[16] *Operation Majnu* was planned by the Uttar Pradesh police as an instructive on-camera event against the *indecency* and *immorality* of local couples who used to meet in various parks. It consisted of beating up couples—married or not—especially women, who were found in these parks.

[17] While political censorship is an important aspect of state regulation, the concern here is with the regulation of representations of the sexual.

as the 'pro-sex'/'anti-censorship' and the 'anti-sex'/'pro-censorship', lobbies. Both of these sides are linked to the women's movement and feminist activism.[18]

Both positions cognize the active influence of representation on how we think, understand the world, and relate to it, even while the 'pro-sex/porn, anti-censorship' lobby has rather paradoxically, also asserted the right to free speech on the basis that representations *do not* influence behavior notwithstanding the advertising proclaimed and established reliance on consumer psychology and media studies analysis of this. Both sides have invoked Mill's harm principle on the one hand, and his notion of moral autonomy, advocacy of tolerance, and freedom of thought and expression on the other, while making their argument. Both sides have dwelt with greater or lesser success on the several philosophical, empirical, legal, and procedural issues involved, notwithstanding the fact that the rather unfortunate caricaturing of each other's positions resulted in the effective loss of some insights.

Bearing the complexities of this debate in mind and glossing them when necessary, one may make the following arguments. The techno-industrial structure of this art form mediates the relationships between representation and reality that are proposed in and by it. The concerns about this relationship were expressed by the women's movement, for instance, must therefore take into account this industrial mediation, to understand the dynamics that determine and shape the appearance (or not) within representation, of women, of sexuality, of violence, all of which were drawn into a continuum in the debates on regulation and harm. While femininity, violence, and 'appropriate' sexuality are all constituted in and as reality, what goes into constituting them, and how they are so constituted, is the matter of mediated representations. Censorship is another element that tries to regulate this mediation, on the premise that the representational—that which exists in representation—can (a) be reproduced in reality, thereby causing actual harm; or (b) affect (or in other ways mediate) social response to that

---

[18] Initially, the women's movement had few disagreements with the state's understanding of mass media. While arguing for the regulation of representation as they did at the time of the Indecent Representation of Women (Prohibition) Act of 1986, they (a) invoked the harm principle in relation to *women as a community* and (b) they excluded representations for *the public good* (the domains of art, religion and education). See section 4(a) of *The Indecent Representation of Women (Prohibition) Act, 1986.*

which is represented, with the same end. It seeks, rather paradoxically, to preempt those possible effects through erasure of the 'source' or 'original' in the representational field.

The issue with unregulated sexual representation is that it may tend to be heteropatriarchal and misogynistic. After all, speech is generated from and received within a larger set of historical contexts, and by specific systems of production. In fact the contexts of production and reception determine the scope of what gets said, who says it, and how it gets said, as the theoretical interventions of feminism, race, postcolonial, subaltern, and Dalit studies have shown.

The key point is *that sex speech about women in the public domain very often tends to proximate hate speech.* The entire spectrum of sentiments—from the erotic to the misogynistic—that are subsumed under the term sexual speech must be acknowledged when debating the emancipatory potential of sexual speech. After all, sexual speech includes 'eve-teasing', or the physical and verbal sexual harassment and intimidation of women in public spaces. It also includes the legal interrogation and intimidation of rape victims, Togadia's remarks on Jyoti Pandey, Modi's remarks on his machismo, Honey Singh's lyrics, the objectification, and commodification of bodies, the commercialization of subjects, the eroticization of alienation and suffering that characterizes the electronic media's representations of women, men, and now children.

Precisely because of the larger, key, though sometimes neglected contexts of cinematic production and reception—some of which have already been set out—content is often scrutinized. This process of scrutiny may sometimes result in the screening of violence and eroticized violence, and the censoring of eroticism and sexual pleasure. Or it may result in the remarkable and instructive intervention that Justice Lentin's dissent in the *Pati Parmeshwar* (My Husband, My Lord: 1989) was.

In 1989, the Censor Board and the Film Certification Appellate Tribunal denied the film, *Pati Parmeshwar* a certificate for public exhibition under Section S 5-B of the Cinematographic Act, 1952. The Tribunal stated that the film was mortifying and offensive to women and derogatory to their dignity. The producers appealed the decision arguing that, "depicting women in ignoble servility did not have anything to do with immorality or indecency since the phrase 'morality' or 'decency' meant sexual morality alone" (Sebastian, 1989: 717). They won. Although the state does act patriarchally, it is not a monolith (Gabriel, 2010: 144). The government went to court and the two-judge bench who heard the case, disagreed with each other.

Justice Lentin who dissented, and wanted to prevent the exhibition of the film, remarked that the heroine's behavior was a glorification of ignoble servility, indecent "to the point of repugnancy" (Sebastian, 1989: 717). He went on to state that servility is always ignoble, and that therefore, the inclusion of the word "ignoble" in the "Guidelines" was superfluous. The points of difference were referred to a third judge, who upheld the verdict in favor of the producers.

Justice Lentin's attempts to dissociate offensiveness and immorality from sexuality and to attach them instead to servility and degradation constitute a remarkable attempt to address the violence inherent in the process of mediation per se because of which, in the context of cinema, the work of the Metzian "outer machine" (the cinema industry), and various macrosystems that give the image its full implications are technologically invisibilized.[19] Hence, it attempts to restore subjectivity and personhood to women and implicitly recommend an alternative framework within which to understand the ethical and sociological implications of alienation, and inequality (Kapur, 1994).[20] The dehumanization and estrangement that violence induces will intensify exponentially in the mechanical and then electronic age and, as Baudrillard's observation about the information age reminds us, "*we no longer partake of the drama of alienation, but are in the ecstasy of an [obscene] communication*" (1988: 21–22, original emphasis). The levels of reification achieved in the new media evidence a grave and possibly gendered predicament.

These tendencies intensify within the dual contexts of a highly patriarchal context and the reigning free-market rightwingism, which has sponsored a highly corrupt state-corporate nexus, unprecedented technologization, the invisibilization of labor exploitation, and the

---

[19] Here, I have drawn on Beller's (2013) compelling analysis of how the cinematic mode of production manifests the logic of the alienation of labor that characterizes post-industrial capitalism.

[20] The consistency with which he did this is evident in his decision as the chairman of Censor Board to permit the exhibition of the *Bandit Queen*, a decision that was challenged but then upheld by the Supreme Court.

armed repression of protest. The state-corporate nexus has unleashed some of the most reactionary tendencies in society, including the fetishization of commodification and intense alienation. As an example, the now-routine item number in cinema, rather than erotically displaying the dancing body, has become a literal itemization of it, the dismemberment of it into component sexualized parts (breast, mouth, belly, navel, thigh, and bottom). It is also deliberately dissociated from narrative so that it can be moved effortlessly from one AV platform to another—from the film to TV ([V] to MTV) to phones, and so on. Such a conceptualization and cinematic rendition of the woman's body manifests a larger tendency to disaggregate, alienate, commodify, and gratuitously consume. More, it creates and produces economies and semiotics of desire that are premised on alienation, ceaseless fragmentation, and commodification. And this becomes fetish as it drives and fuels both a political economy and a gender-sexual politics in which, firstly, "in accordance with the principles of late capitalism, to look is to labor" (Beller, 2013: 250); and secondly, the dismembering, objectification, and subordination (of a woman) becomes an eroticized prerequisite for desirability.

Coleman (2013: 56), writing on the repertoire of sex-games available in the new media, remarks on the Dolcett (code for gynophagia role-play) experience of BDSM (bondage/discipline/sadism/masochism) virtual activity, in which submissive women are depicted "being hanged, cooked and variously penetrated as part of the sexual act." Dolcett fan fiction includes titles like "How to Cook a Woman's Breasts." She goes on to quote from a virtual world blogger's notes

> ... It's kinda weird. I don't like pain. Being whipped, paddled, or tortured really just turns me off. And the idea of snuff play just seems so ... final. But the thought of being prepped, stuffed, basted, roasted and eaten ... that appeals to me. I guess it goes back to my objectification fetish. Being turned into food is just as good as any other type of object.... A few days after joining, I got an IM [instant message] from [a member]. (Coleman, 2013: 57)

The blogger goes on to describe how arousing she found the experience of being tied to a spit and cooked. Coleman remarks that in an important way, the gamers see "their virtual behavior as actual" (2013: 58). Yet they may simultaneously fail to realize that the "generalized blindness with respect to the economization of the senses is constitutive of hegemony" (Beller, 2013: 251).

The techno-industrial-electronic mode tends to valorize objectification and consumption to the extent that being a consumable object is an achievement, when "the thought of being prepped, stuffed, basted, roasted and eaten…. Appeals." It is then not surprising that men are gradually becoming itemized commodities as well. Meanwhile, scant attention is paid to the fact that by and large the owners and decision-makers of this industrial sector continue to be the (mostly male but also female) local and transnational elite who are safely positioned at the top of this patriarchal and predatory pecking order as 'laboring' consumers, and not commodities. But furthermore, the implications of the slippage between visuality and reality, the scopic and the organic, are not encountered equally not least because, as Fisher (2009) reminds us, the equality promised by capital is only a reductive monetary equivalence of all things. And so, actual excesses against women—on or off-screen—are facilitated by their elision as subjects and their transformation into scopic objects of fantasy. The body becomes the issue when transacting fantasy, when moving from the virtual to the actual.

> While fantasy may in fact be empowering and pleasurable in theory, in the process of activating it, of releasing it into the world of consequences and subjectivities, it encounters factors that it must necessarily bypass in order to be successful. These include pain, resistant subjectivities and bodies, statutory law, modifications in logic, and so on. If these are ignored while enacting fantasies—especially those that involve power and pain (domination, rape)—what may be produced is not consensual pleasure, but simply the routine equations between pain–subjugation, pleasure–power. In such a case it is likely that pain and pleasure will remain on two different and gendered sides of the equation, possibly infracting statutory laws but not patriarchal ones (e.g., rape fantasies). Therefore fantasy, sexuality and their pleasures are at once freeing and dangerous, independent and socially determined. (Gabriel, 2010: 149)

The conversion of woman's body into scopic object and fetishized commodity is, therefore, rife with the possibilities that she will remain synonymized with a virtual existence: not organically human, not a feeling, thinking, human subject, with vital organs, a nervous system, a mind, capable of pain, unwilling for pain and subjugation. Perhaps this glitch is what happened with Jyoti Singh Pandey. So, even if Honey Singh enjoys having his mouth pissed in while giving head, or getting sexual desire f*cked right out of him, the gendered recommendation of these signal how this discursive technologic is partly responsible for the exclusion of women from the domain of normative humanity. As Foucault reminds us

> Last but not least, the major enemy, the strategic adversary is fascism … And not only historical fascism, the fascism of Hitler and Mussolini-which was able to mobilize and use the desire of the masses so effectively-but also the fascism in us all, in our heads and in our everyday behavior, the fascism that causes us to love power, to desire the very thing that dominates and exploits us. (Foucault, 1983: xiii)

'Free sexual speech' is an insufficient criterion for a political recovery of pleasure, especially if the very motive of sexual speech is intimidation and social control, and if the troubled idea of 'freedom' is theorized outside of the structural and discursive conditions that facilitate the idea of absolute equality and radical difference.

# References

Barnouw, Erik and S. Krishnaswamy (Eds.). 1963. *Indian Film*. New York, NY: Columbia University Press.

Baudrillard, Jean. 1988. *The Ecstasy of Communication*. Trans. Bernard Schutze and Caroline Schutze. Brooklyn: Semiotext(e).

Beller, Jonathan. 2013. "Kino-I, Kino World: Notes on the cinematic mode of production," in *The Visual Culture Reader*, edited by Nicholas Mirzoeff. New York: Routledge.

Benjamin, Walter. 1970. "Art in the Age of Mechanical Reproduction," *Illuminations*. London: Jonathan Cape.

Coleman, Beth. 2013. "X-Reality: Interview with the Virtual Cannibal," in *The Visual Culture Reader*, edited by Nicholas Mirzoeff. London: Routledge, 2013.

Deleuze, Gilles and Felix Guattari. 1983. *Anti-Oedipus: Capitalism and Schizophrenia*, (trans.) by Robert Hurley, Mark Seem, and Helen R. Lane. USA: University of Minnesota.

Ferro, Mark. 1988. *Cinema and History*, N. Greene (trans.). Detroit, MI: Wayne University Press.

Fisher, Mark. 2009. *Capitalist Realism: Is There No Alternative?* Zero Books: California.

Fiske, John and John Hartley. 2003. *Reading Television*. London and New York: Routledge.

Foucault, Michel. 1983. "Preface," in *Anti-Oedipus: Capitalism and Schizophrenia*, USA: University of Minnesota.

Gabriel, Karen. 2010. *Melodrama and the Nation: The Sexual Economies of Mainstream Bombay Cinema*. New Delhi: Women Unlimited.

Haraway, Donna. 1999. "A Cyborg Manifesto," in Simon During (Ed.). *The Cultural Studies Reader*. London & New York: Routledge.

Kumari, Abhilasha. 2008. *Media: The Key Driver of Consumerism Macro-Micro Linkage and Policy Dimension—A Case Study of FM Radio*, ISID Working Paper.

Mattelart, Michele. 1986. "Women and the Culture Industries," in *Media Culture and Society*, edited by Collins, Curran, Garnham et al.. New Delhi: SAGE Publications.

Metz, Christian. 1982. *Psychoanalysis and Cinema: The Imaginary Signifier*. London: Macmillan.

Rosenstone, Robert A. 1988. "History in Images/History in Words: Reflections on the Possibility of Really Putting History onto Film," *American Historical Review,* 93(5): 1173–1185.

Sebastian, P.A. 1989. "Upholding Ideology of Male Domination," *Economic and Political Weekly*, 24(14): 716–718.

# 16

# The Erotics of Law, Scandal, and Technology

*Lawrence Liang*

A group of diners seated around a dinner table engaged in small talk would be an innocuous scene in any film but when it is a Luis Bunuel film, one can reasonably expect the dinner to take on a strange turn. In his film *The Phantom of Liberty*, Bunuel depicts a group of people seated on lavatories around a dinner table and at some point they begin to excuse themselves to go secretly into a small little room where they eat their dinner in a furtive and guilty manner. Bunuel's inversion of the norms of public and private and what may be seen and what may not within the realm of publicity serves as a useful way of thinking about the somewhat tenuous compact between the public and private in the mediatized world that we live in. A contemporary updating of this scene in India would involve a middle class family gathered in a dinner table oblivious to the hard core pornography playing on the television set and then someone excuses herself to guiltily watch *Kyuki Saas Bhi Kabhi Bahu Thi*. That which was a private secret takes on the shape of a public secret—a truth that is universally recognized even as it cannot be publicly acknowledged. And just as the eruption of scandals is a necessary aspect of serials like *Kyu Ki Saas,* it seems as though the regular eruption of scandals has become such a necessary part of our post-mediatized world that the idea of the scandal as a temporal rupture has itself become meaningless.

The two sites we see this playing out in most often are the Sting Operation's revelation of public corruption and leaked amateur sex scandals (Malhotra, 2011). Collectively they have become important signposts of scandal in contemporary social life. They are also at the heart of legal debates over privacy, media ethics, and legal disorder. The accelerated world of media circulation completely alters our understanding of scandals and the divide between the public and private. If the public–private divide has been at the heart of liberal legal imagination, one of the challenges before us is what happens when we encounter new technologies that render such a divide meaningless. While scandals have always been a crucial site for the production of a discourse on law and its relationship to the public, private, and the secret, they also have the ability to reshape legal discourse in its own image. This paper examines how the discourses of corruption and sexuality in media constantly reference each other as they meet in the "inappropriate overlap of public and private desires" (Miller, 2009) and what this does to legal discourse.

Brought together under the sign of the 'scandal', sting operations and MMS scandals both rely on the technology of the hidden camera and on the surface they seemingly have little to do with each other but as will become evident a number of the political scandals themselves are tainted by the hint of sexual impropriety where the sexual and the political often overlap. I will argue that these new scandals are symptomatic of a much larger shift in modes of public and private spectatorship. Visual technologies do not just allow us to see in ways that were hitherto thought impossible, they also teach us new ways of seeing. If early visual technologies such as photography and movie cameras produced a 'field of the visible' in which direct human vision of events, places, and bodies began to be mediated by an optical apparatus that sees in place of the naked eye, what we seem to have now with the proliferation of hidden cameras is an obsessive production of the unseen and the private in which visual pleasure is referenced through its immersion in the domain of privacy.

Ruth Miller in an important work on contemporary corruption argues that the discourse of corruption has always been underwritten by an erotic charge. This is evidenced in the rhetorical language used to describe the revelation of corruption ('denuding someone', 'naked truth', etc.). For Miller, one of the defining characteristics of the erotic is its disintegration of established boundaries, and historically the idea of bodily disarray has informed anxieties of political or social disarray. She, therefore, argues that the erotic of corruption is a useful way of thinking about how our contemporary lives (personal and political) are brought together in an unholy alliance to create a domain which is not just biological nor just political, but one that is biopolitical. The horrifying images of American soldiers' treatment of prisoners in Abu Ghraib or the parading of young Kashmiris by the Indian army on the one hand and the leaked scandals of politicians like N.D. Tiwari and Abhishek Manu Singhvi on the other, all seem to testify to a new genre—political porn—in which the line between erotic and political disorder is completely erased.

Narratives of corruption also draw heavily from the idea of the diseased body where the body politic is one that is marked by undesirable intermingling of public and private interests. Were the leaked Abhishek Manu Singhvi tapes or Nira Radia's conversations with Ratan Tata a violation of their privacy or a revelation of a compromise of public interest? The fact that they now seem indistinguishable provides us the context to better understand how technologies like the hidden camera have entered our putative consciousness.

The glee with which we listened to the Amar Singh tapes or Nira Radia's conversation with Ratan Tata about Roberto Cavalli gowns is indicative of our fascination and horror with sleaze in a manner that was earlier reserved only for pornography (Vasudevan and Ambapardivala, 2011). Even if some of these revelations justify themselves through a moral language of resistance to power or the revelation of corruption, the fact of the matter is that much of the pleasure that we derived from them had little to do with the illumination that they brought on issues of public interest. We are fascinated with the violation of other people's privacy, even if we don't call it that—and we have all found ourselves riveted with recent media scandals that suggest to us that one of the paradoxes of our time is that even as we see a rise in formal claims of privacy (from our outrage every time Google or Facebook changes its policies to the objections against UID project), we are simultaneously engaged in ordinary practices that relate either to the violation or negation of our own and other peoples' privacy. The infinite regress of privacy (every revelation implies a further concealment, each bit of knowledge uncovered generates the desire for more) finds itself being redeemed in a manner that earlier would have been tainted with guilt. The consumption of pornography for instance always existed within the shadow of guilt, but scandal's reliance on gleeful and not guilty pleasure distinguishes it from pornography.

Narratives of scandalous self-revelation feed the individual reader/ viewer's desire even as any guilt is alleviated by the knowledge that there is wider interpretative community which is part of this infinite regression of privacy. In a post-Facebook world, we are increasingly accustomed to a denial of our own privacy, and it is, therefore, not surprising that the discourse around corruption and sexuality in media constantly reference each other as they meet in the "inappropriate overlap of public and private desires" (Miller, 2009).

Given our contemporary media landscape, it would appear there is a need to rethink the idea of what constitutes pornography and how it can be a useful conceptual category to think about the contemporary techno media landscape. If classical pornography referred to sexually explicit content, it seems almost benignly anachronistic to think of a 'blue film' with its blonde-brunette fornications that people saw on a VCR. Given the intense proliferation of scandals as the lifeline of our post-mediatized lives, the real thrill lies less in direct depictions of sex than in its masking through blurred pixelated images on mainstream television or low-resolution images taken from mobile phones. It makes more sense to speak about contemporary pornography not in terms of a reference to sexual content, but as a form of distribution, circulation and interaction. We often refer to various experiences (often with no connection to sex) as being pornographic and the idea of pornography as a metaphor has now become commonplace enough to reference phenomena marked by a certain excess as being pornographic. In what manner does pornography work as a metaphor, and what is it about forms of excess that make it pornographic? The Internet introduces very tactile forms of fantasy which occupies the space between private fantasy and mass public circulation. Michael Uebel argues that "As the Web becomes increasingly constructed as the imaginary point of the public, we begin to recognize our own desires as they are represented to us in the medias that surround us" (Uebel, 1999). Thus, if the realm of our private sexual fantasies were a point from which we drew a distinction of our interior lives and the exterior world, we now have a scenario where our private desires can be mapped almost immediately upon a public realm in which we see them as mass desires from their inception.

Namita Malhotra in her work on MMS scandals describes this new regime of leaked videos of ordinary sexual acts as one which introduces a new kind of image, and writing about her experience of watching the clip from the Mysore Mallige scandal she says

> When looking at material like Mysore Mallige and DPS MMS clip, the affective relation that predominates is indeed that of its "realness"; for some, this produces a sense of fear, paradoxically a ghostly quality to the image and unease. For me, it was about the uncanniness of the familiar body, which occupies a similar world to yours that is somehow trapped in a video.

She describes the experience as a shocked recognition of yourself and desire to see the images again as a strange combination of, titillation, boredom, and yet an unwillingness to look away because it seems to provide you with a mirror image of what you perhaps look like during sex even as it induces a fear about your own privacy and a disgust for what seems unacceptable.

## The Aesthetics of Pornographic Form?

Building on the argument that scholars like Jean Louis Comolli have made about the intensification of the "field of the visible" produced by technology, as the direct human vision of events, places, and bodies began to be mediated by an optical apparatus that sees in place of the 'naked eye', Linda Williams describes the visual, hard-core knowledge—pleasure produced by the *scientia sexualis* as a "frenzy of the visible." This is best evidenced with the rise of a 'televisual' form of seeing in which the idea of surfing through channels creates a bleeding effect, with each channel seamlessly merging into the other and producing a frenzy of visible, yet indistinguishable images.

The argument of the televisual imagination is that the mode of channel surfing is no longer restricted to TV, and that the ways in which we consume media bleed into other practices. We may, for instance, repress the ritual (watching the screen) but we cannot repress the myth ('watching' the image). If we can switch television off, we cannot switch our televisual imaginary off. The experience of online pornography has similarities as well.

> I caught myself clicking through to a gallery, taking in the contents with a glance, and backing out to click through to the next gallery. I didn't need to

spend much time with the pictures to feel the titillation of porn. That's what gives me a hint about how it must feel to be obsessed with online porn—that the search, as much as (or more than) the pictures, is really what turns you on. No individual picture or video can be as novel or exciting as you hope it will be, so you keep searching and looking, looking and searching. You're never satiated because if you just masturbated to any particular picture or video, you'd miss out on all those other ones. (Lynn, 2005)

In an information crammed society where the televisuality of channel surfing combines with the haptic multitasking function of multiple windows on our computer screens, it is the database and the archive and not the studio which produces our experience of pornography. But what are we to make of this new degraded image that has become almost a default mode of seeing? In thinking about what the introduction of the camera did to consciousness, Walter Benjamin says that the camera introduces us to sensory and psychic experiences allowing us to explore our "optical unconscious" which was not hitherto possible with traditional ways of seeing. Matteo Pasquinelli argues that much before cultural and media theorists started taking the phenomenon of porn as a conceptual category seriously, its affective powers was recognized in science fiction (Pasquinelli, 2009: 159). He argues that what Ballard understood was the need for a post-Freudian exploration of the psyche—one which moved eroticism from interiority to the outer world of reality. Pasquinelli cites one of Ballard's works in which the nervous systems of the characters have been externalized, as part of the reversal of the interior and exterior worlds. Highways, office blocks, faces, and street signs are perceived as if they were elements in a malfunctioning central nervous system. In other works, Ballard spreads a giant pornographic picture of Elizabeth Taylor across hundreds of billboards. Ballard saw the profile of a pornographic 'civilization' in the shadow of the 1950s mediascape, far earlier than the rise of the netporn society.

> Thanks to press, film and television, sex has become a communal and public activity for the first time since the Edens of a more primitive age. In a sense we now all take part in sex whether we want to or not.

Sexual intercourse can no longer be regarded as a personal and isolated activity, but is seen to be a vector in a public complex involving automobile styling, politics, and mass communications. Another crucial aspect of Ballard's work which intrigues Pasquinelli is the mixing of the political and the sexual, or what has also been referred to as warporn. Experimental video artists brought together the spectacle of war, pornography, and sport, in an orgy of images where they become indistinguishable, and in more recent times we have seen the horrors these mixed forms when images of torture became indistinguishable from porn in Abu Ghraib, Kashmir (Sengupta, 2014). We also find the language of war and weapons being recycled in the courts: in *Surya Prakash Khatri* vs. *Madhu Trehan*, the Delhi High Court observed that:

> The power of the Press is almost like nuclear power. It can create and it can destroy. Keeping this in mind, it is imperative for the media to exercise due care and caution before publication of a potentially damaging piece. The court also stated that news reports are like a loaded gun and it may not be appropriate for the media to contend that it not know that the gun was loaded.

What Ballard was interested in was extending the logic of pornography to understand a wider range of phenomena including the laboratory and the studio.

> The apparent scientific detachment, the "analytic activity whose main aim is to isolate objects or events," is compared to the obsessive magnification of detail in pornography: "This obsession with the specific activity of quantified functions is what science shares with pornography." The white coat of the scientist hides an abstract pornographer, while the rationalist anxieties of science are double—bound to a dangerous underworld—we might say: the higher the knowledge, the greater the beast.

He was convinced that there will be a time when science is itself the greatest producer of pornography. Ballard was writing at a time when a lot of the developments in new psychology, with its insistence on reading truth in the skin of the body, were also being tested in legal courtrooms. And there was an almost intimate connection between the laboratory and the court with contested legal battles over technologies such as the polygraph. The polygraph was initially held not to be admissible evidence, but through its popularity in cultural accounts as an aid to investigation, it slowly acquired a legitimacy in law. If the laboratory was a space for the production of a hyper law, then the studio also emerges as an extra legal space that is engaged in the production of its own law. And the form that I am interested in is how accounts of corruption and illegality mirror pornography and its status as the illegal.

# Erotics of Corruption

Ruth Miller in her work on the erotics of corruption (Miller, 2009) traces the link between erotics and corruption to the history of colonial rule, and the anxiety and discourse around corruption in the colonies. She finds that the rhetorical force in the narrative of corruption, bordered on the half-legal, and half-sexual threat to democracy and the rule of law. Miller looks for an erotic basis to the state of exception and specific colonial or postcolonial manifestations of it. She argues that there is a distinct colonial history to the manner in which the idea of corruption gets sexualized, in the context of the colony. She claims that "modern narratives of political corruption have left the realm of bureaucratic decay to enter the realm of erotic disorder." Disagreeing with the claim that the difference between the two zones is that pornographic space allegedly produces desire, while exceptional space does not. She instead argues that exceptional space is as productive of desire as erotic space—that in fact the erotic nature of the corruption discourse is what has made it such a key component of recent debates in globalization and the creation of a free market economy, and how corruption constantly comes in the way of market efficiency.

Miller argues persuasively that what brings corruption and erotic disorder together is the idea of the "corrupt relationship"—that inappropriate overlap, between public and private spheres, on the one hand, and between forms of prohibited cohabitation on the other. Foucault's work demonstrates with respect to modern political structures in general, it was precisely the (public) process of defining the intimate that produced and extended disciplinary power networks over the course of the 19th century. Post 18th century sex could not be thought of outside a discourse of secrecy, and, thus, sexual behavior became a matter for confession, and confession in turn an erotic act. In his discussion of political corruption, Robert Payne makes an explicit, if unintentional, linkage between the stripper and the corrupt state, corruption takes hidden forms and wears brilliant coverings; we can strip it naked and see the horror for what it is. In the spectacle of the striptease, it was not just women's bodies that were spectacularized and eroticized, but the act of revelation, and participation in that revelation, itself which was a part of the erotic game.

When the stamp paper scandal broke out, there was as much attention that was paid to Abdul Karim Telgi as his obsession with dance bar girls, and the crores that he had spent on them. We can now return to our two sites via examples, the DPS MMS case on the one hand and the NDTV BMW sting operation case on the other.

Writing about the media discourse on the DPS MMS case, Nishant Shah says that

> The video in itself had all the makings of a big head-line—underage sex, unsafe sex, "children" identified by their school uniforms, unauthorised recording, distribution, swapping, exchange and circulation of the sexual act and a stunned apparatus unable to deal with the reality of what had just happened.

A comparison can be drawn between the DPS MMS and the NDTV sting operation in the BMW case which saw the collusion between R.K. Anand and I.U. Khan, the public prosecutor in the case. In the SC decision, the account that emerges draws very heavily on the idea of the unholy mixture of the public and the private.

# The Law of Scandal

There have been a number of extremely significant sting operation cases that have reached the judiciary in India. One of these was the Sanjeev Nanda BMW case (NDTV conducted a sting operation in 2007 to reveal a possible collusion between the defense counsel in the case R.K. Anand and the special public prosecutor I.U. Khan). The facts of the case have all the ingredients of a pulp fiction thriller with a mixture of secret meetings, code names, conversations in innuendo. In most of these cases, the court is asked to play a dual role: On the one hand, it has to ascertain the veracity of the tapes and the nature of the underlying conversation and at the same time it has to normatively justify the use of the hidden camera. A reading of some of these cases seems to suggest a new kind of interpretative framework that the courts begin to develop—one which we could call a forensic film studies—where it combines the work of detection with the act of narrative interpretation. In the NDTV case, for instance, there is a detailed examination of conversations in which the mysterious reference to a bada sahib ("Big Boss" a somewhat coincidental reference to a show based on hidden cameras) has to be deciphered by the courts. Reading the transcripts, one cannot but recall a scene from the popular film *Kaho Na Pyar Hai* in which the mysterious villain's identity is stored merely as "sirji" on his sidekick's phone. Another noteworthy case that came up before the courts is Aniruddha Bahal case in which he was prosecuted for his role in the revelation of the 'cash for questions' scandal in parliament.

In all these cases, the courts are faced with the task of making sense of the phenomenon of sting operations and the nature of perception brought about by the hidden camera. While there is a tacit recognition of the dangers of hidden cameras in a mediatized world which demands instant sensationalism of all issues it is also interesting to see a new kind of citizen spectator being propped up. In the Aniruddha Bahal case, for instance, he is hailed as a hero upholding his fundamental duties in the constitution. The court in answering the question about whether citizens have a right to conduct sting operations to reveal corruption holds that the fundamental duties of a citizen includes the duty to "cherish and follow the noble ideals which inspired our national struggle for freedom" (Art 51A(b)) and goes on to say that one of the "noble ideals of our national struggle for freedom was to have an independent and corruption free India" (sic.).

Justice Dhingra says

> Every citizen is duty bound to defend the country and render national service when called upon to do so. I consider that a country cannot be defended only by taking a gun and going to border at the time of war. The country is to be defended day in and day out by being vigil (sic.) and alert to the needs and requirements of the country and to bring forth the corruption at higher level. The duty under Article 51A(h) is to develop a spirit of inquiry and reforms. The duty of a citizen under Article 51A(j) is to strive towards excellence in all spheres so that the nation constantly rises to higher level of endeavour and achievements I consider that it is built-in duties that every citizen must strive for a corruption free society and must expose the corruption whenever it comes to his or her knowledge and try to remove corruption at all levels more so at higher levels of management of the State. I consider that the duties prescribed by the Constitution of India for the citizens of this country do permit citizens to act as agent provocateurs to bring out and expose and uproot the corruption.

What we therefore have is a normative inscribing of the hidden camera within the legal imagination and it is apparent that the idea of a scandal moves from being the exceptional event that shocks our senses to one that now energizes a recalibration of values with the law reinstating the virtues of the hidden camera. A technology that is so morally ambiguous is rendered normal by its insertion into the heart of legal imagination, much as the violation of privacy has been inserted into the heart of the experience of cyberspace via Facebook so that we continue to look even as we cannot bear to see what is before us. But this is not merely a matter of the law adopting or validating a technology. Justice Dingra's paragraph in which we have a language of war, duty, corruption, and exposure creates a liminal zone in which the idea of the hidden camera becomes a mode of seeing which seeps into legal language much as televisuality became the optical unconscious of the late 20th century. When the powers of the hidden camera are celebrated as a virtue in the 'war against corruption', even as much as they secretly document the undeclared wars in zones of exception, the cycle is complete.

The eruption of corruption scandals as well as sexual scandals has provided the occasion for rethinking the relationship between politics and erotics, technology, and the public sphere. Its status as disruptive publicity doubles itself both as a violation as well as a discourse about violation. The 'reality' of these scandals rarely exists as public facts, and if the facts were actually revealed, they would be almost anti-climatic.

I would like to end with two questions which I think require further reflection. Throughout this paper, I have used the idea of the scandal, but I am uncertain if the idea of the scandal is adequate to describe what is taking place in the contemporary context. Similarly, I have my doubts about whether a language of privacy, grounded in a classical understanding of autonomy and personhood can adequately capture the transformation brought about by new technologies in which people participate as willing participants in the compromising of privacy. It were almost as if we are all victims of the Stockholm syndrome with respect to technologies like the hidden camera, where we end up falling in love with that which holds our privacy hostage.

Roland Barthes writing in the late 1950s about the political scandals in France refused to name them scandals arguing that they implicated everybody including the audiences and that any denunciation was hypocritical.

> We know now what a scandal is: it is essentially that which we don't participate in. It is a spectacle but not only that which occupies the scene;

it is rather that thing which pushes the spectator into the shadow of the balcony or the parterre.

It seems to me that rather than the scandal being the event which energizes a certain recalibration of the law, what we are now seeing is the very idea of the indistinction between what may be considered a scandal, and that which is not. And there is a manner in which the law's reinstatement of the virtues of the hidden camera (as evidenced in the sting operation judgments) normalizes what begins as a scandal, by inserting it within the heart of legal imagination, much as the violation of privacy has been inserted into the heart of the experience of cyberspace via Facebook.

# References

Lynn, Regina. 2005. "On how sex and technology come together," in *Naked Ambition: Women Who Are Changing Pornography*, edited by Carly Milne. New York: Seal Press

Malhotra, Namita. 2011. Amateur Video Pornography. In *Downloading the State*. Bangalore: Centre for Internet and Society.

Pasquinelli, Matteo. 2009. *Animal Spirits: A Bestiary of the Commons*. Rotterdam: NAI Publishers.

Sengupta, Shuddhabarata. 2014. "Kashmir's Abu Gharaib?" Available at http://kafila.org/2010/09/10/kashmirs-abu-gharaib/, The BSF as Pornographer: Bravehearts with Bluetooth, available at http://kafila.org/2012/01/20/the-bsf-as-pornographerbravehearts-with-bluetooth/

Uebel, Michael. 1999. "Toward a symptomatology of cyberporn," *Theory & Event*, 3(4).

Vasudevan, Nisha and Zinnia Ambapardiwala. 2011. "Radia Ga Ga," available at https://essays.pad.ma/radia-ga-ga

# A Heteropolitics of Hurt

# 17

## The Engendering of Hurt: A Feminist Analysis of Hurt Sentiments

*Meenakshi Malhotra*

The brutal gang rape of a young woman in Delhi in December 2012 elicited enormous rage and many public protests accompanied by outcries for speedy justice. It also opened up the question of delinquency—is it the age or the extent of violence perpetrated that determines criminality? The law which labels a criminal a juvenile on the basis of age is now sought to be scrutinized with a view to changing the notion of the juvenile.

Another episode which generated outrage, albeit to a limited extent was the suicide of an Indian origin nurse in England who unwittingly fell for a prank perpetrated by two Australian journalists after which she killed herself. While the fact that she may have been suffering from depression in the past is a question that came up, her suicide seemed possibly to be the result of an internalization of guilt/shame. Issues of race, diaspora, and culturally inflected notions of shame intersect with the question of hurt sentiments in this particular case in complicated ways.

This chapter seeks to make sense of/locate and read these events in the light of different articulations within feminist theory. This articulation and conceptualization is necessary in order to move beyond clichés which at best, seek to underline the heroism of the 'victim' and at worst, elicit the most banal and often inane kind of patriarchal pronouncements from politicians. Obviously, civil society and we, as responsible citizens, have to ensure that public opinion is translated into law and socio-legal mechanisms and that promises made to assuage public sentiments are followed up and delivered. The democratic state must stand as a guarantor that the fundamental right to freedom is also freedom from fear for its citizens.

However, there are other views on the question of hurt sentiments and its deployment in developed democracies. Wendy Brown and others like Sara Ahmed and Elspeth Probyn have discussed what can be referred to as "suspect emotions in social theory" (West-Newman). Brown, describing the dangers of what she calls "wounded attachments," deplores the fetishizing of wounds, which she argues has become a characteristic of identity politics in the U.S. (Brown, 1995). Ashish Nandy also mentions similar instances in both the Indian and the global context (Nandy, 2011). Thus, marginalized groups often utilize their victimization in order to forward identity claims. Minority hurt and harm is a real problem but a plethora of 'hurt sentiments' does not always lead to or translate into concrete actions/solutions. The problem of wound or injury does not get addressed by making a martyr out of the victim. Political mobilization should ideally be on lines which do not diffuse collectivities by valorizing the individual as either martyr or hero, in a way that some of our political leaders have done.

The various comments by some parliamentarians (some of them women) are instructive because their statements are premised on twin perceptions: one that the onus of certain kinds of crimes, like rape, lies primarily with the victim and not with the perpetrator and, second, that the internalizing of the wound or injury is a marked characteristic of women. They thus engender hurt in ways that jeopardize an active agential role for women. By extolling tolerance and patience as virtues by saying that "aurat gussa pi jatey hai" (women swallow/drink up their rage), they relegate women to powerlessness and submissiveness. These views embed female nature in passivity and inaction as they reinforce the role of women as upholders of the status quo, charged with maintaining stability, social order, and tradition.

The political mobilization in the aftermath of the recent episode was, thus, carefully and consciously organized around defiant feminist activism evidenced in "take back the night" campaigns. The protests were consciously calibrated to express not only anger and outrage, but also signalled a sense of rights and entitlements that were violated. It suggested that the problem lay not just in violent individuals but in the patriarchal system as also the state which has reneged on its promise of democratic rights to all individuals.

This chapter attempts to look at the expression of hurt sentiments in circulation—in the public sphere and media, in protest marches—in such a way that it provides scope for constructive feminist theorizing, activism, and engagement.

# II

The last few years have witnessed many instances of the outpouring of public protest and anger on the part of aggrieved citizens of India, and more particularly Delhi but none as vociferous as in the Delhi gang-rape case of 'Nirbhaya' (as the young 23-year-old girl came to be designated). Unlike many other protests organized by political parties, this achieved a mass mobilization which was on an unprecedented scale. In spite of the efforts of political parties to appropriate the outrage and use this to sub-serve their own agendas, the event assumed proportions which sent the embarrassed government into a huddle, and made them set up a committee in a very short span of time.

The gang rape and the response to it can be understood as a critical event, not only an event which generates a critical and mass opinion which in turn, forces change in terms of outlook, attitude, and legislation, but also an event which defamiliarizes to an extent where past behaviors and attitudes are held up to scrutiny in such a way so as to force a change. In *Critical Events*, Veena Das talks about violence which enters the "recesses of the ordinary" in such a way as to force a radical revaluation (Das, 1997). In talking about the Partition and the 1984 riots following Indira Gandhi's death, she writes "I want to re enter this scene of devastation to ask how one should inhabit a world that has been made strange through the desolating experience of violence and loss." She further sees this through Stanley Cavell's reading of it as an Emersonian gesture of approaching a world through a kind of mourning for it.

The mourning and outrage generated by this case set off widening circles of protests which were reflected in the international media as well, fitting in with and providing an instance of the human and women's rights violations that are seen as being rampant in our country. The response also seems to chime in with the view that "suffering is the master subject of our mediatized times" which in this particular instance provoked demands of death penalty and castration of the rapists from several quarters. According to an EPW editorial in the immediate aftermath of the event

> The popular press, while they have successfully braved the repression of the government, have themselves contributed to building an atmosphere where in some respects repressive and regressive ideas have found fertile ground to grow.[1]

At least three examples of regressive sentiments can be cited here. The first one came from a woman leader who in all sympathy, talked of the rape as leaving the young woman a "living corpse" (*zinda laash*). This response, apart from being a stock response of our parliamentarians, as Flavia Agnes points out, also betrays a mindset where all is lost when one is shamed and all honor lost. The woman 'Nirbhaya' who many wished would be called a rape survivor, revealed her wish to live fully, during her brief spells of consciousness, from her hospital bed. She, it seemed, was prepared to live with the consequences of rape, go forward in life, and it is possible that, with her fearless attitude, she would have forged ahead on her chosen path without carrying the burden of constructed notions of purity and pollution. The attribution of immorality which clouded earlier legislation and judgements of rape probably did not occlude her vision. The reference to her as a living corpse enshrines a further irony in as much it sets up a mind–body dichotomy, between her fearless mind (*Nirbhaya*) and her brutalized body which took her life and rendered her a victim of senseless and gratuitous violence. Pointing to a comparable dichotomy in the Sathin Bhanwari rape, Taisha Abraham avers that "the doublespeak and patriarchal mindset of the centre/state machinery is visible in the splitting of mind and body, where the divide-and-rule macrocosmic policy of patriarchy reveals its microcosmic form" (Abraham, 2012). Through this mind–body split, the politics of patriarchal structures tries "to both disembody and silence women" (Abraham, 2012). By saluting/ extolling one woman's spirit as fearless, it is easy to paper over the

[1] Editorial page. 2013. *Economic and Political Weekly*, 48(2): 1–2.

cracks in the system which is one of pervasive and fear-inducing violence, particularly directed against women.

The other puerile responses offering another instance of a retrogressive thinking and in its turn betraying a regressive mindset came from claims that located episodes of sexual harassment and rapes as those that happened in India, not 'Bharat', a factual error which can be statistically borne out. The difference, if any, probably lies in the fact that fewer cases get reported, a fact that, in its turn, casts aspersions on the redressal mechanisms in place. This attribution of all ills to the incursion of Westernized modernity, echoes the state's attempt in the last century to attribute all ills to the foreign hand. Equally absurd was the response which attempted to place the onus of the guilt on the raped woman by arguing that it was her defiant attitude that spurred on the rapists to brutalize her and that had she pleaded with her rapists and referred to them as brothers, she might have got off lightly.

This case, in many ways, has been a test case and has generated numerous debates on issues of sexual violence both against women and transgenders, issues of rape laws and problems therein. It has given rise to a chorus of voices claiming hurt sentiments. In this babel, it is easy to lose sight of the multifarious hurt sentiments at stake. Whose sentiments were hurt? At the broadest macro level, urban India, especially its youth, protested against this horrific event. We, as a nation, were ashamed and outraged that such a thing could happen in the heart of south Delhi. This was no remote village in Jharkhand or Chhattisgarh. The subject (not the victim—and the choice of the term has a significance) who by all accounts, resisted objectification by asserting her subject status—through her and her family's willingness to speak—was an aspirant, through education and hard work, to upward mobility. Further, she was almost a role model in her community where she lived and tutored other children to supplement the family income. It was her desire for a better life, for upward mobility, that struck a chord in the hearts of millions who read about her. She was not a silenced, illiterate subaltern, but the very embodiment of newly emerging Indian youth, visiting malls and multiplexes while dreaming of a better life. The media, the middle classes (admitting many exclusions of rural, uneducated, and backward classes) sought legitimacy for a plethora of hurt sentiments in the wake of the Delhi rape case. Additionally, we, in a sense, bore collective witness to this tragic saga of a young, motivated girl and mourned her passing. Moreover, beyond sentimentalizing, it is important to see how she—and to some extent, her parents—attempted to break the mold of victimhood.

While there are religious/community, class, and caste ramifications to almost every situation in which rape takes place, the point about this particular case is not simply the fact that the rapists were from a lower socio-economic strata. Unlike the earlier cases of Rameeza Bi and Sathin Bhanwari, images and updates about the case circulated in social media and provided an instance of citation/reiteration leading to a situation where simmering anger was brought to a boil, as it were. The public protests sought to legitimize emotion and affect and it is worthwhile to remember that 2012 also witnessed an unprecedented show of solidarity with Anna Hazare as he registered outrage at corruption. The question is not simply whether Dalit rapes perpetrated by upper castes are reported or not, but also that the literally gut-wrenching saga of 'Nirbhaya' struck a chord with urban youth in and around Delhi. There seems to be a level of identification and the feeling that it could well have been any of the thousands of young girls who migrate to cities in search of a better life. The ascribed identity of 'Nirbhaya' distinguished her from the many other (albeit unacknowledged) nameless victims of rape.

The idea of the name here is perhaps important, as the designated identity Nirbhaya did not seek to breach her privacy or anonymity but also sought to distinguish her from the many 'victims' of violence and rape. The idea of nomenclature and changes in the same acquire a particular resonance in the context of humiliated groups or communities. One well-known instance is the question of nomenclature that assumes a political valence, like that of designations of queer or Dalits. Another instance of the political implications of nomenclature and of changing names is that of African Americans. Ashish Nandy voices his discomfort with "American Blacks changing the name of their community according to their changing ideas" of what constitutes humiliation. In the change from Negroes associated with "slavery and racial discrimination" to Blacks which "ironed away ethnic distinctions" to African Americans, he sees a "kind of response" which "declares the locus of control to be outside oneself" (Nandy, 2011: 264). Further, there is a positive charge to the identities discussed above which gets blurred with the designated name of

African American. Does this renaming indicate that the memories of slavery and racism are more shameful for the former slave than for the 'master'? Nandy opines that normatively and cognitively it is better to be a slave than a master, a point reinforced by feminist epistemology.

Ironically, however, the loudest voices speaking on the case, claiming collective hurt, were based on a series of what can be seen as false claims. It is here that the question of suspect emotions in social theory is of relevance. While more than one human right was violated, a fine distinction has to be made where wounds are not fetishized or made to seem a badge of identity. As theorists in many transnational contexts have pointed out, this is not to deny that historically, wrongs have been perpetrated but the problem with the fetishization of wounds is that it freezes and negates all other aspects of identity. As Nandy, inter alia, has pointed out in the context of questions of humiliation, trauma becomes a badge of identity and certifies one's membership of a social group: it becomes the mark of one's identity and self-definition. This is not to mistrust the account of historically oppressed groups but to keep in mind the fact that feelings of hurt/humiliation can also be part of a political programme in the furthering of ostensibly democratic but actually fascist politics. Nandy offers the example of different Jewish communities each claiming a history of persecution (Nandy, 2011: 270). He also cites the instance of ethno-nationalists and of Hindu nationalism as a case study where wrongs were claimed and attributed, with varying measures of truth.

Statements of the kind routinely made by our politicians and cited above expose an atavistic mindset and are based on spurious identitarian claims. Attempts at appropriation of this kind, while demonstrating the urge to forge communities and commonalities, operate on the basis of what can be called a reverse metonymy. That is, the sentiments of a small, often fringe group are reported in such a way that they are made to stand in for the whole. Groups, whether right wing or regional, apparently become the spokesmen and custodians of (outdated) morality, discover that even negative reporting serves as a means of mobilization, effecting ideological interpellation of disaffected groups. It seems that even the most outlandish and aberrant sentiments have takers somehow, somewhere.

It is in the context of whipping up frenzied public opinion that the question of capital punishment must be viewed. A lot of people, including the girl's parents, have demanded that capital punishment be meted out to the rapists. The notion of death penalty, as also its concomitants of hanging, castration, is based on the concept of retributive justice, which according to feminist and other legal theorists, do not necessarily address the complex issues involved in a case of this kind. As Flavia Agnes reminds us, "the insertion" of sharp-edged objects such as wooden splinters, iron rods, glass bottles, knives and swords can cause far more damage to the "female anatomy, but does not warrant the same kind of punishment as rape" since it is not perceived as a "state worse than death" (Agnes, 2013). What colors this terminology is the patriarchal premise of "vaginal purity" and the misogynistic and murderous intent underlying other kinds of assault like acid attacks, slashing of the face and insertion of objects which do not constitute penetration but are as damaging as rape. These acts of violence are not bracketed with rape but can actually be much worse (Agnes, 2013: 12). Any grievous exercise of violence inflicted with the intention of torturing, chastising, and humiliating women is no less gruesome. A fact that redounds to the credit of the Justice Verma committee report is that it takes all these offences into cognizance.

The demand for death penalty rests, according to legal theorists like Flavia Agnes, on a notion of retributive justice which on one hand can assume dimensions/proportions which may seem barbaric and regressive, adopted by societies where versions of rough and ready instant justice seem to prevail, without resolving many of the issues involved, in the long term. Apart from being short-sighted, the demand for capital punishment "obscures the routineness of the violence that takes place in our societies, in our homes, in our private spaces and makes it seem like a rare aberration" (Agnes, 2013). It also somewhat obscures the insidious and pervasive nature of violence, the fact that it is not episodic but a structural fact in many societies. Horrific narratives of the partition and of genocide in Bosnia remind us that questions of sexual violence are intertwined with issues of power.

The limitations of the death penalty in spite of the growing public demand for it, was realized by the law makers in the Justice Verma Committee. The committee, which was set up by the government as a face-saving measure to update and revise the rape laws in response to the situation prevailing in the wake of the gang rape, has eschewed the death penalty, seeing it as counterproductive. The committee discussed and deliberated on the demand but then put forward a reasoned argument about the problems that beset such a move. The first problem, in a seeming paradox, has to do with the low rate of convictions in rape cases, a fact pointed out also by Flavia Agnes and elsewhere by Brinda Karat (Karat, 2013). The uncertainty of conviction and, therefore, punishment would become even more uncertain, with more cases being given the 'benefit of doubt' Death penalty might temporarily quell public outcry, but will fail to have deterrent impact at ground level. At a practical level, it might lead the rapists to kill victims in order to ensure that there are no witnesses.

The other problem is the conviction of impunity, which according to V. Geetha keeps "unequal class and gender arrangements in place." She also poses a question that forms a persistent thread in most feminist interrogations. This is about the everyday existence of sexual violence and brutality in our many contexts, violence that does not get addressed and escapes with impunity. Thus, as she points out, verbal abuse of women, lewd gestures, stalking, and sexual threats mark and make our experience of public spaces; while humiliating speech acts and routine unwelcome sex, if not sexual torture, define conjugal authority and rights (Geetha, V. 2013).

It is in this context that we must appreciate the recommendations of the Verma Committee which is a comprehensive attempt not only to revise rape laws, but also to address multifarious issues that have come up in the wake of rapidly changing social arrangements. First, it corroborates and extends the dominant feminist understanding that rape is about power. It also brings up the question of marital rape and conveys a nuanced understanding of the demand for sexual autonomy in changing social contexts. It is also instructive here to remember that a substantial number of 'rape' cases are charges levelled by 'hurt' parents of girls who have chosen to exercise their sexual autonomy and eloped.

Some gaps notwithstanding, in the area of judiciary reform and rehabilitation of rape survivors who are made to relive their trauma in their interface with family, and with legal and medical systems in the course of 'redressal'—the Justice Verma committee report demonstrates its awareness of multiple discourses which are now in circulation in the public domain (and which have led advanced societies to lay down certain protocols) like the sexual autonomy and rights of both women and transgendered peoples. The committee also showed its awareness of the glaring gaps in Indian law on matters of child abuse and trafficking and attempted to address some of these issues. As Brinda Karat reports, India has been among the few countries with no laws or protocols against child sexual abuse (Karat, 2013). Similarly, the bill on prevention of sexual harassment at the workplace (Vishakha Judgment, 2005), formulated by a bench headed by Justice Verma earlier, is still pending. However, the ordinance that has been formulated in response to the committee's recommendations, and has now become law, seems to have taken several steps backwards. It has also lost an opportunity to tailor legislation which would answer to the needs of a demographically sizeable group whose voices are increasingly beginning to be heard. This group is that of women who are vociferously demanding legislation which is responsive to their needs. The problem with the ordinance seems to be one besetting the government's approach to many issues—apathy on the one hand and the desire to address diverse constituencies including that of rural patriarchs who advocate the banning of 'western' food items like noodles which are supposed to induce raging hormones, that according to them has led to an increase in the occurrence of rapes. It is perhaps relevant in this context to note that the *khap panchayats* meting out rough and ready retributive justice operate in this gap/space created by the failure of the government to reach and address the problems spawned by the effects of a rapidly urbanizing society.

Modernity or modernities in India are uneven, fractured, and heterogenous as are the stakeholders in this process. It is, thus, difficult to formulate and even more difficult to execute laws addressing the differential and widely varying social spectrum. The Verma Committee's framing of issues is resonant with the needs of a rapidly modernizing society but has now been put on the back-burner apparently in the face of the exigencies of electoral and vote-bank politics. Women, and by that I cover women across a broad spectrum of classes, and their requirements are again getting subsumed and swallowed by other interests. Far from making women-centric laws, or those that reflect the mood of the nation, the laws that are made take us back several decades as they try to cater to different interests groups and constituencies.

Further, this is not an isolated case, but a symptom of a deeper malaise, where the individual is cast into the mold of either victim or martyr. By drawing sympathy for the individual case, where the government undertakes a few token measures, larger questions are put on the back-burner. Legal bodies and government agencies which are directly responsible count on public apathy to evade and avoid being called to give an account of their (c)omissions.

Also one of the issues highlighted by this case is that one criminal misdemeanor often serves to highlight not just the issue of rape as in this instance but also related issues of pornography and paedophilia, resulting in an increase in incidents and cases of child rape. In the era of Internet availability where porn clips can be downloaded virtually free of cost, control and legislation are problematic both in terms of conceptualization and implementation. On the one hand, we realize the importance of safeguarding freedom of speech and expression as a democratic right, but should also able to understand its interface with and impact on other issues.

As far as the issue of pornography is concerned, the perspective of the radical feminists which relates issues of power, violence, and rape to patriarchy is a structurally coherent one. Social attitudes, overt and insidious, emanating from and naturalized by patriarchy (and rendered acceptable by it) are reasons for increased incidents of rape and violence. But statistics detailing increase in the number of incidents getting reported can also be an indicator of growing intolerance for crimes, which previously went unreported due to fear of shame and stigma.

The case of 'Nirbhaya' has also opened up the question of justice at several levels—whether justice should be retributive or reformative. On the face of it, the latter would be preferable to the former. Yet, when one examines the issue of juvenile justice, several problems beleaguer the case, making any snap decision difficult. While age forms the basis of determining and understanding who is a juvenile, the issue of age has to be viewed as one of the many complex parameters for determining punishment. Age is or should not be understood merely in terms of chronology or as an invariable. Rather the extent of delinquency and the grievousness of the crime committed should be the determining factors. The 'Nirbhaya' case has trained the spotlight both on issues of juvenile justice as well as questions of capital punishment. There are many underage offenders who are in remand homes in situations which are, as per evidence, neither reformative nor retributive.

# III

At the outset, I had also referred to the case of the London-based nurse of Indian origin, Jacinta Saldanha, who unwittingly fell a prey to a hoax call made by two Australian radio-journalists, and committed suicide in the wake of the media publicity. This case raises a number of issues which can be discussed. My point, however, in bringing up this case is not to compare the two cases as much as to extend a few arguments applicable to the issue of the engendering of hurt sentiments.

The first point is that the perception of humiliation is a subjective one. Further, woven into this subjectivity may be issues of race, questions of diasporic identity, leading to and possibly causing exceptional psychological vulnerability (Jacintha was reportedly suffering from depression). One of the ways to approach this case is through the idea of intersectionality, which would involve an analysis of the situation through the complex lens of gender, race, and diaspora *simultaneously*, without privileging one category of analysis.

The second issue is the internalization of the humiliation so that it becomes a wound. This wound is magnified to such an extent that self-annihilation appears to the afflicted individual as the only way out. Ironically, Jacintha constructs herself as a victim/martyr in her self-inflicted death, instead of externalizing or voicing her feeling of insult and injury.

In such a situation, it appears that guilt and shame become a marker and badge of identity, to the detriment of all other aspects. This is one of the problems with the notion of victimhood where all other markers are lost, and socially attributed identity is so deeply internalized that it takes over all aspects of subjectivity. Without going into the dynamics of pain—physical, psychological or both, one is brought back to the body as the site of selfhood. Thus destroying the body is a hopeless attempt to wipe out hurt and humiliation. In one case, we see an attempt to resist—however unsuccessfully—social attributions of victimhood, the other sees the subject appropriating the identity of victim over all others.

Some of these ideas of hurt, humiliation have been discussed mostly within the framework of caste and Dalit humiliation in the Indian context, notably by Gopal Guru and Sundar Sarrukai. However, more work needs to be done at the interface of issues of gender, class, and caste. In a recent review, Kavita Krishnan has discussed two recent articles by Prabhat Patnaik and Maya John which look at the interrelationship of class and gender through a Marxist lens. While she critiques and disputes several aspects of their arguments, she accepts that these are all attempts to "assimilate and analyze the valuable lessons emerging from December 16, and understand the intersections of class, caste, patriarchy globally as well as specifically in the Indian context" (Krishan, 2013).

# References

Agnes, Flavia. 2013. "No Shortcuts on Rape: Making the Legal System Work," *Economic and Political Weekly*, 48(2).

Brown, Wendy. 1995. *States of Injury: Power and Freedom in Late Modernity*. Princeton: Princeton University Press.

Das, Veena. 1997. *Critical Events*. New Delhi: Oxford University Press, pp. 7–8.

——— 2000. "On Bodily Love and Hurt," in *A Question of Silence: The Sexual Economies of Modern India*, edited by Nair, Janaki and Mary John. London: Zed Books.

Geetha, V. 2013. "On Impunity," *Economic and Political Weekly*, 48(2) 12 January.

Guru, Gopal (Ed.). 2008. *Humiliation: Claims and Context,* New Delhi: Oxford University Press.

Karat, Brinda. 2013. "Report In, Action Awaited," *Indian Express*, February 2.

Krishan, Kavita. 2013. Capitalism, Sexual Violence and Sexism. Available at Kafila. org/2013/05/2013 (accessed on July 10, 2013).

Lane West-Newman, Catherine. "Suspect Emotions in Social Theory." Available at www. tasa.org.au/co, p 1-2 (accessed on July 10, 2013).

Nandy, Ashish. 2011. "Humiliation: The Politics and Cultural Psychology of the Limits of Human Degradation," in *The Indian Postcolonial*: *A Critical Reader*, edited by Elleke Boehmer and Rosinka Chaudhuri. London and NY: Routledge.

Taisha, Abraham. 2012. "Sathin Bhanwari Revisited," *Indian Journal of Gender Studies*, 19(1): 149–157.

# 18

# On the Question of Free Speech and Censorship

*Krishna Menon*

One of the most contentious issues facing liberal democracies the world over is that of freedom of speech and the possible limits and regulations that this might be subjected to. It is contentious because liberal societies attach special significance to free speech. It would be worth our while to ponder very briefly as to why liberal-democratic societies do this?

It is a fact that most liberal-democratic societies value free speech and expression as a liberty in itself, and not as a mere subset of the general conception of freedom (Mill, 1998). Liberals tend to defend freedom generally, and free speech in particular, for a variety of reasons; they argue that free speech fosters genius, creativity, individuality, and human flourishing.

The simplest argument for defending freedom of speech and expression is of course the belief that "sticks and stones can break my bones, but words can never harm me." This argument has a limited validity, as it is obvious that real and threatening consequences could follow unregulated speech.

One of the most persuasive defenses of the idea of free speech comes from John Stuart Mill (1998) who argued that free speech is essential because it is only through this that a society can arrive at the 'truth'. Excluding Mathematics, Mill argued that on every other subject, truth can be arrived at only by listening to all manners of conflicting and dissenting opinions, and then striking a balance. He also suggests that since human beings are of diverse nature, it is important that their diverse opinions be heard. The problem with Mill's argument is that it ignores the asymmetry of power that exists in society and thus precludes the possibility of such a free flowing expression of ideas and thoughts in an equal manner.

Besides, more often than not, individuals do not share the same political, moral, or ethical universe, this makes it rather difficult for individuals to talk and understand each other, sometimes with rather violent and serious consequence. In any case, we know better now than to assume that truth is constant and stable.

Thomas Scanlon (1972) in *A Theory of Freedom of Expression* makes the quintessential liberal argument linking freedom of speech with individual rationality. In exercising free speech, the autonomous individual would also take responsibility for his/her actions. This is in keeping with the liberal idea of the sovereign individual; the state cannot direct such an individual to any one belief or opinion. In this framework, free speech is essential because it is a vindication of the individual's autonomy.

A more contemporary justification of free speech comes from Lee Bollinger who suggests that free speech needs to be defended because it leads to a more tolerant society. By listening to diverse and contradictory opinions, he argues that people develop a zone of tolerance. However, it is not clear in his argument as to why tolerance should be valued to begin with; also there is a clear danger of unrestricted free speech sometimes resulting in the opposite of tolerance.

The topic of free speech is one of the most contentious issues in liberal societies. Free speech becomes a volatile issue when it is highly valued because only then do the limitations placed upon it become controversial. The first thing to note in any sensible discussion of freedom of speech is that it will have to be limited. Every society places some limits on the exercise of speech because speech always takes place within a context of competing values. Speech is important because we are socially situated and, thus, it makes little sense to say that Robinson Crusoe has a right to free speech, since such a right is validated only within a social setting. At a minimum, speech will have to be limited for the sake of order. If we all speak at once, we end up with an incoherent cacophony. Without some rules and procedures, we cannot have a conversation at all and consequently speech has to be limited by protocols of basic civility.

For Mill, any doctrine should be allowed the light of day no matter how immoral it may seem.

> If all mankind minus one were of one opinion, and only one person was of the contrary opinion, mankind would be no more justified in silencing that one person than he, if he had the power, would be justified in silencing mankind. (Mill, 1998)

Such liberty should exist with every subject matter so that we have "absolute freedom of opinion and sentiment on all subjects, practical or speculative, scientific, moral or theological" (Mill, 1998). Such liberty of expression is necessary, he suggests, for the dignity of persons.

Despite this strong defense of free speech, Mill also suggests that we need some rules of conduct to regulate the actions of members of a political community. The limitation he places on free expression is "one very simple principle," now usually referred to as the *Harm Principle*, which states that "The only purpose for which power can be rightfully exercised over any member of a civilized community, against his will, is to prevent harm to others" (Mill, 1998).

Mill is usually understood to have meant that an action has to directly invade the rights of a person. The limits on free speech will be very narrow because it is difficult to support the claim that most speech causes harm to the rights of others. Liberals find it difficult to defend free speech once it can be demonstrated that its practice does actually invade the rights of other individuals.

What types of speech, if any, cause harm according to Mill? The example Mill uses to illustrate his understanding is with reference to corn dealers: he suggests that it is acceptable to claim that corn dealers starve the poor if such a view is expressed through the medium of the printed page. It is not acceptable to express the same view to an angry mob, ready to explode, that has gathered outside the house of the corn dealer. The difference between the two is that the latter places the rights and possibly the life, of the corn dealer in danger. It is only when speech causes a direct and clear violation of rights that it can be limited.

If we base our defense of speech on the 'harm principle', we are going to have very few sanctions imposed on the spoken and written word. It is only when we can show direct harm to rights, which will almost always mean when an attack is made against a specific individual or a small group of persons, that it is legitimate to impose a sanction.

If we can expand the harm principle from the physical to the mental realm, more options might become available for prohibiting speech that is sexist, homophobic, or casteist.

There are two basic responses to the harm principle as a means of limiting speech. One is that it is too narrow; the other is that it is too broad. Joel Feinberg suggests that the harm principle cannot shoulder all of the work necessary for a principle of free speech and, hence, offers an offense principle that can act as a guide to public censure. The basic idea is that the harm principle sets the bar too high and that we can legitimately prohibit some forms of expression because they are very offensive. Offending someone is less serious than harming someone, so the penalties imposed should be less severe than those for causing harm.

Such a principle is difficult to apply because many people take offense as the result of an overly sensitive disposition, or worse, because of bigotry and unjustified prejudice. A further difficulty is that some people can be deeply offended by statements that others find mildly amusing. Despite the difficulty of applying a standard of this kind, something like the offense principle operates widely in liberal democracies where citizens are penalized for a variety of activities, including speech that would escape prosecution under the harm principle. Wandering around the local shopping mall naked, or engaging in sexual acts in public places are two obvious examples.

Very few liberals take the Millian view that only speech causing direct harm should be prohibited and most support some form of the offense principle. Some are willing to extend the realm of state interference further and argue that hate speech should be banned even if it does not cause harm or unavoidable offense. The reason it should be banned is that it is inconsistent with the underlying values of liberal democracy to brand some citizens as inferior to others on the grounds of their caste, religion, or sexual orientation. To argue the case above, one has to dilute one's support for freedom of expression in favor of other principles, such as equal respect for all citizens. The task we face is not to arrive at hard and fast principles that govern all speech. Instead, we have to find a workable compromise that gives due weight to a variety of values. For instance, we have to decide whether it is better to place a higher value on speech than on the value of privacy, security, equality, or the prevention of harm.

The argument is that speech can be limited for the sake of other liberal values, particularly the concern for democratic equality; the claim is not that speech should always lose out when it clashes with other fundamental principles that underpin modern liberal democracies, but that it should not be automatically privileged. To extend prohibitions on speech, it is suggested that the state should decide what is acceptable for the safety and moral instruction of citizens. This has certainly been the practice of most societies, even liberal-democratic ones, to impose some paternalistic restrictions on behavior and to limit speech because it causes offense or might create harm or violate the basic values of democratic citizenship.

Feminist theory debates the question of restrictions on free speech most specifically in the context of the issue of pornography and censorship, and there is no one position within feminist theory on this issue since feminists differ in their understanding of issues such as body, work, sexuality, rape, and violence—some of the key issues involved in the various feminist positions on censorship and pornography. Feminist positions on pornography currently break down into three rough categories. The most common one and in some senses the most predictable one is that pornography is an expression of male culture through which women are commodified and exploited and, hence, should be subjected to strict censorship. A view, the liberal position, combines a respect for free speech with the principle 'a woman's body, a woman's right' and thus produces a defense of pornography along the lines of, "I don't approve of it, but everyone has the right to consume or produce words and images." The stress is upon the act of choosing, rather than upon the content of any choice. Liberal feminists share the general liberal bias toward free speech, but maintain a complicated position on pornography. "As a woman I am appalled by Playboy ... but as a writer I understand the need for free expression." Such arguments are not pro-pornography but induced rather from anticensorship ones based on several grounds, including: great works of art and literature would be banned; political expression would be suppressed; and a creative culture requires freedom of speech.

A third view—a true defense of pornography—arises from feminists who have been labeled 'pro-sex' and who argue that women should have the choice to participate in and to consume pornography. Pro-sex arguments sometimes seem to overlap with liberal feminist ones. For example, both express concern over who will act as censor because subjective words, such as 'degrading', will be interpreted to mean whatever the censor wishes. On the dangers of censoring pornography, pro-sex and liberal feminists often agree. On the possible benefits of pornography to women, they part company. The third position argues rather persuasively that inevitably, censorship will be used against the least popular views, against the weakest members of society. The third position is arguing that pornography is free speech applied to the sexual realm. Freedom of speech is the ally of those who seek change: it is the enemy of those who seek to maintain control. Pornography, along with all other forms of sexual heresy, such as homosexuality, should have the same legal protection as political heresy. This protection is especially important to women, whose sexuality has been regulated by censorship.

The feminist position more generally on free speech and censorship might, thus, be summed up as—countering hate speech with more speech to quote Ratna Kapur. What she implies is that the best antidote to hate speech of any kind is most certainly not law, for that has only a limited application and would always operate within a domain of power- thus banning certain speech as objectionable and allowing certain others depending on the play of power.

Thus, the third group of feminists recognizes and acknowledges that certain kinds of speech and depiction might cause offense and even has the potential to create harm and could possibly be against the tenets of democratic citizenship. However, the legal machinery of the state already circumscribed by certain assumptions of class, caste, and sexuality can hardly be trusted to play the role of a neutral umpire. Indeed a neutral umpire is not possible; hence, Shohini Ghosh (1999), for instance, has argued that as feminists the demand should be for opening up spaces for multiple representations, interpretations and responses rather than silences.

In the context of the debate around what has come to be called the Ambedkar Cartoon Controversy, I would like to examine the issue of whether cartoon and jokes could create harm, cause offense, or be against the principles of democratic citizenship? If they are then should it be banned would be the next obvious question. Humor is empowering. This is so because humor can uphold dominance or humor is social, because it generally arises in social situations, it works within and upon historically specific social situations, and therefore it has a social function. Humor can be used as a means to maintain interpersonal relationships, to assert power over others, to defend oneself against dominance, to affirm personal and collective identities, to question cultural forms, and so on.

It is precisely this social, critical, self-asserting nature of humor that has made it inappropriate for women in patriarchal society. The act of holding the floor, calling people's attention, and showing off one's wit does not fit into the traditional notion of femininity.

Yet this does not mean that women lack a sense of humor or that they have never made use of humor in public contexts such as literature. Feminist criticism has demonstrated how women writers have often used humor to express their resistance to the social oppression they have suffered.

It is not that feminists do not love a good laugh, but they do not appreciate being the butt of all jokes. Sexist jokes provide a socially acceptable situation where one is allowed, even encouraged, to laugh at something outright misogynistic and yet, flying under the guise of a joke, cannot be taken seriously or as solid truth. For instance, jokes about incapable female drivers and accountants—the humor's incongruity lies in the notion that women, despite the natural deficiencies of their sex, might actually attempt something in a field where men are innately superior. Responding negatively to a sexist joke appears an offence.

Nonetheless, jokes remain a socially sanctioned space to attack all groups on the margins. Telling a sexist joke assures all that you are not a feminist and makes clear that your beliefs align with the current patriarchal system.

On the other hand, a member of the dominant group can handle a bit of jousting thrown his or her way because they know that the derisive elements contained in the joke will not last forever. Conversely a sexist joke is not an isolated event in which a woman is harmlessly teased or ridiculed; it is rather one instance among many in which women are belittled or disparaged. Jokes become a way to gauge the climate of a particular social and cultural moment. It is not that feminists are not funny, but, as poignantly expressed, "nobody laughs at the sight of their own blood."

Shankar Pillai's cartoon in 2012 has evoked very different responses from Dalit groups, than from when it was drawn in the early 1950s. In 2012, many Dalit groups argued that the said cartoon was offensive, it could lead to harm and was most certainly against the values of democratic citizenship. Does this mean that 60 odd years after independence Dalits no longer appreciate humor?

Feminists have long been used to being told that they don't get the joke. This is very similar to the oft repeated statement that Nehru asked Shankar the cartoonist not to spare him. Being sure of one's position in society seems to be directly proportionate to the kind of jokes that one can accept in good humor about oneself. Dalit groups that have expressed their discomfort with this cartoon are articulating a deeper anxiety—that of being on the margins and trying very hard to move center stage. Under these circumstances, it is difficult to get the joke.

Most Dalit groups are not objecting to a critique of Ambedkar's role in the making of the Indian Constitution; however, the nature of that criticism, who is making that criticism and its context have all to be accounted for. These voices have suggested that no one group can accord to itself the power to decide what is funny and what is not (Sukumar, 2012).

It is equally offensive to be told that Dalits are incapable of reason. The repeated references to Dalit 'hurt' suggest that Dalits do not have reasoned arguments against the cartoon but only an emotional and passionate response to it. Replacing the former with the latter is a way of depoliticizing the Dalit objection, and somehow makes it seem less threatening in the context of post-Mandal India. Thus, the state's 'positive response' of removing the offending cartoon and the textbook is more a gesture of assuaging hurt Dalit feelings, rather than a response to the political assertion of a till recently voiceless group that has only recently become politically significant, assertive, and powerful (Guru, 2012).

K. Satyanarayana has argued that intellectuals were hasty in their response to the Ambedkar cartoon controversy when they dug in their heels and refused to entertain the voices of discomfort regarding the cartoon. Instead of addressing the concerns articulated by some Dalit groups, the discourse was deflected to the issue of free speech and censorship. Thus, what could have been an opportunity to discuss

Ambedkar's role in the drafting of the Indian Constitution and the various deprecatory descriptions of his role was lost and Dalit groups that raised objections were projected as being anti-free speech. By not allowing this, they made it possible for the state to usurp the terrain and do what the state does best, flex its muscle. It is after all in the nature of the state to look for opportunities to exercise power. In this instance, it did so by censoring the textbook that has not only the contentious cartoon but many other uncomfortable issues as well.

Ambedkar's representation in post-independence India is politically charged, given the fact that he was, unlike Gandhi or Nehru, never officially represented. No parks, stadia, airports, or flyovers were named after him. Dalits kept him alive through iconization. Ambedkar was kept alive by Dalit efforts, his icons dotted the rural and small town landscape in many parts of India, despite the repeated acts of vandalism directed at these installations. Ambedkar's contribution to the drafting of the Constitution is at best paid lip service to and at worst denied or even ridiculed. Dalit collective memory kept him alive and one of the most popular images has been of Ambedkar with the Constitution in his hand. From the 1990s, Dalit politics especially in north India has undergone a complete transformation, and this combined with the contentious understanding of Ambedkar's role in the making of the Indian Constitution is the specific context of the cartoon controversy.

Charu Gupta has argued that traditionally the Hindu upper caste construction of the Dalit male has been problematic. This cartoon seems to echo some of those assumptions. On the one hand, Dalit men are often portrayed by Hindu upper castes as strong but stupid, with inferior intellectual abilities, ready to serve their masters. Or else, Dalit men are projected as dangerous and violent who lust after upper caste women (Gupta, 2011).

If we revisit the Shankar cartoon, the former kind of representation is too obvious to be missed, here is Dalit Ambedkar serving his upper caste master Nehru, but the servant is slow and incapable and needs some goading. Surely the Dalit groups that objected to this cartoon have a point. Satyanaryana has suggested that what we need is a substantive engagement with Ambedkar and Dalit politics and a formal engagement of the kind that the current textbooks engage would inevitable throw up issues such as the cartoon controversy.

We need to recognize that speech and speech acts have very real consequences for people and their lives, and therefore we need to consider this impact very seriously. Can speech that incites violence and hatred be allowed? The next question would be who decides what is the kind of speech that incites violence and hatred? An equally significant issue is of silence that could lead to violence and hatred. On occasions, silence can result in more harm than speech.

These are questions that cannot have fully formed and stable answers. The answers would depend on the context, on who is speaking or keeping silent and who is being spoken to and indeed where are the words beings uttered?

The fact is that speech, however hateful and violent it might be, can at least be countered, but a society under censorship would be a dangerous place with simmering unarticulated hatred and violence that cannot be heard or responded to, but can be felt. Censorship has a tendency especially in unequal societies to strengthen the hands of those groups that have access to power; hence, for those on the margins, it would always be the safest to strengthen anti-censorship politics.

In an unequal society, certain codes and norms governing free speech would be needed; however, the state need not be the sovereign body in charge of this, it is for the citizens to decide the appropriate code and norms in response to specific issues and contexts arrived at not by banning, burning, or censoring but by listening to multiple voices and debating.

# Bibliography

Figueroa Dorrego, Jorge. 2015. "Disputing Patriarchy, Disrupting Romance—Humor in Behn's *The Lucky Mistake* and 'The Wandering Beauty'," Available at *Universidade de Vigo* http://webs.uvigo.es/angelestome/disputing.pdf (accessed on July 18, 2015).

Ghosh, Shohini. 1999. "The troubled existence of sex and sexuality: Feminists engage with censorship," in *Image Journeys: Audio-Visual Media and Cultural Change in India*, edited by Christiane Brosius and Melissa Butcher. New Delhi: SAGE Publications.

Gupta, Charu. 2011. Paper Presented at IAFFE Conference, China, June 24–26, 2011. "Body Blues: Representations of Dalit Male Bodies in Colonial India." Available at https://editorialexpress.com/.../conference/download.cgi?...IAFFE2011... (accessed on July 18, 2015).

Guru, Gopal. 2012. "Foregrounding Insult: Gopal Guru." Available at http://kafila.org/2012/06/02/foregrounding-insult-gopal-guru/ (accessed on July 18, 2015).

McElroy, Wendy. 1997. "A feminist defense of pornography," *Free Inquiry Magazine,* 174. Available at http://jlampl.net/A%20Feminist%20Defense%20of%20Pornography.pdf (accessed on July 18, 2004).

Mill, John Stuart. 1998. *On Liberty and Other Essays.* New York: Oxford University Press.

Satyanarayana, K. "Ambedkar Cartoon Controversy: A Dalit View." Available at http://www. youtube.com/watch?v=WHRN30NATe0 (accessed on July 18, 2015).

Scanlon, Thomas. 1972. "A theory of freedom of expression," *Philosophy and Public Affairs,* 1(2): 204–226.

Sukumar, N. 2012. "The Cartoon, the Classroom and the Idea of India." Available at http:// roundtableindia.co.in/index.php?option=com_content&view=article&id=5144:the-cartoon-the-classroom-and-the-idea-of-india&catid=119:feature&Itemid=132 (accessed on July 18, 2015).

# Coda

# 19

# The Lines of Control

*Vishwajyoti Ghosh*

## I

Before being a cartoonist/graphic novelist, I am a citizen first: A citizen with the freedom to have feelings, if not the freedom to free speech. Now, the former is far easier than the latter. I have the freedom to have feelings and the freedom to deal with those who hurt my feelings. And on that note, I want Sarojini Naidu arrested. Posthumously, so be it. But I want her arrested. In a broadcast over All India Radio she referred to Mahtama Gandhi as "this tiny creature whom once in a mood of loving irreverence, I called Mickey Mouse of a man." Can you imagine? She called Bapu a Mickey Mouse because of his big ears. On Bapu's 70th birthday, the *Civil and Military Gazette*, Lahore, published a caricature of the same. It is said Bapu had a good laugh. A good laugh over a political cartoon? Totally unacceptable. A good laugh hurts me, insults my sentiments, and punctures my pride. However trivial it might be, my compromised sense of humor (however negligible) is totally negotiable based on my personal convenience. So, I revise my stand. I want Sarojini Naidu arrested, the Gazette banned and *Bapu* booked for conspiring with those who hurt my feelings for the father of the nation. But alas, that is unlikely to happen, not because the three are long dead but more importantly my sentiments do not have a mob following; nor do they have any institutional political validity. Had that been the case, the newspaper house would have been brought down, effigies burnt, streets gutted with fellow sentimentalists canoodling with television crews. And if you keep a close eye you might just notice a pattern there. Getting hurt or expressing one's protest and pain usually comes with a sharp media plan. And that happens on a Friday. The casual mob arrives in its Friday dressing and takes over the headlines. Prime time is sorted. The following Saturday abounds in crisp justifications from either side justifying vandalism as an expression-of-sentiment-of-the-masses. And finally, it all comes together beautifully in the Sunday prime time debate. A good media weekend never hurt anyone. Neither the hurt nor the headlines. Besides being hurt, I would also be famous. Once again, the freedom to express with sticks and stones would be far easier than the freedom of expression with a pen or a brush; which brings me to the point I began with, that of a cartoonist.

# II

Sometime back, the young workers of a political party arrived late in the evening to deal with a professor. One, who dared to forward a political cartoon—a crime isn't it? The midnight knock does not need a uniform anymore, it is a civil prerogative. The Emergency of the 1970s makes a daily comeback, embedded in a 21st century democracy. Before the lawmakers arrive, this issue needs to be handled in its own way. So, the young workers do what they have to do, intimidate him to confess that he has political affiliations of another color. "Now that you know how to forward a jpeg, we will tell you how to sign a confession." Soon, the lawmakers arrive, and arrests are made. Once the issue has been handled in its own way, the law will take its own course; that too for forwarding a political satire. I stare into my drawing board. In another city, a political party discovers a cartoon in a textbook. Published over 60 years ago, the cartoon has been re-published in a textbook explaining a moment of the nation's political history. But no, it is unacceptable again because apparently the leader depicted is the marble monolith of the community with different factions claiming him with a different branding. "Ban the cartoon!" says one, "Ban the cartoon!!" say all. It takes less than a gulp for the Parliament to be hurt in unison and, thus, cartoons are banned from school textbooks of the land. Final and forever. Politics and cartoons are two different things, I must remember. In fact, one leader tells me on television that the mind should be used for good things. So, am I to understand that the political cartoon is a product of the perverted? Later that night over another television debate, a social worker asks the anchor innocently "why do cartoons always have to be so critical, why can't they show something *nice*?" They are surely telling me something I missed all the while. Beware or else the sentiment of the masses will follow. Put off the lights, close the windows. It happens all the time in another City Maximum, where two political parties are led by none other than two political cartoonists. And trust their workers to get hurt all the time, expressing their pain on the streets, on Fridays. The lovely contradictions that make our democracy just so endearing! Like me, everybody knows that political parties without exception often benevolently practice the theory of 'expression of mass sentiment' I am scared to look back at my drawing board now. I look out at the streets below—empty. The walls bare. Nothing compared to the ones in the City of Joy (and not Humor), full of multi-colored political graffiti, raw satire, and crude caricatures. Walk around the city and you will realize—when a jpeg file can be so defamatory what damage would those walls do to the moral fabric of that metropolis? Those walls need to be whitewashed and so does our democracy. Maybe I too could draw cartoons for a greeting card company—'something nice'. Oh dear, it's midnight now, hope nobody knocks. And if they do, I will be famous. Then, do not waste your time signing release petitions for me. Instead bring out your cell phone and vote for me when I make it to the Big Boss house.

Goodnight.

# About the Editors and Contributors

## Editors

**Rina Ramdev** is Associate Professor, Department of English, Sri Venkateswara College, University of Delhi and the Secretary of Indian Association of Commonwealth Literature and Language Studies (IACLALS). She has worked on the politics of post-coloniality, the writings of Arundhati Roy and the relationship between literature and social movements. She is also interested and involved in exploring the intersections of academic practice and political resistance within institutional spaces.

**Sandhya Devesan Nambiar** is Assistant Professor, Department of English, Jesus and Mary College, University of Delhi. She has studied English Literature and Philosophy at Lady Shri Ram College, University of Delhi and Jawaharlal Nehru University. Her doctoral thesis was an exploration of conceptual structures in Continental Philosophy and of Deleuzean modes of philosophical thought in particular. She currently resides in New Delhi.

**Debaditya Bhattacharya** is Assistant Professor, Department of English, Bhagini Nivedita College, University of Calcutta. His doctoral work engaged with the relationship between literature and death. The other areas of his research interest include continental philosophy, Renaissance studies, popular culture and the philosophy of technology.

## Contributors

**Tapan Basu** is Associate Professor, Department of English, University of Delhi. Prior to this, he taught for 28 years in the Department of

English, Hindu College, Delhi, before he joined as Associate Professor in the Department of English, University of Delhi. He has a keen interest in the study of the politics of identity-constructions and identity-confrontations, especially along religious and caste lines, in contemporary India. He has edited *Translating Caste* (2002), an anthology of fictional and non-fictional narratives of caste and caste-consciousness, and is the author of an unpublished monograph on *The Writings of B.R. Ambedkar and the Construction of a Dalit Cultural Identity*, written under the aegis of a fellowship he received from the Social Science Research Council, New York.

**Prasanta Chakravarty** is Associate Professor of English at the University of Delhi. He works at the cusp of arts and political philosophy. His principal research interest lies in heterodox and non-conformist political and religious writings/movements of early modern Europe. His publications include *Parchment in the Fire: Literature and Radicalism in the English Civil War* (2006) and an edited volume, *Shrapnel Minima: Writings from Humanities Underground* (2014). He is also deeply invested in contemporary debates on humanities studies—globally and in South Asia.

**Giti Chandra** is Associate Professor, Department of English, St Stephen's College, University of Delhi. She is the author of three books, including *Narratives of Violence and Collective Identities: To Witness These Wrongs Unspeakable* (2009).

**Vinita Chandra** is Associate Professor, Department of English, Ramjas College, University of Delhi. Her PhD from Rutgers University, USA, is titled *Constructing Nationalities: Indo-Anglian Fiction*. Her area of specialization is Post-colonial Theory and Fiction. She is also deeply invested in the theoretical and practical aspects of the politics of protest.

**Radhika Chopra** is the author of *Militant and Migrant: The Politics and Social History of Punjab* (2011), editor of *Reframing Masculinities: Narrating the Supportive Practices of Men* (2006), and co-editor of *South Asian Masculinities: Contexts of Change, Sites of Continuity* (2004). Her recent publications include *Ziddi Mundeh: Political Asylum, Transnational Movement and the Migrations of Men* (2015); *A Museum, a Memorial and a Martyr: Politics of Memory in the*

*Sikh Golden Temple* (2013), *Commemorating Hurt: Memorialising Operation Bluestar* (2010), among others.

**Soumyabrata Choudhury** is Associate Professor, School of Arts and Aesthetics, Jawaharlal Nehru University, New Delhi. He was a Fellow at the Indian Institute of Advanced Study, Shimla, till 2012 and a Visiting Fellow at CSDS, Delhi in 2012–2013 before joining the Centre for Studies in Social Sciences, Kolkata. He has authored the book *Theatre, Number, Event: Three Studies on the Relationship of Sovereignty, Power and Truth* which came out in March 2013.

**Anup Dhar** is Associate Professor, School of Human Studies, Ambedkar University, Delhi. A trained medical doctor, he has been a Research Fellow in Women's Studies at The Asiatic Society, Kolkata, and a Fellow in Cultural Studies at the Centre for the Study of Culture and Society (CSCS), Bangalore. His publications include *Dislocation and Resettlement in Development: From Third World to World of the Third* (2009, co-authored with A. Chakrabarti) and *World of the Third and Global Capitalism* (2011, co-authored with A. Chakrabarti and S. Cullenberg). He is currently completing a book titled *The Secret Politics of Ab-Original Psychoanalysis: Fort-Da between the Windscreen and the Rear-view Mirror.*

**Karen Gabriel** is Associate Professor, Department of English, and Director, Centre for the Study of Gender, Culture and Social Processes, St Stephen's College, University of Delhi. She has written extensively on issues of gender, sexuality, nation, and representation. Her second book *Melodrama and the Nation: The Sexual Economies of Bombay Cinema 1970–2000* was published in 2010. She is currently working on the political economy of terrorism and the media and visual cultures.

**Shohini Ghosh** is Sajjad Zaheer Professor, AJK Mass Communication Research Centre, Jamia Millia Islamia, New Delhi. She is the author of *Fire: A Queer Classic* (2010) and the director of *Tales of the Night Fairies*, a documentary on the sex-workers' movement for decriminalization. Her current work is titled *Violence and the Spectral Muslim: Action, Affect and Bombay Cinema at the Turn of the 21st Century.*

**Vishwajyoti Ghosh** is the author of the graphic novel *Delhi Calm* (2010), a political graphic novel set in the 1970s and a visual book of postcards *Times New Roman & Countrymen*. He is the curator of *This Side That Side: Restorying Partition* (2013), an anthology of graphic narratives from Pakistan, India and Bangladesh. Ghosh has also been the creator of cartoon columns like "Full Toss" in *Hindustan Times*, "Acid Test" in *Down to Earth* and "Backlog" in *The Little Magazine*. His comics are regularly published in various journals and anthologies, both in India and abroad. Associated with "Inverted Commas" a communications initiative, he is currently working on a mapping project in the workers' clusters of Gurgaon. As a founder member of the Pao Collective, he also remains an active and dynamic participant in graphic/comics artists' collective projects and often works with graphic artists from different parts of South Asia.

**Mushirul Hasan** is a Jawaharlal Nehru Fellow, Jawaharlal Nehru Memorial Fund, New Delhi. He is former Vice Chancellor and Professor of History, Jamia Millia Islamia, New Delhi. He is also former Director General, National Archives of India, New Delhi. He was awarded the Padma Shri in 2007. His publications include *Nationalism and Communal Politics in India 1885-1930* (1991), *The Legacy of a Divided Nation: India's Muslims since Independence* (1997), *John Company to the Republic: A Story of Modern India* (2001), *Making Sense of History: Society, Culture and Politics* (2003), *From Pluralism to Separatism: Qasbas in Colonial Awadh* (2004), *A Moral Reckoning: Muslim Intellectuals in Nineteenth Century Delhi* (2005) and *Wit and Humour in Colonial North India* (2007), among others.

**Akhil Katyal** is Assistant Professor, Department of English, Shiv Nadar University. He finished his Ph.D titled 'The Double Game of Sexuality: Idioms of Same-Sex Desire in Modern India' at SOAS, University of London. His article 'Laundebazi: Habits and Politics in North India' came out in *Interventions*, a journal of postcolonial studies, in 2013. His first book of poems *Night Charge Extra* came out with Writers Workshop in 2015.

**Sunalini Kumar** is Assistant Professor, Department of Political Science at Lady Shri Ram College, University of Delhi. She has a PhD in urban planning and political science from the University of Delhi and has published in edited volumes, academic journals as well as popular magazines such as *Tehelka* and *Motherland*, apart from being a blogger on the popular site Kafila. Her most recent publication is titled "Chronicle of a Death Untold: The Lethal Geographies of Delhi's Periphery" and appeared in a volume titled *Critical Studies in Politics: Sites, Selves, Power* (2014). Sunalini is currently working on a book on the National Capital Region of India.

**Lawrence Liang** is an independent lawyer and researcher who worked with the Alternative Law Forum which he helped co-found. He also moonlights as a film and media scholar. He has recently finished a book on libraries and the future of reading and is completing another one on law and justice in Indian cinema. He writes for a number of places including e-flux and Kafila, and has taught and lectured at many universities in India, the US, and Europe.

**Meenakshi Malhotra** is Associate Professor, Department of English, Hansraj College, University of Delhi. She has worked and published on gender and literary theory.

**Krishna Menon** is Associate Professor, Department of Political Science at Lady Shri Ram College, University of Delhi. She has contributed essays for *Political Theory: An Introduction* (2008), *Human Rights, Gender and Environment* (2009), *Applied Ethics and Human Rights* (2010), *Women's Studies in India* (2014), and *Gender and Identity: A Case Study of Nurses from Kerala in Delhi* (2008). She is a trained Carnatic musician and a Bharata Natyam dancer and has also been the classical dance critic for *The Indian Express* between 1992 and 1995.

**Siddharth Narrain** is a lawyer and Research Associate at Sarai, Centre for the Study of Developing Societies (CSDS), New Delhi, where he is working on issues related to law, social media, and violence. He has previously worked with the Alternative Law Forum, Bangalore, and as a journalist with The Hindu Group of Publications in Delhi. He has co-edited *The Shifting Scales of Justice: The Supreme Court in Neoliberal India* (2014).

**Mukund Padmanabhan** is the Editor of *The Hindu BusinessLine*, the business daily brought out by The Hindu Group of Publications and published in 17 towns and cities all over India. An MPhil in Philosophy, he worked briefly as a lecturer in University of Delhi before switching to journalism. He worked for the magazine *Sunday* in Calcutta and the *Indian Express* before joining *The Hindu*. He is interested and has written about politics, legal affairs and literature. He is an adjunct faculty of the Ateneo de Manila University in the Philippines, where he teaches law and advanced writing to post-graduate students. He curates two festivals of theater and music on behalf of his newspaper group – The Hindu Theatre Fest, and The Hindu November Fest.

**Manas Ray** teaches Cultural Studies and Sociology at the Centre for Studies in Social Sciences, Kolkata. He is currently working on two anthologies of his essays: (a) *Displaced: Lives on the Move* and (b) *Foucault Contra Agamben: Essays on Biopolitics and Liberal Rule*.

**Dilip Simeon** is a Delhi-based historian and writer. His publications include a monograph on the labor history of Jharkhand; the novel *Revolution Highway*, and numerous academic articles and opinion pieces. He is a member of the governing body of the Aman Trust, which works to understand and reduce violent conflict.

# Index